$100

	DATE DUE		

MURDERED BY HIS WIFE

MURDERED BY HIS WIFE

———◆———

A history with documentation of the
Joshua Spooner murder and execution of
his wife, Bathsheba, who was hanged in
Worcester, Massachusetts, 2 July 1778.

———◆———

Deborah Navas

University of Massachusetts Press
AMHERST

Library of Congress Cataloging-in-Publication Data
Navas, Deborah.
Murdered by his wife / Deborah Navas.
p.   cm.
"A history with documentation of the Joshua Spooner murder and
execution of his wife, Bathsheba, who was hanged in Worcester,
Massachusetts July 2, 1778."
Includes bibliographical references.
ISBN 1-55849-227-5 (alk. paper)
1. Murder — Massachusetts — Brookfield (Town) — Case studies.
2. Spooner, Bathsheba, 1746–1778.
3. Spooner, Joshua.   I. Title.
HV6534.B755N38   1999
364.15′23′097443 — dc21   99-15160
CIP

British Library Cataloguing in Publication data are available.

Portions of Chapter 9 were published in
Proceedings 108 (1998) by the
Massachusetts Historical Society, Boston

For my mother,

DOROTHY ETHEL HUNT,

a Worcester girl

Contents

Contents

MURDERED BY HIS WIFE

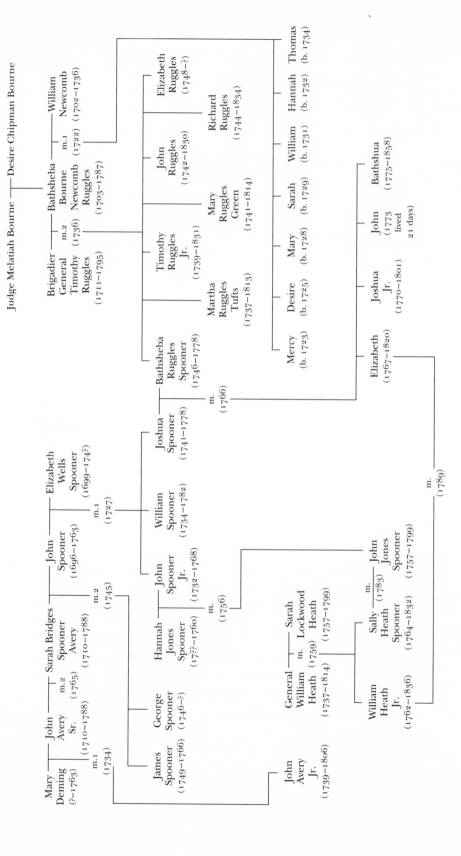

Introduction

O N A MOONLESS March night in 1778, Joshua Spooner of Brookfield, Massachusetts, was murdered in his dooryard and his body stuffed down his well. The next day in Worcester, his murderers were caught, identified because they were wearing Spooner's clothes and silver shoe buckles. The three men, who were Revolutionary War soldiers, quickly confessed their guilt and implicated Spooner's wife, Bathsheba, as the instigator of the crime. All four were tried and found guilty. Four months later, the three soldiers and Bathsheba Spooner were hanged together in Worcester, Massachusetts, despite repeated appeals to the state for a stay of execution.

Supported by her prison confessor, Bathsheba Spooner had asked to be given time to deliver the child she was carrying, but the state denied her. A postexecution autopsy revealed she was indeed pregnant with a five-month male fetus; the State of Massachusetts was guilty of committing a murder while in the act of punishing a murder. This grim discovery might ordinarily have brought the curtain down on what was a sad and shameful episode of Massachusetts's revolutionary history.

But the story refused a decent burial. Accounts of it appeared in diary entries and letters, and it lived on in memory and local legend, told and retold around hearths in earlier days. The year 1844 saw the story's first published appearance among two volumes of famous murder cases by a noted Worcester lawyer, Peleg W. Chandler. A century later the story was fictionalized as *The General's Lady* by Esther Forbes, and it has also been recapitulated in enumerable monographs and newspaper and magazine articles published over two centuries.

This 220-year-old murder remains one of New England's most enduring mysteries, though it has never been a mystery in the whodunit sense. We know who did it: two British soldiers, Sergeant James Buchanan and William Brooks, and a young Continental soldier named Ezra Ross wrote a full confession of the crime. They freely admitted their guilt and were deeply penitent. And there is little doubt that Bathsheba Spooner, Joshua's wife, was the chief perpetrator, though she made no public confession or act of contrition. Neither is there a great deal of mystery surrounding the facts. A detailed account of events can be reconstructed from the prisoners' confession, trial notes, court records, and other documents, all of which are published in the appendixes.

In its own time the murder of Joshua Spooner was characterized as "the most extraordinary crime ever perpetrated in New England."[1] But if the murder were all, the story would have been long forgotten. It is also a love story with tragic consequences and timeless implications.

From the records we know that Bathsheba Ruggles Spooner was beautiful, intelligent, high spirited, and witty. She was thirty-two years old at the time of the murder, a mother of three young children and extremely unhappy in her marriage. In her own words she felt "an utter aversion" to her husband. And, as the favorite daughter of Massachusetts's most despised Loyalist, Brig. Gen. Timothy Ruggles, she was on the wrong side of the political fence in patriotic Massachusetts, caught up in the midst of the Revolution.

A year before the murder, in March 1777, fate intervened by delivering Ezra Ross to Bathsheba Spooner's care. At sixteen, Ross had just finished his first year's enlistment fighting with the Continental army under General Washington. He was ill, walking home to Ipswich from New Jersey by way of the great post road that passed through Brookfield within a few feet of the Spooner gate. Bathsheba took him in and nursed him back to health. Ezra Ross returned to visit the Spooners the following summer and again in December. Evidence strongly suggests that Ezra and Bathsheba became lovers and conceived a child and that Bathsheba's pregnancy ultimately led to the ill-conceived murder.

The real mystery at the heart of this story is Bathsheba Spooner herself. Was she a cold-blooded murderess or the victim of a misogynist culture and justice system? Because she refused to repent publicly or explain herself, her silence has invited two centuries of reading between the lines.

"The past is always changing," the writer May Sarton once observed, meaning that one's perception of the past is changeable, reshaped by new information and new insights. Accordingly, Bathsheba Spooner has changed over two hundred years. The eighteenth and nineteenth centuries most often vilified her. To Rev. Ebenezer Parkman, who visited her in prison and delivered a sermon after her execution, she was an evil woman, an adulteress guilty of "cruel, unnatural, loathsome murder . . . detestable uncleanness, . . . multiplied acts of unfaithfulness to the conjugal bonds and defiling the marriage bed."[2] In the nineteenth century, Peleg Chandler spoke of her "obdurate wickedness" and made this observation based on his reading of her character: "no criminals are so hardened . . . or endure a death of shame with more calmness or apparent innocence than women."[3]

It took an early feminist—a leader of the women's suffrage movement—to view Bathsheba's story with sympathy. In 1899, Elizabeth Cady Stanton published an article in the *New York World* entitled "The Fatal Mistake that Stopped the Hanging of Women in Massachusetts," and started a revisionist trend. Twentieth-century writers have followed suit, sometimes lavishing sympathy to the point of ignoring altogether troublesome facts about the murder. Esther Forbes's Bathsheba Spooner did not plot to murder her husband, nor did she cuckold him, as the flesh-and-blood Bathsheba surely did. To be fair to Esther Forbes, readers in 1938 (when *The General's Lady* was written) would have been no more sympathetic to wayward female sexual behavior than their eighteenth- and nineteenth-century forebears.

Along with changing perceptions of women in general, the historical record itself has been altered by new information recently come to light. Traditional accounts perpetuated a number of erroneous assumptions, passing them down over time as fact. One such inaccurate but widely held belief is that Joshua Spooner was much older than his wife. This misunderstanding was perhaps based on the prisoners' confession, in which Sgt. Buchanan refers to Joshua as "the old fellow" and Bathsheba is quoted as calling him "Old Bogus." But the Spooner genealogy lists Joshua Spooner's birth date as 1741, making him only five years older than Bathsheba, who was born on 15 February 1746.[4]

However, it is very possible that Joshua looked and acted much older than his chronological age. One source—apparently quoting Bathsheba—accuses him of being unmanly, and his behavior is represented as fearful and prissy in others. These unappealing traits present a far more complex and interesting ground for ill will between husband and wife, compared to his simply being an old man (with the cold-blooded implication made by some writers that his advanced age was reason enough to murder him).

In addition, two accounts of the Spooner trial that were not generally known before add significantly to the little we know of Joshua Spooner's character. According to one witness whose testimony was recorded in notes written by prosecutor Robert Treat Paine, Spooner was bad to his wife and frequently drunk.[5] Another set of trial notes written by Associate Justice Nathaniel Peaslee Sargeant suggest that he may have kept a mistress.[6]

Most important, there is new evidence that points to a truly reprehensible conflict of interest within the Massachusetts Council, upon whose judgment the life of Bathsheba's unborn baby depended. The decision against a delay of execution until the child could be delivered appears to have been prompted by personal vengeance on the part of the state's second highest legislative official.

It seems time, then, to reexamine this old story of love, betrayal, and murder by the light of the late twentieth century and to make the record as accurate as possible. Bathsheba Spooner will continue to seduce readers and writers on into the twenty-first century and perhaps as long as there *are* readers and writers. But one must first do justice to the empirical truth in facts, as they come to be known, in order to intuit the far more profound, disturbing, and mysterious truths of the heart.

1

Unnatural Murder

THE NATURAL darkness of an eighteenth-century night is hard to imagine in our highly illuminated present day. The night of 1 March 1778 in Brookfield, Massachusetts, was darker yet, for the moon had set early. Nearly new, its thin crescent had slipped below the horizon at 8:32 P.M., leaving only the infinitesimal, cold light of stars — if they were visible at all — to lend the snow-covered ground definition. In the utter darkness of that long-ago Sabbath evening, a man was about to be murdered in his dooryard.

That it was a moonless night must have seemed pure good luck to the murderer who, crouching beside the kitchen garden gate, would have been invisible to his victim. It is likely that no light was given off from the house's windows. Interior shutters would have been carefully closed and latched to contain the soft glow from the kitchen fire as well as to shut out the brutal event soon to take place outside.

The victim's name was Joshua Spooner, a thirty-seven-year-old well-to-do farmer and businessman. As the murderer kept watch awaiting his coming, Spooner was walking up the mild incline where the great road, as the post road was commonly called, ran alongside the front of his house. It was something after nine o'clock and most of Brookfield's residents had banked their fires and retired to the warmth of their goose down bedding on that cold late-winter night.

The road would have been treacherous with frozen ruts at that time of year, and so Joshua Spooner probably carried a hand lantern with an enclosed candle to light his way in the near pitch-darkness. It may have been the flicker of light that signaled Spooner's approach to his murderer, who then ran through the house and out to the back dooryard to wait by the kitchen garden gate.

Spooner had just spent several hours drinking at his neighbor

Ephraim Cooley's tavern, accompanied by his friends, Dr. and Mrs. Jonathan King, who, like himself, were among Brookfield's most prominent citizens. His thoughts were apt to be happily engaged with the conversation just passed rather than with any anticipated pleasures at home. He and his wife, Bathsheba, did not get along. Lately she had been keeping two disreputable-looking British soldiers in the house, and they had taken advantage of his hospitality by eating from his stores, drinking his rum, and running up bills for grog at the local taverns. They were escaped prisoners-of-war, among the hundreds of Gen. Burgoyne's captured troops who were notorious for committing highway robberies and other crimes throughout Massachusetts at that time. He had not liked their looks, and he had asked his wife to get rid of them.

On the night of his murder, Joshua Spooner probably assumed that the British soldiers were long gone. In the two weeks following his ultimatum, the soldiers had been kept out of his sight. Bathsheba Spooner had put them up in the barn, fed them and brought them drink, and invited them into the house when her husband was asleep or gone from home. During those two weeks she had been furiously engaged with them concocting improbable schemes for murdering her husband. On the moonless Sabbath evening when Joshua Spooner walked home from Cooley's tavern, he had no idea of her deadly intentions.

William Brooks was the murderer who crouched by the kitchen garden gate awaiting Joshua Spooner. Very soon Brooks would hear Spooner's footsteps ascend the four granite steps that led from the road to the dooryard and then the unmistakable sound of the front gate's latch. Following the homely rattle of the latch would come the damp thunk of fist hitting flesh and a cry for help that went unanswered.

Bathsheba in the sitting room — separated from the murderous beating by only a few short feet, a wooden louvered shutter, the thickness of a pane of glass — surely caught her husband's dying call. When William Brooks was finished and the body pushed down into the well, he and his two cohorts went inside the house to find Bathsheba stunned and in a state of confusion.

Later, her neighbors insisted that she view the corpse, against her wishes. When she saw the reality of what her plotting had wrought, she touched her husband's bruised forehead and exclaimed, "Poor little man." It was a cry of the heart that rings true two hundred and twenty years later, expressing shock and perhaps some sympathy, if not grief.

Joshua Spooner's murder was a brutal, poorly planned, and senseless act which three of its perpetrators would go on record as regretting profoundly. All four would pay for it with their lives. It caused the death of a child in utero and orphaned at least four others. And it so easily might never have happened, if the moon had been full on 1 March 1778 or if Joshua Spooner had not carried a light.

Or if divorce had been an option for eighteenth-century women.

That it was thought to be "the most extraordinary crime ever perpetrated in New England" is a measure of the profound fear and horror excited throughout the infant nation — in the midst of a war to throw off the yoke of oppression — by the murder of a man by his wife.

2

By the Lot of Providence

TUCKED AWAY in western Massachusetts, the small town of Brookfield is all but invisible to those traveling through it. Brookfield's narrow common sits well off the highway, a grassy island of tranquility with its white-spired Congregational Church at one end and carefully preserved Victorian homes lining either side. If time has not stopped here according to the romantic conceit, it has been arrested for the last hundred years. Two centuries earlier, however, Brookfield was the star of Worcester County, a bustling center for farming, rural commerce, and industry, and a popular stopping place for any number of travelers along the great east-west highway between Boston and New York.

In 1777, one among the many travelers passing through Brookfield was a young American soldier named Ezra Ross. Described by one eyewitness, Maj. Benjamin Russell, as "a fine looking youth,"[1] Ross had finished his first year's campaign in the Continental army and was walking home along the post road, through Brookfield, from Gen. George Washington's winter encampment at Morristown, New Jersey.

His elderly parents, Jabez and Johana Ross, awaited him from their home in Ipswich; probably his older sister Joanna, a spinster, lived in the family home as well. The Ross family lived in the village of Linebrook, located in the extreme western part of Ipswich. Linebrook was a modest farming community with homes predominantly built along the Linebrook Road (which was also the Boston post road).

The Jabez Ross family were members of the small Linebrook parish, whose membership at its peak was less than one hundred. Linebrook's pastor, George Lesslie, would prove extraordinarily loyal to Ezra and his family. Mr. Lesslie signed the Ross's petition asking the council to spare Ezra's life, and he also made the journey to Worcester to minister to him in prison.

From the petition submitted by the elder Rosses to the Massachusetts Council in May 1778, we know that the Rosses were an extraordinarily patriotic family who suffered more than their share of misfortune.[2] Of their seventeen children, only six sons and three daughters survived.[3] Five sons had entered the service; four of them — Jabez Jr., Nathaniel, Benjamin, and Kneeland — signed on as minutemen "at the first instance of bloodshed," and as soon as the alarm reached Ipswich on 19 April 1775, they marched to Lexington (too late in the day to hinder the British retreat to Boston).

However, before the Ipswich minutemen returned home from Lexington, two ships were sighted at the head of the Ipswich River on the morning of 21 April. Rumors that the British were coming, "cutting and slashing and killing all before them," drove Ipswich residents into a panic, causing them to hide their valuables and flee up the Merrimack Valley.[4] The alarm was spread to neighboring towns, and the roads were quickly filled with hastily packed carts and families on foot carrying what household goods they had been able to snatch up before abandoning their homes.

According to one early historian of Newbury, Massachusetts: "[One] woman . . . having run four or five miles, in great trepidation, stopped on the steps of Mr. Noble's meeting house to nurse her child and found to her great horror that she had brought off the cat and left the child at home." Another man, "having placed his family on board of a boat to go to Ram Island for safety, was so annoyed with the crying of one of his children that he exclaimed in great fright, 'Do throw that squalling brat overboard or we shall all be discovered.'"[5]

Fourteen-year-old Ezra was left at home while his brothers were off doing battle in Lexington and later on at Cambridge and Bunker Hill. We have no way of knowing if he took part in the infamous "Ipswich Fright," but he surely would have been present to see the two battalions of musketmen and riflemen under the command of Col. Benedict Arnold that camped in Ipswich in mid-September 1775 on their way north to Quebec.

Arnold's Second Battalion included the famous Capt. Daniel Morgan and his Virginia riflemen, dressed in fur caps and deerskin, who put on a sharpshooting exhibition that astonished and impressed Ipswich citizens. The pageantry of battle flags, fife and drum, and marching soldiers was likely irresistible to a young boy from such a patriotic family. On 19 December, Ezra Ross joined his three brothers in the war, signing on at age fifteen as a private in Capt. Thomas Mighill's company, serving in Woburn's Col. Loammi Baldwin's Twenty-sixth Massachusetts Regiment.

The Ross's petition said, "Three [sons] marched to the southward with General Washington, of which number was [Ezra], who engaged for one, the other two for three years. A fourth mingled at the northward his bones with the dust of the earth." The identity of the son who was killed in the north is uncertain. One Ross son whose death on a northern battlefield is documented was Abner, born twenty-one years before Ezra. But Abner Ross was killed during the French and Indian wars (1758) at Fort Louisbourg on Cape Breton Island in Nova Scotia. It is a curious coincidence that he fought under or alongside Bathsheba's father, Col. Timothy Ruggles, who was appointed Brigadier General in charge of the Massachusetts forces later in 1758.

Ezra Ross's first year of military service must surely have disabused him of any romantic notions about war. He would witness more gore, suffering, and death than he could have imagined possible as a young boy of fifteen. His regiment fought under General Washington at Cambridge until the evacuation of the British from Boston in March 1776. His company had followed Washington to Long Island and on to New York and New Jersey, suffering a series of bitter defeats[6] until the successful surprise attack on Trenton (Christmas night 1776), immortalized in the famous painting depicting Washington crossing the Delaware. The Twenty-sixth Regiment had battled the elements as well as enemy forces; according to Colonel Baldwin's biography in Clifford K. Shipton's *Sibley's Harvard Graduates*, his men suffered from the lack of tents. Despite his youth, Ezra Ross was a seasoned veteran who had served under some of the most demoralizing and brutal circumstances of the Revolutionary War.

In March 1777, when Ezra Ross and Bathsheba Spooner first met, Ross had been discharged at the end of the campaign in December

1776, most likely beginning his journey homeward from Washington's Morristown encampment where smallpox, dysentery, and influenza were rampant. His 240-mile-walk to Linebrook parish was made in the harshest of winter weather.[7] It is possible that he was ill when he left Morristown, and, if so, the bitter cold and rigors of traveling on foot would have exacerbated his condition by the time he reached the Spooner house in March. Though a battle-proven soldier, he was still a sixteen-year-old boy, severely ill and trying to make his way home on numb, and very likely frostbitten, feet. Perhaps he had stopped at the Spooner house for food or lodging, or perhaps someone — Bathsheba herself — might have looked from a front window to see him stumbling along the road. And so he was taken in and nursed back to health by a remarkably beautiful woman, in what would be considered luxurious surroundings compared with his own more modest home in Linebrook.

Ross's parents' petition is most affecting for the parental love it portrays as well as for their understanding of their young son's vulnerability in such a situation: "On his return, from the first year's campaign, he was by the lot of Providence, cast upon Mrs. Spooner, in a severe fit for sickness from whom he received every kind office and mark of tenderness, that could endear and make gratefull a child of sixteen, sick, destitute, in a strange place, at a distance from friend and acquaintance. . . ."

And what of Bathsheba's state of mind and spirit at the time? We know she had turned thirty-one just a month before Ross's visit and that she was profoundly unhappy in her marriage and felt an "utter aversion" to her husband. It is one of the few direct quotations of hers to be recorded, and its vehemence resonates across centuries.[8] Given her acute unhappiness and likely repressed sexuality ("aversion" strongly implying a lack of sexual intimacy), she would have been extraordinarily vulnerable herself, caring for a handsome young man who was seriously ill.

It was a romantic situation made to order, heightened by the tender ministrations of nursing. It is no surprise that the two would form "a very warm attachment," as Peleg Chandler delicately put it nearly a century later. Given their vulnerabilities and the intimate situation, it is hardly possible to imagine that either could have done otherwise.

Ezra Ross stayed with the Spooners for an unspecified period in

March 1777, until he recovered and went on home to Linebrook. It is likely that he and Bathsheba would never have met again if the war had not intervened. In early July 1777, General Burgoyne was forcing American troops out of key strategic military positions from Lake Champlain southward. His plan was to secure the Champlain-Hudson line by seizing Crown Point and then Fort Ticonderoga, which was to be used as a base of operations for the eventual junction with an army under General Howe sailing northward up the Hudson River. The two British armies were to meet at Albany, effectively dividing and conquering the colonies.[9] Had they been successful, the American Revolution would in all likelihood have ended ingloriously in September 1777. New Englanders and the new Continental Congress saw the American abandonment of Fort Ticonderoga as an alarming and utterly humiliating defeat.

In August, Congress issued levies for fresh troops to reinforce the northern army, and to encourage enlistment the town of Ipswich voted to offer willing recruits bounties of up to eighteen pounds. On 9 August the town ordered "one sixth part of the able-bodied men of the training band and alarm lists, not already engaged, be at once drafted and marched for the relief of the Northern Army under General Gates."[10]

Though he had just returned from a year's service, Ezra Ross re-enlisted (or was drafted) in Capt. Robert Dodge's company, under Col. Samuel Johnson's regiment. Given his earlier voluntary service, it is more likely he went voluntarily again, but we can only speculate as to whether he was prompted by patriotism, a generous bounty, or a desire to travel through Brookfield and visit the Spooners on his journey northward. We do know, according to his parent's petition, that he called upon Bathsheba to express his gratitude for past favors. Imagine Bathsheba's delight in seeing him again, in mid-August at the height of summer — that most metaphorical of seasons. She "then added to the number of her kindnesses, and engaged a visit on his return."

Ezra Ross served four months in the northern campaign and fought under Col. Samuel Johnson at the 18 September battle to recapture Ticonderoga. Though the effort was ultimately unsuccessful, over one hundred American prisoners of war were liberated and a vast number of British troops, bateaux, gunboats, and armaments were captured, providing a much needed boost to American morale. Johnson's regiment went on to join with the main body of Continental forces under Gen. Horatio Gates to win the critical victory over General Burgoyne at Saratoga in mid-October 1777. The fighting was extraordinarily bloody, according to British Sgt. Roger Lamb, who was present as a soldier and medic: "A constant blaze of fire was kept up, and both armies seemed to be determined on death or victory."[11] It is possible that in the course of the battle of Saratoga Ross fired upon his future cohorts in crime, British Sgt. James Buchanan and Private William Brooks.

Ezra did return to the Spooners in December, after surviving the attacks on Fort Ticonderoga and Mount Independence, the second battle at Freeman's Farm, and Saratoga. He quickly became a member of the household and apparent friend and traveling companion to Joshua, while at the same time lover to Bathsheba.

[3]

A Bad Conjugal Example

PELEG W. CHANDLER, writing about Bathsheba Spooner's life and death eighty years later, strongly disapproved of her upbringing. "The circumstances of her birth and early education were not favorable to that delicacy and refinement, which constitute the greatest charm of the sex . . .." Chandler wrote. "It is said that General Ruggles and his wife did not set a good example to their children in their conjugal relations."[1]

If we can overlook the tinge of self-righteousness and quaint chauvinism informing these opinions, they do provoke some interesting questions about the family life of this woman "whose passions had never been properly restrained."

Bathsheba Ruggles Spooner was born 15 February 1746, in Sandwich, Massachusetts, the sixth child of Timothy Ruggles and Bathsheba Bourne Newcomb Ruggles.[2] Both the Ruggleses and the Bournes were prominent Massachusetts families, and so it would seem that Bathsheba Ruggles's life lacked for nothing, with the advantages of wealth, education, beauty, and social position as her birthright.

Timothy Ruggles was a fifth-generation descendant of distinguished colonial settlers who, by intermarriage with other prominent New England aristocrats, boasted a lineage traceable back to European royalty. Born 20 October 1711 to Rev. Timothy Ruggles and Mary White of Rochester, the eldest son of twelve children, he attended Harvard in 1728 where he was fined for card playing and reprimanded for provoking another student into hitting him. Stories abound illustrating Ruggles's wry humor, and one of the more amusing shows that he came by his wit naturally. According to Clifford Shipton (*Sibley's Harvard Graduates*), once when buying a horse he verbally agreed to pay on Election Day but made the note payable on

Resurrection Day. The owner of the note did not notice the substitution until he sought payment, upon which young Ruggles responded that it still had some time to run. His father, the parson, intervened, saying "Timothy, pay him. You will have enough else to attend to at the Resurrection, besides paying for old horses."[3]

The dramatic impact Ruggles made on his contemporaries, even as a young undergraduate, is borne out by the wealth of documented stories illustrating his personality and later his professional achievements. He was an outsized, extraordinary man in every respect, including physical appearance. According to James Ruggles, a nineteenth-century family biographer, he was "a person of gigantic proportions; over six-feet high and of Herculean strength. His face of dark complexion was of beautiful proportions, and indicated a mind of stern resolve and fixed principles."[4] Other references describe him as "handsome, with a strong and commanding face. He . . . was social, witty, profane, and wise about human nature, . . . a man of few words who never said anything silly."[5] He also showed remarkable self-restraint in a culture where excessive eating and drinking were the norm; Ruggles was a vegetarian and drank nothing stronger than small beer.

Timothy Ruggles graduated from Harvard in 1732 but did not bother to receive his M.A., which was automatic if the fee was paid. This omission prompted Clifford Shipton to make the following telling observation respecting Ruggles's character: "In a man committed to obscurity this neglect was not unnatural, but in a man of his prominence it was evidence of that disregard of custom and public opinion which was to shape his life."[6]

Within a year of graduating, Ruggles was admitted to the bar at Plymouth, and in 1734 he was elected district representative to the General Court from Rochester, beginning twenty-three years of distinguished service in the Massachusetts legislature.

On 18 September 1736, Timothy Ruggles married Bathsheba Bourne Newcomb (born 11 November 1704), the daughter of Judge Melatiah and Desire Bourne of Sandwich and a member of the most prominent family dynasty in that historic Cape Cod town. Melatiah was the grandson of Rev. Richard Bourne, a founder of Sandwich who mastered the Indian tongue and became a missionary to the Mashpee tribe and founder of their legal reservation. It was an amazing feat of scholarship and dedication as well as open-mindedness in a time when Indians were universally feared and reviled. The Bourne family were direct descendants of the Plymouth Pilgrims John Howland and Elizabeth Tilley, and their name is even to this day exalted, at least to the height of the Bourne Bridge that spans Buzzards Bay, linking Plymouth with the Cape.[7]

When Timothy Ruggles and Bathsheba Bourne Newcomb met, she was a recent widow with seven young children aged two to thirteen (Thomas, Hannah, William, Sarah, Mary, Desire, and Mercy Newcomb). Her first husband, William Newcomb, had died in 1736 in his early thirties (from unspecified causes), leaving her and their children a good-sized estate: the Newcomb public house and two shops were valued at £2,759, and there was also over £1,000 in uncollected debts.

Very little is known about William Newcomb, but what little is documented reveals something of Bathsheba Bourne Newcomb's taste in men and, implicitly, her own personality. That she possessed a fiery disposition is substantiated in later tales circulated about the Ruggles marriage. According to *Sibley's Harvard Graduates*, William Newcomb was a notorious hell-raiser who, as a freshman, broke window glass costing more than his combined rent, study, and tuition for a quarter term. Upon graduation he celebrated by breaking glass worth nine shillings more. He married Bathsheba Bourne immediately after college without returning for his M.A. degree, and he worked in Sandwich as innkeeper at the inn he inherited from his father.

After Newcomb's death Bathsheba Newcomb immediately set to work as innkeeper with the help of her older children, who would later take over the job entirely when they were grown. It was Bathsheba Newcomb's pluckiness in assuming her dead husband's duties behind the bar that later gave playwright Mercy Otis Warren material for a scurrilous caricature in a satire entitled *The Group*.[8] The play was used as anti-Loyalist propaganda on the eve of the Revolution, escalating tensions that would explode into war on Lexington green just three months later. The character named General Hate-All (that is, Brig. Gen. Timothy Ruggles) says,

> When young, indeed, I wedded nut brown Kate,
> (Blyth buxom Dowager, the jockey's prey)

But all I wish'd was to secure her dower
I broke her spirits when I'd won her purse;
For which I'll give a recipe most sure
To ev'ry hen peck'd husband round the board;
If crabbed words or surly looks won't tame
The haughty shrew, nor bend the stubborn mind,
Then the green Hick'ry, or the willow twig,
Will prove a curse for each rebellious dame
Who dare oppose her lord's superior will.

Mercy Warren portrayed Ruggles as the cruelest and most blood-thirsty of the Loyalists she lampooned in *The Group,* and she made him a wife-beater as well. Though wholesale character assassination was prevalent at that time, such accusations have a nasty way of sticking, or, at the least, provoking doubts about a man's character even some two hundred years afterward. However, other stories recorded about Bathsheba Newcomb Ruggles show clearly that she was not broken in spirit, suggesting that the wife-beating accusation may very likely have been part of the whole defamatory purpose of the satire.

Mercy Warren did later admit to some qualms of conscience about *The Group* to her friend John Adams. Though she was perhaps justified in savaging leading Tories such as Ruggles and Gov. Thomas Hutchinson, who she and her husband, James Warren, believed supported tyranny, there is no political justification for the acrimonious portrayal of Bathsheba Ruggles—whose politics were, if anything, more likely patriotic—as a brow-beaten tavern slut. The attack was most likely personal.

Mercy Warren was born Mercy Otis in Barnstable—just a few miles down the road from Sandwich. She would have known Bathsheba Bourne personally, though Mercy was twenty-four years younger. The fathers of both women were judges who founded powerful family dynasties in their respective towns. The Bournes were far more distinguished, however; their men were Harvard educated. Mercy's father was descended from yeoman stock but saw to it that his son James went to Harvard.[9] Also, in a highly unusual step for his day, Judge Otis allowed his daughter Mercy to attend the tutorial sessions in mathematics, history, and the classics as James was prepared by the local minister for his Harvard entrance.

[17]

Physically and temperamentally the two women were as different as could be. Bathsheba Bourne was dark, pretty, robust in health, and very likely an extrovert who probably never read a book in her life. Mercy Otis was fair, with an intellectual and interesting rather than pretty face, well educated and a writer, shy, depressive, and subject to numerous physical complaints. It is hard to imagine that they would have approved of each other, and it is highly likely that personal animosity played a role in Mercy Otis Warren's creation of nut-brown Kate, the jockey's prey.

Thus it was from behind the Newcomb tavern bar that Bathsheba Bourne Newcomb first caught Timothy Ruggles's eye, presumably as he rode the country court circuit between Plymouth and Barnstable. When they married Bathsheba was seven years older than her husband, thirty-two to his twenty-five. The rigors of daily work and child-bearing aged women early in eighteenth-century New England. By thirty-two they were apt to look much older, and because of loss of calcium during pregnancy they often were very nearly toothless (a tooth per child was the law of nature for mothers). However, at thirty-two Bathsheba Newcomb was very likely an outstanding exception to this rule (just as her daughter and namesake was a noted beauty at the same age). However, her substantial property may have caught Timothy Ruggles's eye as well; he was notorious for being a shrewd businessman.

The Ruggles-Newcomb marriage was probably a love match in that the ceremony took place only five months after William Newcomb's death, and neither poverty on Bathsheba Newcomb's part, nor pregnancy (their first child, Martha, was born eleven months later) prompted so short a mourning period. The haste was most likely dictated by passion — both were strong-willed, passionate people. It can be argued that their stubborn, intense natures would later contribute to the demise of their marriage and perhaps to their daughter Bathsheba's undoing as well.

The Ruggles's early years in Sandwich, from 1736 to 1753, were probably their happiest. Timothy Ruggles hung his lawyer's shingle on the Newcomb inn and joined his wife behind the bar when he wasn't attending the state legislature or court. He personally attended both bar and stable, believing that no man should be above his own business. He umpired at quoit pitching and foot races as well and would later revive this interest in athletic competitions when he instituted the Hardwick Fair.

Even as a young man, Ruggles engaged in exploits that were legendary. He was infamous for his profanity, which shocked many of his contemporaries. (It was considered all the more shocking in his daughter Bathsheba, who came by the habit naturally.)[10] As he matured his wit became more biting and sarcastic. Once when representing a client in Taunton, Massachusetts, an elderly female witness entered the crowded courthouse and was unsure where to sit. Ruggles escorted her to the judge's empty seat. The judge arrived shortly and became indignant upon learning that Ruggles had put her in his chair, to which Ruggles responded, "May it please the Court, I thought that the place for an old woman."[11]

Though he often used his humor to deflate pomposity, he was also unusually gracious (for the time) to those below his station, once tipping his hat to a passing Indian "to let him know I am as polite as he is."

Ruggles's height — nearly a foot above the average for the age — and presence alone set him apart from his contemporaries. He was literally and figuratively larger than life and provoked outsized emotions — from the profoundest love and loyalty in his daughter Bathsheba, who appears to have modeled her personal style after his, to a murderous hatred from his political enemies, who would become legion.

Young John Adams was an admirer of Ruggles before their politics divided them. In 1756, after Adams graduated from Harvard, he worked for a brief time as a schoolmaster in Worcester under Rev. Thaddeus Maccarty. Adams was a liberal in ecclesiastical matters and found Maccarty quaint. Maccarty, for his part, found John Adams to be a poor teacher, sitting at his desk engaged with his private writing while his students taught themselves. Adams quickly tired of overseeing the "little runtlings" and changed to law, studying with a prominent lawyer, James Putnam. He came to know Ruggles during this three-year stay in Worcester.

"Ruggles' grandeur consists in the quickness of his apprehension, steadiness of his attention, boldness and strength of his thoughts and expressions, his strict honor, conscious superiority and contempt of meanness," Adams wrote. He went on to describe the effect of such an imposing presence: "People approach him in dread and terror."[12] The fear Ruggles inspired no doubt fueled the intense hatred visited upon him later, which by association would be visited on his daughter Bathsheba as well.

And so young Bathsheba Ruggles grew up within a large, extended household in Sandwich, living at the town's social center among a bevy of siblings and rambunctious older step-siblings. A lively, pretty little girl, she was very likely indulged by her family, stepfamily, and visitors to the inn as well. She was an accomplished horsewoman later and was probably something of a tomboy as a child. She would have learned to ride early, and she was said (by Levi Lincoln, attorney for the defense, in his notes on his summary to the jury) to be her father's favorite. She very likely shared his interests and attitude — in particular his "conscious superiority" and utter disregard for the opinion of others — which would not serve her well in a culture that believed women were designed by God to be modest, subservient domestic beings.

The cozy and familiar life of Sandwich ended in 1753 when Bathsheba was seven years old. Ruggles moved his wife and their children in concert with several other Ruggles households to the sparsely settled township of Hardwick, twenty miles northwest of Worcester. Timothy and his wife Bathsheba, now age forty-two and forty-nine, brought only their seven Ruggles children, leaving in Sandwich Bathsheba's seven surviving children by William Newcomb, who ranged in age from nineteen to thirty. Three Newcomb daughters were married by then, and William Jr. was old enough at twenty-three to take charge of the Newcomb tavern and inn, which was his by right of primogeniture.

The Ruggles clan had long possessed a grant of nearly one hundred square miles, and the move to settle this plantation was a coordinated effort involving twenty-four related families. Seven-year-old Bathsheba was old enough to have developed cherished connections with Sandwich. Whatever she may have thought about this move, it must certainly have been a hardship for her mother. In middle age Bathsheba Newcomb Ruggles was leaving her birthplace, family, and the settled comforts of a long-established community where she was a highly regarded member to set out for the wilderness with seven children, ranging in age from five to sixteen, and only her husband's kin for company.

Timothy Ruggles built a fine two-story Georgian-style house in Hardwick with a deer park and imported hunting and riding horses, as well as prize bulls for selective breeding of his dairy herd.[13] He planted a large orchard with a variety of fruit trees and improved his crops according to the latest farming methods. He also kept hunting hounds for the entertainment of his guests (he didn't hunt himself) and became known for his lavish and generous hospitality. The Ruggles house no longer exists, but a large boulder with a deep drilled hole about twenty inches wide remains at the Hardwick site where a massive flagpole, reputedly higher than any in the county, once bore aloft the Union Jack.

From 1754 through 1759, Ruggles was away on five campaigns in the French and Indian wars. He fought the French at Crown Point as a colonel under Sir William Johnson, whom he personally criticized for needlessly sacrificing troops by marching them against entrenched enemy positions. He served as second in command at Lake George in the defeat of Baron Dieskau and also served as brigadier general under Lord Jeffery Amherst in 1759.

Ruggles earned a preeminent position of leadership in every area of endeavor. After returning home from the Canada wars, he was awarded a fifteen-hundred-acre tract of "potash lands" in Princeton by the General Court in honor of his many years of military service (interestingly enough, during his term as Speaker of the House). Some ten years later (in 1772) Joshua Spooner bought 550 acres of this land for £720, for which he owed Ruggles £190 at his death.

According to Francis Everett Blake's *History of the Town of Princeton*, the potash farm appears to have been an unprofitable and troublesome piece of property that produced a very small amount of inferior-grade potash. The state couldn't sell it so awarded it to Ruggles.[14] Ruggles was a canny businessman and would have seen the depositions attesting to the land's poor return that were filed with his deed in Worcester. He nonetheless charged Spooner a rather substantial sum for his portion. Ruggles's own remaining larger parcel of 580 acres of potash land was assessed at only £500 in a 1777 inventory of his estate, suggesting that he might knowingly have taken advantage of his son-in-law in the business deal.

In 1762 Timothy Ruggles was appointed chief justice for Worcester's Court of Common Pleas. As a long-standing member of the state legislature, he was the acknowledged leader of the king's party throughout the state. His last honorific would be fateful, however: in 1765 he was elected president of the first Provincial Congress, or "Stamp Act Congress" as it was later called, and this marked the beginning of his downfall.

The Stamp Act, which was enacted by Britain's parliament to take effect in November 1765, followed on the heels of the equally unpopular Sugar Act of 1764. These tariffs and taxes, levied to recoup British expenses from the long, drawn-out French and Indian wars (lasting from 1754 to 1763), provoked outrage in Boston. Even before enactment, rumors of the Stamp Act moved Boston to riot; mobs rampaged through the houses of appointed stamp collector Andrew Oliver and Lt. Gov. Thomas Hutchinson. More important, the taxes became a rallying point for organized resistance that would, in ten years, lead to open war.

On 8 October, representatives from nine provinces arrived in New York to begin formulating a response to England. Timothy Ruggles was one of the three Massachusetts delegates, and it is indicative of the degree of Loyalist sympathy prevalent at that time that he, the leader of the king's party, was voted president of the congress (by one vote) over the fiery patriot James Otis. A declaration of rights was drafted, which stated that "two privileges are essential to freedom, and which all Englishmen have ever considered their best birthright — that of being free from all taxes but such as they have consented to in person or by their representatives, and of trial by their peers."

Timothy Ruggles was one of only two delegates who refused to sign the declaration, and he left the congress before adjournment early in the morning of 24 October, the day of the signing. When news of his defection reached Boston, radicals on the General Court moved to expel him but compromised on a letter of censure, which was publicly read by the Speaker of the House of Representatives in February 1766. Ruggles wasn't given the opportunity he requested to record the reasons for his voting position, though he did publish them later on in a May issue of the *Boston Post-Boy*. In this open letter he offered several carefully wrought legal arguments for withholding his signature, capped by the reason that for him was most critical: "If I had signed it I must have acted in direct opposition to . . . the reproaches of my own conscience, a tribunal to me more awful than this (however great) by which I have been condemned."

The Boston papers responded by listing him among "enemies to their country [whose] names ought to be hung up and exposed to contempt."

Over the next few years Ruggles defended the king's position fearlessly, contemptuous of the "patriotic element," which he believed to be the worst sort of lawless mob, manipulated by unprincipled individuals (such as John Hancock) who encouraged the break with England for their own profit. Attacks against him in and out of the legislature became ever more virulent. Despite his great and growing unpopularity, his own town of Hardwick remained loyal to him for five more years and annually elected him representative to the General Court until 1771, when no one was sent. From 1772 on, Hardwick sent patriots to the legislature.

Brig. Timothy Ruggles was forced to leave Hardwick, never to return, in August 1774. British Lt. Gen. Thomas Gage, acting as royal governor of Massachusetts, had appointed Ruggles to the prestigious Mandamus Council with an annual stipend of £300. The right to name these thirty-six Mandamus Counselors had been taken away from the overwhelmingly patriotic legislature, and consequently Gage's appointments were singled out for violent retribution. Many appointees declined the honor, but not Timothy Ruggles.

When the rumor went out around Hardwick that Ruggles would be riding to Boston to take his oath of office as a Mandamus Counselor, the townspeople gathered along the road at the Old Furnace bridge, and the town militia was called out to arrest him. He was met at the bridge by his younger brother Benjamin Ruggles, captain of the militia, who told him that if he crossed the bridge he would never be permitted to return to Hardwick. Brigadier Ruggles answered, "Brother Benjamin, I shall come back, at the head of five hundred soldiers, if necessary." To which Capt. Benjamin Ruggles replied, "Brother Timothy, if you cross that bridge, this morning, you will certainly never cross it again, alive."[15]

Dressed in full military regalia, sitting astride his black war horse,

Brig. Timothy Ruggles "took off his cap with a military gesture to the people, and they, overawed by his appearance, immediately gave way and uncovered their heads to him as he passed unmolested through the ranks."[16]

This scene, recorded a century later by a Ruggles descendant, is certainly romanticized but probably essentially true, and true in spirit to the awe and respect that Ruggles inspired. As it turned out, he never did cross the Old Furnace bridge again. By leaving Hardwick he gave up all of his substantial property (a 400-acre homestead farm in Hardwick, the remaining 580 acres of potash land in Princeton, and five other farms in various locations throughout Massachusetts as well as a long list of personal property).[17] In 1778 he, along with Gov. Hutchinson and Stamp Collector Andrew Oliver, led the list of three hundred Tories who were officially exiled and forbidden to return to Massachusetts on pain of death. His threat to come back at the head of an army would ultimately prove empty, but it was very likely not forgotten.

The awe and reluctant respect shown him by his neighbors at the Old Furnace bridge dissipated quickly. *The Boston Evening-Post* cried for his blood, virtually inviting political assassination: "You have given the finishing stroke to your tatter'd Reputation, and are now driven out from your inheritance, the Society of your good Friends and Neighbors, and like the cursed Fratricide of old, fear that everyone who finds you shall slay you."[18]

Ruggles stayed within the British encampment in Boston, where he began what would turn out to be a series of unsuccessful efforts to gain British support for a Loyalist company. His history of informing British officers of their stupidity undermined his cause with the British generals in Boston and later in New York, who controlled his fate.[19] A young Loyalist by the name of Edward Winslow, who had joined in petition with Ruggles for a British-sponsored Loyalist Cavalry, characterized him thus: "There was such a mixture of virtue even with his obstinacy that while we deprecated it as unfortunate to ourselves we dared not oppose it."

Gen. Timothy Ruggles evacuated Boston with the British troops in 1776 and was put in charge of a colony of Loyalist refugees on Staten Island, New York. It was demeaning work for a man of his position, intelligence, and military experience. He stayed there until 1780, when he was relieved from active duty and moved to Long Island.

Life in Hardwick for young Bathsheba Ruggles would have been luxurious by the standards of the day. She probably attended school, learning to spell, read, and write the fine calligraphic hand she possessed as an adult. Insulated from the political ferment in Boston, her life very likely felt secure in its privilege up until October 1765, when her father left the Stamp Act Congress, resulting in public censure that began the free fall of his reputation and career.

Family life at home, however, probably was a battlefield in miniature long before then because of the bitter animosity between the Ruggles parents. It might have begun with Ruggles's lengthy absences during the French and Indian campaigns. His wife, Bathsheba, would have assumed the position of head of the household and perhaps was reluctant to give it up when he returned. Or it may be that she found her husband's native obstinacy (John Adams called it "an inflexible oddity [that] renders him a disagreeable companion in business")[20] increasingly difficult to live with. In any case, Brigadier and Mrs. Ruggles's fights became the stuff of Hardwick legend.

Bathsheba Newcomb Ruggles was described (in James Ruggles's memoir) as a "termagant scold" and "Xanthippe," who reputedly served up her husband's favorite dog to him in a pie. Given that Timothy Ruggles was a vegetarian, this incident is most likely apocryphal, typical of an era characterized by misogyny in religion, politics, and culture, and also typical of the exaggerated accusations leveled at both Ruggleses. One frequently reported incident, however, does have the heft and feel of real life. A shortened form of the story, taken from James Ruggles's family memoir, *The Offering*, contains this parable:

> While once the Brigadier was selling a cow to another man, his wife came out of the house and began to expostulate to him on the foolishness in selling so good an animal, so cheap. The Brigadier thundered forth, "If you mean to rule in the house and out of doors too, you must wear some breeches," and directing another person where to find a

pair of short-legged buckskin trousers told him to bring them at once. She, seeing the dreams of her ambition verified in a different way than what she had ever expected, began to tell him of his wickedness, and that "as for putting on breeches, she shouldn't." It was not his nature to order twice, and taking her into the house, he helped her exchange her apparel for the buck-skins in short notice, and then told her she was at liberty to get such a price for the cow as she saw fit.

James Ruggles concludes that if all hen-pecked husbands resorted to the same means the result would prove a blessing to themselves and make their homes a heaven and their wives angels. Being forced into her husband's pants did not have so favorable an impact on Bathsheba Ruggles, however. It appears that in effect she left him. When he rode out of Hardwick in 1774 for the last time, she did not accompany him, and when in 1782 he moved to his land in Wilmot, Nova Scotia (given to him along with an annual stipend by George III for his loyalty), she did not join him there.

The animosity in the Ruggles family came to a head when Timothy Ruggles left Hardwick in 1774. The larger war made the inner family war manifest, and the children were forced to choose sides. Ruggles took two sons (John and Richard) with him and left his wife and eldest son, Timothy, behind. Bathsheba Newcomb Ruggles would live with her son Timothy in Hardwick until her death at age eighty-three in 1787.

Young Bathsheba may have chosen between her father and mother early on, or else she had been chosen herself long before the war irrevocably divided the family. That she was her father's favorite may not have endeared her to her mother. There is reason to believe that mother and daughter were alienated in that nothing in the historical record shows that Bathsheba Newcomb Ruggles ever visited, or wrote, or had anything to do with her daughter during the time she was locked in Worcester's jail, though the mother lived less than twenty miles away.

On 16 January 1776, Ruggles's livestock, including thirty horses and thirty head of cattle, sheep, and swine were auctioned off. Timothy Ruggles Jr. and his mother were allowed to stay in his house until the final estate settlement in 1779. In 1777 Timothy Jr. petitioned the legislature not to include his own property ("a small estate in Hardwick which formerly belonged to Isaac Thomas") with his father's confiscated property. He later withdrew the petition before the legislature acted on it. Whether this property was separate from his father's four hundred–acre farm is unclear, but because Tim Jr. and his mother continued to live in Hardwick, they must have remained at this location, wherever it was.

A mysterious penciled notation among the Worcester probate records pertaining to Brig. Timothy Ruggles declares that record number 51497, a "Decree for an Allowance to Wife," 16 March 1778, is missing. Why this record is missing is a mystery in itself, but the greater mystery is the filing date, which was fifteen days after Joshua Spooner's murder, when the brigadier was behind British lines on Staten Island and unaware of his daughter's plight. Perhaps he had instructed a Worcester friend by letter to file the decree for him. In any case, the existence of such a decree suggests that even in 1778 (or, more likely sometime before that date) Ruggles acknowledged the separation from his wife to be permanent.

It is clear from the stories passed down about her that Bathsheba Newcomb Ruggles refused to defer. Whether because she was older than her husband, independent in spirit, or simply as stubborn as he was, she flouted the behavior prescribed for wives by law, church, and society and engaged in a Homeric battle of wills whose ultimate end could only be separation or murder. This lesson her daughter and namesake must have absorbed, unconsciously or otherwise.

As Peleg Chandler pointed out, Bathsheba Ruggles Spooner must have been fundamentally affected by her extraordinary and controversial family. If she wasn't exposed to a model of female decorum and deference in her mother, she also did not learn flexibility or restraint from her father, who acted on the strength of his convictions utterly heedless of consequences (as she would later act). More to the point, as her father's favorite, she would have emulated him consciously or simply have inherited his powerful personality with no acceptable way, as a woman in eighteenth-century Massachusetts, to exercise it.

Pondering the Ruggles family history fails to answer the most critical question of all, however: How did Bathsheba come to marry

Joshua Spooner, a man whom she quickly grew to loathe? Most twentieth-century conjecture around this point fixes the blame on Brig. Timothy Ruggles, accusing him (on the basis of no real evidence) of arranging the loveless match.[21] After all, Joshua Spooner was the son of a wealthy Boston merchant and owned at least a partial interest in several Middleborough mills; he would have been considered a good catch by a prospective father-in-law.[22] Ruggles, whose real estate holdings amounted to some £30,000 (by conservative estimate more than a million dollars today), had a great regard for property himself.

Writers more sympathetic to Ruggles have suggested that he may have arranged the match hurriedly to secure his daughter's future in the face of his own uncertain future and pending censure by the General Court for his refusal to sign the Stamp Act protest in late October 1765. (Bathsheba's marriage took place a little over two months later, on 15 January 1766.)

However, we can only speculate as to why Bathsheba married Joshua Spooner. Brig. Gen. Timothy Ruggles certainly appears to have been a calculating businessman with a forceful and perhaps overbearing personality who might well have influenced his daughter's choice. But it is also entirely possible that Bathsheba accepted Joshua of her own free will, perhaps for the second most common reason women marry in haste: to escape an embattled and unhappy family.

[4]

Irrevocably Joined in Marriage

I N THE eighteenth century, a married woman had few legal rights. According to William Blackstone's *Commentaries on the Laws of England* (1765), "By marriage, the husband and wife are one person in law; that is, the very being or legal existence of the woman is suspended during marriage, or at least is incorporated and consolidated into that of the husband; under whose wing, protection, and cover, she performs everything."[1]

Escape from an unhappy marriage was virtually impossible. The courts would grant a bill of divorcement only in cases where impotency, extreme physical cruelty, or adultery could be proven. To leave her husband without a legal divorce, Bathsheba Spooner would have had to abandon her children and the considerable goods and money she was likely to have brought to the marriage as dowry.

From Rev. Thaddeus Maccarty's "Account of the Behaviour of Mrs. Spooner" we know that Bathsheba's distaste for the marriage developed early on. "Domestic dissensions soon took place, and went on from step to step, till she conceived an utter aversion to him." That Bathsheba began to dislike Joshua so early gives some credence to the theory that the marriage was arranged rather than driven by romantic love or physical passion. Upper-class families, then as now, prefer to marry their own, and the Spooners were prominent members of Boston's wealthy merchant class. Perhaps equally important, from Timothy Ruggles's point of view, the Spooners were affiliated with prominent Loyalists. Two years after Joshua and Bathsheba's marriage, Joshua's eldest brother, John Spooner Jr., would be forced to leave Boston with his son Andrew and Loyalist wife Margaret Oliver Spooner after her father, Andrew Oliver (the crown-appointed stamp tax collector), had his house ransacked and was hanged in effigy by the Sons of Liberty.[2]

Joshua's father, John Spooner, was a wealthy Boston merchant trading in pitch, tar, silver, brass, pewter, fabric, and furs, among other commodities, according to a record book from the American Antiquarian Society archives.[3] John Spooner was born in 1696 in Yorkshire, England, and married Elizabeth Wells in 1727. They had six children, of whom John (born 1 September 1732), William (born 24 October 1734), and Joshua (born in 1741) survived to adulthood. Elizabeth Spooner died around 1744, and John Sr. then married Sarah Bridges in 1745. The Spooner patriarch had two more sons, George and James Spooner, before his death in 1763.[4] His widow, Sarah Bridges Spooner, went on to marry John Avery, Esq. in 1765, and this marriage would turn out to be fateful for Bathsheba in her efforts to secure a stay of execution.

According to the law of primogeniture, John Spooner Jr., as oldest surviving son and heir, received the lion's share of his father's estate: "all my real estate with the appurtenances thereto belonging." The bequest included all rents and profits, with the exception of the widow's right of dower to Sarah Bridges Spooner, which consisted of a £400 bequest and £120 annual stipend (reduced to £80 if she should remarry), a horse and chaise, Spooner's two black slaves, Prince and Venus, and £70 in linen, plate, and furniture.[5]

John Spooner Jr.'s inheritance made him a very wealthy man. That he led an aristocratic life is borne out by his portrait, painted by John Singleton Copley.[6] Spooner's carefully coiffed and powdered wig, fashionable gold-braided waistcoat, and pose are all indicative of a British gentleman of high social rank. John Spooner Jr. escaped the prerevolutionary violence in Boston, only to die within six months of his arrival in England "of a mortification of the Bowels," according to *John Boyles Journal of Occurrences*. His funeral, costing £59.10, was grand indeed.[7] His estate then fell to his oldest son, John Jones Spooner, who would later become the guardian of Bathsheba and Joshua Spooner's orphaned children.

John Spooner Sr.'s other sons, William, Joshua, George, and James received separate bequests of £4000 each. Though in no way comparable to John Spooner Jr.'s inheritance, it was still a healthy business stake, roughly equivalent to something like a quarter million dollars by today's standards.

Joshua Spooner was certainly well-to-do, well connected, and a gentleman (of the gentry) in the social order of the day. Whether Bathsheba married him at her father's behest, out of desperation to escape her family, out of infatuation abetted by her precipitous nature, or because his wealth was his chief attraction, we have no way of knowing for certain. On 8 January 1766, marriage banns were published, and on 15 January Bathsheba Ruggles and Joshua Spooner were married in Brookfield. They became members of the third precinct church, where the Reverend Nathan Fiske was pastor. Joshua appeared to be a prominent member of Brookfield society: at some point he acted as treasurer of Brookfield's third precinct and he also served as a selectman for Brookfield in 1772 and 1773.[8]

It is not clear where the Spooners lived for the first six years of their marriage; the twenty-acre lot on which their last house was built was purchased for £150 from John Rich, 25 November 1771.[9] According to tax records, the house was forty-two feet long and thirty feet deep, two-storied, with an attached shed or small room off the back. The architecture was very likely classic Georgian / New England farmhouse or saltbox style. We know from an inventory taken immediately after Joshua's murder that the first floor was divided into a kitchen, probably along the back of the house, an east parlor (sitting room), and a west parlor (for entertaining). Three chambers (bedrooms) made up the second floor.[10]

Before the Revolution, two-storied houses were a mark of affluence in rural Massachusetts. That the Spooners were considered wealthy by their neighbors is borne out in Joshua's burial sermon, delivered by the Reverend Nathan Fiske: "This awful catastrophe reads us a solemn lecture upon the insufficiency of wealth, or elegant accommodations, or of gaiety or gaudiness of dress, to make people secure in their persons, or contented or happy in their minds."[11] Fiske's pejorative "gaudiness of dress" probably applied to Joshua, with his silver shoe buckles, as much as to Bathsheba. According to Nathaniel Peaslee Sargeant's notes on the trial, even the Spooner daughters, Elizabeth and baby Bathshua, wore silver shoe buckles like their father's.

The Spooner house site may be seen today, located on the north side of Elm Hill Road about a mile off Route 9 in Brookfield. Near it is a red shale marker, set there in 1763 at the behest of Benjamin Franklin when he was postmaster general. The marker originally read "65 miles to Boston," though only the word "Boston" can be made out now. The house is long gone, believed to have burned down sometime in the late nineteenth century after years of abandonment.[12] The only remaining artifacts are the well, rubble from a central chimney, the indentation of a cellar hole, and four steps made of broad flat stones that lead directly from the road to the little rise where the house once stood near the road and facing south. A good-sized barn behind the Spooner house survived until sometime into the twentieth century. Only part of the foundation — two joined walls of stones flecked with gray-green lichen — remain now.

The well lies a few feet beyond the stone steps, its opening flush with the ground. Back when it provided fresh water for the Spooner household, one or two tiers of stones would have formed a curb around the opening. A stone slab caps it now, admitting just enough light to reveal a narrow interior lined with unmortared stones. It is difficult to imagine an adult body fitting in it; even by the physical standards of the eighteenth century, when men were shorter and more slender than they are today, Joshua Spooner must not have been a large man.

Bathsheba and Joshua Spooner had four children, three of whom survived. Elizabeth was born 8 April 1767; Joshua on 21 February 1770; John on 26 February 1773 (he died about a month later, either on 19 March or 17 April; and Bathshua on 17 January 1775. "Bathshua" was apparently a common diminutive for "Bathsheba"; Bathsheba herself signed "Bathshua" on her petitions to the council.

Any affection that Bathsheba might have felt for her husband apparently dissipated quickly. We can only speculate at what her "utter aversion" to Joshua was made of, but the record does offer some clues. Robert Treat Paine's minutes of the trial supply some information characterizing Spooner as an abusive drunkard. A trial witness, Sally Bragg, whose testimony appears in his notes, said that "a fortnight before then Jesse Parker was saying how bad a man Mr. Spooner was, bad to his Wife. Had just got him[self] drunk. . . . Mr. Spooner will not get drunk many times more. . . ."

That Joshua was a bad drunk is reason enough for his wife to have found him odious, but other unpleasant qualities as well may be gleaned from the record. This characterization of Joshua was reported in a 5 May *Massachusetts Spy* account (believed to have been written by James Sullivan, an associate judge for the trial): "His only fault appears to be not supporting a manly importance as head of his family, and not regulating the government of it." This information would logically have come from Bathsheba, possibly when the prisoners were questioned by the judges before the trial. In Sargeant's notes Ephraim Cooley testified: "I heard his son call his father Old Bogus," indicating that Joshua was unable to command the respect of his children or his wife.

The *Spy*'s allegation of unmanliness is supported by two accounts of Joshua's cowardly behavior with the two British soldiers who were taking advantage of his hospitality. In Alexander Cummings's testimony from Foster's trial notes, Cummings says that "he sat up with Spooner at his request, who said he did not love to have Brooks in the house[,] he did [not] like the looks of the man. He [Spooner] desired his wife to get [the British soldiers] off. He said if she did not he would send for the committee next morning." It is clear that Joshua was intimidated by the soldiers and unwilling to confront them.

Other witnesses attest to Joshua's fearfulness that night. In the confession written by Buchanan, Brooks, and Ross entitled "The Dying Declaration" (included here in appendix A), James Buchanan wrote that on the night Joshua returned from Princeton, he discovered how much Buchanan and Brooks had drunk at the local taverns at his expense and asked them to leave immediately. The soldiers talked him into letting them stay by the fire until morning, but it is clear that Joshua did so reluctantly. Joshua stayed in the sitting room and was joined by Reuben Old (or Olds), a neighbor who had apparently come to see Joshua on business. According to Buchanan, Old visited back and forth between the sitting room and kitchen (where the soldiers were making merry by the kitchen fire, presumably drinking Spooner's rum). Old reported to Buchanan that Spooner was afraid the soldiers meant to rob him and that he believed they had already taken a silver spoon and a great deal of pewter. But Cummings then convinced Joshua that none of the pewter was missing, and Joshua himself found the spoon where he had hidden it. "Mr. Spooner went up stairs and brought down a box, which he had his money in, and laid down on the floor with it under his head," Buchanan wrote. "Every thing Mr. Spooner did or said, Old came and told us."

These comments reveal clearly and dramatically how fearful and panicky Joshua was, feelings that were, as it would turn out, entirely justified. Even more revealing is the fact that Reuben Old, who was Joshua's friend, joined the soldiers in the kitchen making fun of him. Joshua appeared to be the very opposite of manly in the eyes of the British soldiers and Reuben Old, and doubtless in Bathsheba's eyes as well.

It is a pity that no portrait of Joshua Spooner (or of Bathsheba) is known to exist, but Copley's portrait of Joshua's brother, John Spooner Jr., reveals a rather weak, soft, pompous-appearing man. It is reasonable to assume that the brothers favored each other in character as well as appearance; altogether, Joshua would have embodied a most unappealing contrast to Bathsheba's father, according to whom she most likely patterned her standard of manhood.

Finally, one secondary source has suggested that Joshua Spooner may have been an adulterer as well as an unmanly drunk. An anonymous entry in a nineteenth century history of Worcester County mentions a rumor — said to have originated with Bathsheba's family — that Joshua had a mistress who was a servant living in the house: "The argument of her counsel not obscurely intimates that this woman — perhaps more than one — was a servant in the kitchen." Defense lawyer Levi Lincoln's trial notes (included here in appendix E) do not record any such argument on his part, but a page or more appears to be missing from the end of the original manuscript. It is very possible that the nineteenth-century historian had Lincoln's complete notes or some other reliable source for this remarkably specific allegation of unfaithfulness.[13]

A primary source recently come to light, Nathaniel Peaslee Sargeant's trial notes, appears to add substance to this rumor. Sargeant's case notes are far more detailed than Foster's or Paine's, and he is the only trial official we know of who recorded the following exchange between Dr. Jonathan King and Spooner while they were drinking together at Cooley's tavern: "I told him I feared his negro woman would hurt him — he said he did not fear her." This enigmatic remark could very well allude to a servant who apparently had some sort of intimate relationship with Joshua—for what other reason would she want to hurt him? And if the rumor was indeed true, the insult and humiliation to Bathsheba would have been immense and ample justification for her loathing.

Dr. King's remark provides admittedly inconclusive evidence of adultery, but other indirect references suggest Joshua was guilty of something. In his execution sermon, Reverend Maccarty said, "In vain must it be to plead one crime in excuse for another. . . . What must be the case of a wicked man, who is suddenly deprived of life by the hand of violence? . . . All opportunity for [repentance] wholly ceases . . . [and] the immortal soul is in a sense destroyed, as well as the body." Rev. Nathan Fiske in his burial sermon also made a similar reference: "And if the victim that is at any time slain by murderers, is under the guilt of unrepented and unpardoned sin, this indeed is an awful thought!" It seems that the community was aware of some wrongdoing of Joshua's—whether it was his drunkenness, his adultery, or something else we will perhaps never know for certain.

All this is speculation, of course. Yet even if we grant it to be true, or a credible approximation of the truth, hatred and revulsion do not necessarily result in murder. Millions of women have endured marriages to men whom they abhor, without conniving to murder them. Possibly Bathsheba would have lived long to suffer and endure her unhappy marriage, too, if Ezra Ross had not appeared in her life and altered its course irredeemably.

[5]

Seduced from Virtue and Prudence

BATHSHEBA SPOONER'S initial feelings for Ezra Ross were apparently warm. According to the Rosses' petition, she had shown him "every kind office and mark of tenderness" while nursing him back to health, but it is likely that when he left her house in the spring of 1777 she never expected to see him again. And they might never have reunited, if he had not reenlisted after the American army was forced to evacuate Fort Ticonderoga the following July. That Ross stopped to visit Bathsheba in August on his way north to report for duty in New York suggests that her warm feelings were reciprocated and that he had thought about her during those intervening four months.

She appeared very glad to see him, "add[ing] to the number of her kindnesses and engag[ing] a visit on his return." This second encounter, occurring at the height of summer, was fateful. Probably their mutual attraction proved irresistible by the end of the visit.

Ross went on from the Spooners to serve his second enlistment, which lasted about four months.[1] Warfare in the North proved even more dangerous and grisly than the terrible defeats Ross had survived in New York and New Jersey during the previous year's campaign. Burgoyne had allied himself with several Indian tribes, and it was believed he was paying his Indian confederates for American scalps.[2] In fact, he had given his Indian allies permission to take the scalps of the dead, and he proved unable (or unwilling) to restrain their numerous atrocities committed against the living. One of the more notorious examples was the scalping of Jane McCrae, a young Loyalist engaged to an American officer in Burgoyne's Loyalist Auxiliary Corps. Burgoyne pardoned the Indians responsible lest they defect from his ranks.

Burgoyne's troops had successfully run American forces out of Fort Ticonderoga, continuing to inflict a series of defeats as they forced the patriots southward to Fort Schuyler (Stanwix), some one hundred miles north of Albany. However, the tide began to turn when American Brig. Gen. John Stark defeated a Hessian supply raid at Bennington, Vermont, on 16 August. From Bennington onward the Americans halted the British advance, winning two significant victories at Freeman's Farm in mid-September.

Ezra Ross's company (under Col. Samuel Johnson's regiment) was attached to the army led by Maj. Gen. Benjamin Lincoln, whose strategy was to harass the posts at Burgoyne's flank and rear in order to divide and weaken the British army that was already suffering from a lack of supplies and reinforcements. Ross took part in the attack on Mount Independence in aid of the devastating Fort Ticonderoga raid on 18 September, and afterward joined with the combined American forces to overwhelm the British at Saratoga. On 17 October Burgoyne surrendered his army of some six thousand soldiers to the American general, Horatio Gates.

The infant American nation was beside itself with joy over this dramatic triumph. It marked the most significant achievement in the country's crusade for political autonomy since the Declaration of Independence a year earlier, in that Burgoyne's defeat persuaded France to recognize America as an independent nation and grant it military aid.

The *Massachusetts Spy* announced two Thanksgivings for the year 1777. The first was the traditional holiday proclaimed by the State of Massachusetts Bay to be held on Thursday, 20 November in thanksgiving for the blessings of nature's abundance and most especially for the Saratoga victory, "against the arbitrary claims and military violence of Britain; and especially in a late instance of divine interposition, in which the arm of the LORD of hosts, and GOD of armies, very conspicuously appears, hath given us a compleat victory, over a whole army of our enemies." On 27 November, however, the Continental Congress proclaimed another Thursday, 18 December, "as a day of public thanksgiving, throughout the United American States."[3]

The problem of conflicting Thanksgiving dates was one of the more trivial clashes arising at that time between the authority of the state and the new Continental Congress; Massachusetts citizens apparently solved the problem by celebrating both Thanksgivings. According to the trial testimony of Sarah Stratton (a servant who occasionally lived at the Spooner house), Ezra Ross returned from his northern enlistment to the Spooner household "in the fall of the year between the two thanksgivings."[4]

Ross apparently stayed on with the Spooners, occasionally making short business trips with Joshua, until sometime in late January or early February. A number of sources indicate that Bathsheba and Ezra became lovers soon after his return from the war.

Most writers who have taken up the Spooner story have assumed that Ezra Ross was the father of Bathsheba's unborn child. Though the assumption is supported by circumstantial evidence as well as a kind of universal romantic yearning that love — and perhaps especially a risky, illicit love — be true, we can't be absolutely certain who the father of Bathsheba's baby was. Bathsheba's only comment on the baby's paternity was that it "was lawfully begotten," which she was likely to have represented to the council no matter who the father was in order to save its life. However, she implicated Ezra as the father when she told constable Elisha Hamilton, "it [the murder] happened by means of Ross's being sick at our house."[5]

Other circumstantial evidence points to Ezra Ross as the most likely candidate as well. We know that he was intimate with Bathsheba by his own confession, recorded by the Rev. Ebenezer Parkman, the minister at Westborough (some ten miles west of Worcester). At the time of the Spooner murder trial and execution, Parkman, a conservative theologian and follower of Jonathan Edwards, was in his mid-seventies. He nonetheless took an intense interest in the murder case, riding in from Westborough on horseback to visit Bathsheba and the male prisoners in Worcester's jail.

Ebenezer Parkman's interest in the prisoners seems to have been prompted by the sensationalistic nature of the case as much as his concern for the state of their souls. Fortunately for us (and for American historical scholarship in general) he kept a life-long, meticulously detailed diary in which he transcribed a confession solicited from Ross, complete with his comments on Ezra's manner of speech and spelling:[6]

The following is the first of [Bathsheba's] promoting her husband's Death. As she was going to Hardwick she asked me the reason of my being so low spirited? I made answer It was my long absence from home. She replied that her opinion was I wanted someone to lodge with. I told her it would be agreeable. She asked me if such a One as herself would do? I made answer If she was agreeable, I was. (The Dialect was so.) Upon which she said after she came off her journey she would see.

NB. After her return she gave me an invitation to Defile her Marriage Bed; which I Excepted (The spelling is so). And after that she proposed constantly every sheam [scheme] for her husband's death. Ezra Ross.

Even though this confession is filtered through Parkman's exceedingly Calvinistic point of view, there is little doubt about its authenticity since it so credibly reflects the artless sensibility of a seventeen-year-old boy. Ezra's ingenuousness is affecting to this day, and in his own day he won the sympathy of Ebenezer Parkman, who scathingly denounced Bathsheba as the agent of Ross's destruction in a post-execution sermon delivered 5 July entitled "The Adultress Shall Hunt for the Precious Life":

a woman who . . . violates the solemnities, cools in her Esteem & regard for her Husband . . . not only hates him, but allows her loose imagination to range and wander after Others, nay not a few, & rove from him to pollute & defile the marriage bed [indulging] her own wanton salacious desires. . . . How loathsome are all such, and how directly opposite the pure & holy Nature, Law, and Will of God.

So keep thee from the Evil woman, from the flattery of the tongue of a strange woman. Neither let her take thee with her eyelids. There are a thousand dangers, that poor young wretches are in by reason of the snares & traps which are everywhere laid . . . particularly the poor beardless youth not quite 18.

Parkman was not the only observer convinced that Bathsheba and Ezra were lovers; calmer heads came to the same conclusion. In his notes outlining his trial arguments, Levi Lincoln based his defense of Bathsheba on insanity. As part of that plea, he argued that "with her address, and engaging appearance she might have had any gallant she pleased, not [such] as Ross." And according to the *Massachusetts Spy*,

> She became acquainted with Ross, to whom she made some amorous overtures, and told him that if he would kill her husband, she would become his lawful wife: It appears, by the examination of Ross, before the Justices, that his conscience at first started at the appearance of so much guilt; but upon her persuasions and the fancied happiness of marrying a woman so much above his rank in life, and the allurements of wallowing in Mr. Spooner's wealth he fatally consented.[7]

Some sources suggest that Ezra Ross wasn't Bathsheba's only sexual conquest, though given the sensationalistic nature of the murder, it is very difficult to distinguish reliable knowledge of the situation from prejudice, hearsay, and malicious gossip. Ebenezer Parkman's suggestion that Bathsheba had wandered from her husband toward other lovers, "nay not a few," makes clear his opinion on the matter. But is it a trustworthy opinion? His diary as a whole is a detailed, factual, and literal record of his life and times; based on context, the small portion dealing with the Spooner murder is likely to be reliable as the truth he knew and experienced. As an orthodox theologian, however, he was predisposed to judge Bathsheba harshly, and he did. He was not the humanitarian Thaddeus Maccarty was, whose intelligent, graceful, and sympathetic discourse on essentially the same Calvinistic tenets of faith contrast sharply with Parkman's hellfire-and-brimstone judgments.

We have no way of assessing, however, what the "nay not a few" in his post-execution sermon was based on. It may have reflected Parkman's own knowledge gained from his solicitation of confessions from the male prisoners, or it may simply have reflected his prejudice (and that of his age) against women who defied the rules of sexual conduct prescribed to them.

The possibility of other affairs is implied in other sources as well, which will be explored more fully in the next chapter. But these "infamous prostitutions" (as the *Spy* put it), whether real or collectively imagined, would have taken place only after Bathsheba realized she was pregnant. The timing of the baby's conception, with its discovery and Bathsheba's immediate frenzied reaction, most strongly supports Ezra Ross's paternity.

At the autopsy performed 2 July, "a perfect male fetus of the growth of five months, or near it" was taken from her.[8] The fetus's age is also supported by Bathsheba's statement in her petition to the council, dated 16 June, that she was above four months advanced in a pregnant state. Therefore, the infant would have been conceived somewhere toward the end of January. Allowing for a week to ten days after conception for her to notice the telltale food aversions and swelling of breasts (undeniable symptoms for those experienced in pregnancy), at the very end of January or around the first of February she realized she was pregnant and panicked.

According to this scenario, if Bathsheba and Ezra conceived the child sometime between 20 and 25 January, it would have taken possibly another ten days for her to detect the early signs of pregnancy. No hard evidence has yet appeared to prove it was the pregnancy that set off her deranged murder plotting, but it is the most likely cause of her bizarre behavior and frantic desire for her husband's death.

On the face of it, such a radical leap from pregnancy to murder appears entirely illogical, crazy. But it does have a certain emotional logic for someone who perceives that her back is to the wall and her survival is at stake. In 1777 the punishment for a convicted adulteress in Massachusetts was a public whipping of up to thirty lashes while the subject was stripped naked to the waist. Bathsheba very likely had not been sleeping with Joshua, given her professed aversion to him. Consequently, it was reasonable for her to fear that he would prosecute her as an adulteress out of revenge (he was even known to be "bad to his wife"), in order to subject her to the public humiliation and extreme pain of a flogging.

Also, a public whipping was not the only possible consequence. The rabid anti-Tory sentiment prevalent throughout Massachusetts made the brutal tar-and-feathering of Loyalists commonplace. In 1777, Baroness von Riedesel noted in her diary that the wife and fifteen-year-old daughter of a Captain Fenton, a Boston Loyalist, were both stripped naked, tarred and feathered, and paraded through the city.[9] And much closer to home, the minister of Brookfield's second parish, Eli Forbes, had his chaise stoned and was driven from town for his Loyalist sympathies.

Given these examples, as well as that of her own father under threat of death from the patriot mobs, Bathsheba surely would have understood that as a convicted adulteress her life as well as her dignity might be imperiled. For someone with her pride and spirit, however, the humiliation of being beaten half-naked before her jeering neighbors might have seemed a punishment worse than death.

By late January she had possibly three months before her pregnancy would become apparent, with no real alternatives for escaping Joshua available to her. Divorces were a rarity in the eighteenth century and rarer yet when initiated by the wife. Bathsheba had no apparent grounds except, possibly, her husband's adulterous relationship with a servant. In any case, her pregnancy would be revealed before any such action could be taken.

Abortion at that time was both legally and morally acceptable because a fetus wasn't considered alive until "quickening," usually in the fourth month. There were a number of procedures to release "obstructed menses," including blood letting, hot baths, douches, and commonly found purgatives such as juniper berry extract or calomel.[10] However, these methods were not any more reliable than abortion was in the present century before modern surgical techniques were developed.

The possibility of leaving her husband and joining her father was presented during the trial by defense attorney Levi Lincoln, which he cited to illustrate Bathsheba's deranged thinking. More than one witness at the trial testified that Bathsheba had considered leaving Joshua. According to Justice Sargeant's notes, Susanna (or Susannah) Wilson, a neighbor, heard Bathsheba say two months before the murder, "she was mad & had a good mind to go-off." Bathsheba had apparently considered leaving Joshua seriously enough to discuss moving arrangements with another neighbor. In Sargeant's notes Reuben Old(s) testified that "Mrs. Spooner said, [sometime that winter,] I will go thro my Plan now. I thou't she meant to go to her father for she asked me sometime before to carry away some things for her."

Though going off to live with her father was probably Bathsheba's most fervent fantasy, it was not really a practical choice and may well have been logistically impossible. Without a legal divorce, fleeing to her father would have meant abandoning her children and her home and braving New England winter weather to travel some two hundred miles on horseback and cross enemy lines to join him — and doing so at a time when Brigadier Ruggles himself had very little left in the way of property or wealth to support her. And as for her family in Hardwick, her brother Timothy and mother were facing eviction from the family homestead.

In late 1777 and early 1778, just before the murder took place, Ruggles was with the British on Staten Island in charge of four hundred Loyalist refugees. He had been trying and failing repeatedly to gain British backing for a Loyalist cavalry corps. Having had all of his considerable wealth and holdings in Massachusetts confiscated because of his loyalty to the crown, he was at that time subject to the condescending authority of the British general Sir Henry Clinton, a vain, petulant man who apparently viewed him as a nuisance.[11]

Bathsheba was inescapably bound by marriage to a man she hated, and soon to have another man's child. Very soon her adultery would become obvious, incurring painfully humiliating and possibly mortal consequences. Murder, then, might have seemed the only possible and logical solution to a person in the grip of panic and whose character (like her father's and mother's before her) was absolutely incapable of submitting.

That her behavior became suddenly irrational is well documented.[12] First, she tried to convince Ezra Ross to poison Joshua, but Ross appeared reluctant. He did slip some aqua fortis into Joshua's grog on the night before their Princeton trip, causing Joshua to spit it out and say that "if he had enemies in the house he should think they intended to poison him."[13] Aqua fortis, or nitric acid, was in itself an illogical choice of poison because its extremely bitter taste would make any tainted potion undrinkable. Arsenic, which was commonly available as a pesticide, would have been the rational choice for a calculating murderer.

According to Alexander Cummings, Ross brought a full bottle of aqua fortis with him on the Princeton trip with Joshua but would later explain to Bathsheba that he had no opportunity to use it. Levi Lincoln's defense of Ross, that "his neglecting various opportunities [to murder Joshua] . . . showed that he had no real design to do it, but only wished to keep up the appearance of an intention" seems astute.

Because of Bathsheba's frantic sense of urgency, it is reasonable to assume that Ross's one poisoning effort occurred very shortly after her discovery of pregnancy. Parkman's diary relates that Bathsheba also urged Ezra to poison a Brookfield neighbor, Jabez Crosby. Crosby had lost two sons in the war and had accrued fifteen months of military service, himself.[14] He may very well have been an outspoken patriot, but what he did to excite Bathsheba's hatred will probably never be known. However, if Parkman (and Ezra) are to be trusted, her intention to murder a neighbor as well as her husband further attests to her deranged thinking at that time.

The day after the attempted poisoning in early February, Ezra Ross left Brookfield with Joshua for an extended business trip to the potash farm in Princeton.[15] Joshua, it seems, had no idea of Ross's liaison with his wife. This obliviousness, along with his response to the poison in his drink suggests that he was unusually obtuse, or perhaps he was blinded by his own affection for Ross. Ezra Ross, for his part, was probably greatly relieved to leave the Spooner household and his mistress who was suddenly bent on turning him into a cold-blooded murderer. In fact, Ezra didn't return to the Spooner house, but left on a horse borrowed from Joshua to see his father at home in Linebrook.[16] He would not reappear in Brookfield again for nearly a month, until the night before the murder.

Though Ezra brought the bottle of nitric acid with him on the trip to Princeton, Bathsheba clearly doubted that he would accomplish the job. Eager to enlist more reliable perpetrators, she asked her servant Alexander Cummings to call in British troops passing by on the road. In Sgt. James Buchanan and Pvt. William Brooks, she would find what she was looking for.

[6]

Burgoin People

BRITISH SOLDIERS wandering about the Massachusetts countryside were commonplace at the beginning of 1778. In the fall of 1777, after Lt. Gen. John Burgoyne's 17 October defeat at Saratoga, Massachusetts was overburdened with the upkeep of nearly six thousand British troops.[1] Burgoyne's entire army was marched to Boston, originally to await transportation back to England. But the Continental Congress objected to the overly generous terms of the articles of surrender (called the "Convention") worked out between Generals Gates and Burgoyne, and General Washington also feared that the repatriated British troops would enable fresh troops to be dispatched back to the war in America. Consequently, most of the British "prisoners of the Convention" were stranded in America until the war's end.

Burgoyne and his officers (as well as Gen. Adolf von Riedesel, commander of the German Brunswick army, his wife, the baroness, and their three young daughters) wintered in Cambridge, attending dinners and entertainments and hobnobbing with Boston's upper crust, prompting the *Massachusetts Spy* of 22 January 1778 to complain,

> In a late London paper was a paragraph informing the world, that a number of feather beds, bottles of Lethe, spirits of hartshorn, and lavender &c. was preparing to be sent to the British troops serving in America. . . . It is shrewdly suspected that Burgoyne's troops have . . . procured and taken large draughts of Lethe, for the commanders have taken to *dancing*, and the privates to robbing and deserting, the former forgetting their men, and the latter their officers; and the whole forgetting they are prisoners.

While their officers were handsomely entertained in Boston and Cambridge, some five thousand British regulars were put up in internment camps on Winter Hill and Prospect Hill in Charlestown and in other Massachusetts locations. Nearly six thousand prisoners of war were a severe strain on Massachusetts's resources and supplies, already stretched thin by three years of British blockade and two years of war. Consequently, the camps were poorly appointed, overcrowded breeding grounds for small pox, dysentery, and other pestilence.

Sgt. Roger Lamb of the British Ninth Regiment of Foot, who was a prisoner of war quartered at the Prospect Hill camp and then later on in Rutland (ten miles northeast of Worcester), described vividly the impoverished camp conditions: "It was not infrequent for thirty or forty persons, men, women, and children, to be indiscriminately crowded together in one small, miserable, open hut, their provisions and firewood on short allowance; and a scanty portion of straw their bed, their own blankets their only covering. In the night time, those that could lie down, and the many who sat up from the cold, were obliged frequently to rise and shake from them the snow which the wind drifted in at the openings. . . ."[2]

Even if the immediate threat of British attack was over in Massachusetts, (the British army having evacuated Boston in 1776), the prisoners-of-war camps were a continual threat to domestic security and peace of mind. In vast numbers, British soldiers escaped from them to pilfer food and clothing throughout the Massachusetts countryside, and more than a few were locked up in town jails for exhibiting gross misbehavior at local taverns and for highway robbery.

Sgt. James Buchanan was a Burgoyne prisoner of war who, as traditional accounts have had it, escaped from the prison camp at Rutland before meeting up with Bathsheba. Sergeant Lamb apparently had been kept in the same prison camp as Buchanan, and he recorded the Spooner story in his *Memoir of His Own Life*, printed in Dublin in 1811. In his *Memoir*, Lamb says that Buchanan and he were at Rutland when Buchanan escaped, although in his earlier book *An Original and Authentic Journal of Occurrences during the Late American War* (originally published in 1809), Lamb states, "In the summer of 1778, the captured army was ordered to remove from Prospect-hill [in Charlestown] to Rutland County." The Rutland barracks were apparently still under construction at the time of the murder, 1 March. According to a 4 December 1777 issue of the *Massachusetts Spy* advertising for "industrious and enterprising" carpenters and masons, at that time only one of three barracks had been built.[3] A 9 April 1778 *Spy* report stated, "We hear that a number of Burgoyn's troops are on their way to the Barracks in Rutland," suggesting that British soldiers probably were not kept there until after the murder, and that Lamb confused the location in his memoir. Also, the indictment and death warrant both listed Buchanan's and Brooks's residence as "Charlestown."

At any rate, according to Lamb's memoir, Buchanan did not exactly desert from the internment camp but left under less-than-honorable circumstances:

> A sergeant Buchanan received cash from his officer, to provide shoes for the company, but unfortunately squandered it. Apprehensive of punishment, he went away privately, to a place about 40 miles from Boston, and worked at his trade to provide as much as he lavished, in order to make good his account. Having saved much, he was returning to his regiment, and by accident met with a soldier, who informed him that a sergeant was appointed in his place, it being concluded that he deserted. Being so advised he resolved to escape to Montreal (where he left behind him his wife and child) in the hope of obtaining pardon by means of Sir General Guy Carleton then Governor of Canada. On his route to Canada he passed through Brookfield, and there, unhappily for the parties, was noticed by a Mrs. Spooner, daughter of General Ruggles, who held a command in the former provincial war.[4]

In James Buchanan's own words, however, he was in the company of William Brooks, another Burgoyne deserter, when they left Worcester on 8 February, intending to go to Springfield to find work. Very little is known about Brooks other than an incident recorded by Sergeant Lamb in *Occurrences*. Lamb relates that he and Brooks sailed on the same troop ship from Ireland to Quebec, and the ship had to put about mid-crossing because Brooks had leapt overboard in fear of punishment for stealing a shirt from one of his mess mates. The incident reveals Brooks's poor character as well as a certain lack of intelligence in seeking escape by jumping into the middle of the Atlantic Ocean.

Sgt. James Buchanan's recapitulation of events is recorded in the male prisoners' confession, "The Dying Declaration of James Buchanan, Ezra Ross, and William Brooks, Who were executed at Worcester, July 2, 1778, for the murder of Mr. Joshua Spooner." It was written from Buchanan's point of view and signed by all three (by Brooks with an X, "his mark"). This account was not the legal confession made before William Young when the men were first apprehended and examined, but a document written at the behest of Isaiah Thomas, publisher of the *Massachusetts Spy,* who intended to sell it on the day of the hanging. In a notice published in a 11 June issue of the *Spy,* Thomas announced: "The poor unhappy men under sentence of death in this town; deeply impressed with a sense of their guilt, have delivered a true and circumstantial account of the proceedings in that horrid murder for which they are to suffer, to the Printer hereof." And, Thomas might have added, for which he himself was to gain. The "Dying Declaration" would sell for two shillings and a poem on the subject for one shilling.

"Last speeches," though they originated as religious documents in the English literary tradition, became increasingly secular in tone and were undoubtedly read for entertainment more than religious edification by the crowds attending eighteenth-century executions in both England and America. Whatever the motives of those selling and buying this particular "Dying Declaration," however, there seems no reason to doubt the earnestness and veracity of the three prisoners' confessions. A week after their first examination before the constable, Ross and Brooks were so concerned with their confessions' truthfulness that they amended them to correct earlier lies and mistakes.[5] Because their only hope of eternal life depended upon a true confession of guilt, "The Dying Declaration" is in all likelihood as factually accurate and truthful as the three men could make it and a highly reliable documentation of events.[6]

According to Buchanan, he and William Brooks passed the Spooner house and were called in by a servant named Alexander Cummings (himself a young Scottish soldier who had been one of Burgoyne's troops and had known Buchanan in Canada).[7] Cummings invited the two British soldiers to warm themselves by the Spooner kitchen fire and told them his master was away on business, but his mistress had a great regard for the British army and would be very glad to meet them.

Bathsheba was indeed glad to see them. She greeted them with a flattering, How do you do, Gentlemen? and proceeded to entertain them lavishly.[8] Such hospitality and luxury: a warm fire, good rum, and dinner prepared for them and served in the sitting room where the best company ate, accompanied by a beautiful woman of wealth and position. It was not at all the treatment that British enlisted men were accustomed to in patriotic Massachusetts. "[We] were never in better quarters, little thinking of the bait the seducer of souls was laying for us," Sergeant Buchanan later confessed.

According to "The Dying Declaration," because the weather was very bad, Bathsheba invited Buchanan and Brooks to stay in the house with her until it should clear. Within the first or second day, Bathsheba confided to Buchanan that she and her husband did not agree, and that Joshua was away on a journey to Princeton and she didn't expect him home soon. As it snowed heavily and the soldiers stayed on from day to day, Bathsheba's and Buchanan's conversations grew increasingly personal. She confided that a Mr. Ross accompanied her husband and intended to poison him, and she asked Buchanan to stay until they saw whether Joshua returned or not. Alexander Cummings said he overheard her say to Buchanan, "they could enjoy one another" if her husband were out of the way.[9]

Fine food, all the drink he could want, and the delectable prospect of sex with the beautiful and charming mistress of the house: it was a difficult situation to resist, especially for a man who had shown himself susceptible to temptation.

Joshua returned home without Ross about a week after the British soldiers arrived, and Bathsheba, having sent Ezra off with a bottle of nitric acid, expressed her great surprise.[10] The servant Jesse Parker's assertion (from Foster's notes), "When Mr. Spooner came from Princeton Mrs. Spooner said she never was so stumped in her life," jumps out amid the mass of detailed and often repetitious testimony that has survived from the Spooner murder trial. The idiomatic "stumped" lends authenticity; doubtless Bathsheba really made this callous remark. Also there can be little doubt that the trial judges, jury, and spectators viewed it as evidence of her black and detestable character, as her neighbor Dwight Foster described her in a letter detailing the Spooner murder.[11]

When one considers the context, however, her "stumped" remark reveals a more complicated mind set than blatant insensitivity alone. Obviously the statement is a lie, because if she truly never expected to see Joshua again she would not have solicited the services of Buchanan and Brooks. The exaggeration and callous bravado inherent in exclaiming "[I] was never so stumped in my life" bespeaks a pose that is evocative of the darkly ironic humor of soldiers, for example, distancing themselves from the horrors of battle.

Assuming Bathsheba's point of view at that time can perhaps illuminate the complex quality of mind that produced the remark. Only fifteen days earlier she had discovered she was pregnant, and her fear of exposure and punishment convinced her that her husband's death was an urgent necessity. Incapable of murdering him herself, she talked Ezra into a failed attempt to poison Joshua. Though Ezra took the poison with him when he accompanied Joshua to Princeton, she doubted the outcome sufficiently to line up two passers-by to do the job if Ezra failed. Even Buchanan (in "The Dying Declaration") commented on her recklessness: "The reader must needs think this is a very strange circumstance, that she should make such a discovery to an entire stranger."

But it is very likely that in her emotionally-charged, desperate state, Bathsheba didn't think of Buchanan as a stranger at all. He was a soldier and officer of the Crown—very like her father whom she missed ardently. She was predisposed to seek help and strike up an instant intimacy with a man whose politics, rank, and habit of command seemed most familiar and dear to her. Thus her callous bravado was probably a pose unconsciously struck for Buchanan's benefit, perhaps mirroring his as well as her father's sardonic, soldierly style of wit—which she had made her own style too. Exclaiming that she was "stumped" to see her husband return alive also served to make light of a deadly serious matter by turning it into a kind of joke.

That such a posture signified a reprehensible lack of human sympathy rather than humor clearly did not register with her, which shows just how out of touch she was with the reality of the murder she was actively plotting. Also, Buchanan's apparent encouragement of the plan gave it credibility so that it would ultimately develop a life and momentum of its own.

Soon after he arrived home from Princeton Joshua learned from his neighbors the extent of the soldiers' tavern bills and spent an anxious night guarding his money box in the sitting room, accompanied by Reuben Old. The next day Spooner gave Cummings five dollars with which to treat Buchanan (whom Bathsheba had represented as Cummings's cousin), perhaps hoping a little pay-off would persuade the soldiers to go peacefully.

Brooks and Buchanan did not go far. They spent the day at Mrs. Stratton's house several miles away in Western (now Warren, Massachusetts). From there they went to Cooley's tavern, at only a quarter-mile distance from the Spooner house, and then to Dr. Foxcroft's across the road.[12] When Cummings came to tell them that Joshua had gone to bed, they returned to the house for supper and liquor and retired to the barn for the night.

The next day (Tuesday, 17 February), Buchanan and Brooks went to visit Mrs. Berry and Mrs. Tufts, who apparently wanted to hire them to do some work. Mrs. Tufts was Bathsheba's oldest sister, Martha, who lived with her family on a farm three miles southwest of the Spooner house on the Old Brimfield Road near the Quaboag River.[13] Bathsheba accompanied Buchanan and Brooks and "[they] all stayed at Mr. Green's, drinking until late." Whether "Mr. Green's" was a local Brookfield public house or the house of Bathsheba's brother-in-law John Green in Worcester is unclear. Since the trip to Worcester would have taken four hours by horseback and five by walking, the Brookfield location seems most likely.

In "The Dying Declaration," Buchanan included an account of the following incident, which took place as Bathsheba, Buchanan, and Brooks set out for home that night: "Some distance from thence, she said she had given a handkerchief to a British soldier that had some words in anger with me, Buchanan, upon which Brooks went back on the horse, and she and I went home. Brooks missed his road on his return, but got to the house sometime after us; but he did not get the handkerchief, as the soldier would not deliver it, until he saw Mrs.

Spooner." This passage strongly implies that Bathsheba had been flirting with another British soldier at the tavern, incurring Buchanan's
anger, which was most likely prompted by jealousy. She seems to have
abandoned all sense of propriety or caution in that she was drinking
publicly and flirting with enemy soldiers.

From the letter written by Dwight Foster (Judge Jedediah Foster's
son) to a J. Clarke soon after the murder, we know that she was being
talked about by her Brookfield neighbors: "You are already acquainted with the character of Mrs. Spooner which has long labored
under aspersions highly to her disadvantage. . . ."[14]

As well as appearing to have a reckless disregard for propriety, Bathsheba seems also to have lost her wits in risking the ire of Sergeant
Buchanan, her best hope of achieving her murderous ends. Or perhaps her flirtation was an effort to seduce another back-up murderer
or to spark Buchanan to action. This other British soldier, unnamed
in Buchanan's account, might have been Samuel Woods who may also
have been privy to Bathsheba's murder plans. The following letter
discussing Samuel Woods was written on 5 March 1778, four days after
the murder, by the Committee of Correspondence for Worcester to
the Massachusetts Council:

> The Committee and many others have for some time dreaded
> the Consequence of such numbers of Burgoin people pass-
> ing through the country being fearfull some unhappy con-
> sequences would result from it — the late unhappy murder
> of Mr. Spooner has shewn their fears were not ground-
> less. . . .
>
> A Sergeant named Sam' Woods who kept at the same house
> [Walker's] with these murderers . . . as by his own confession
> & the declaration of the people of the house he was as inti-
> mate with Mrs. Spooner who was at this house the most of
> Frayday & part of Saturday before the murder . . . , the Jus-
> tice as their [*sic*] was no direct proof was inclined to re-
> lease him, but the Committee apprehending he might throw
> some light upon this matter committed him as a Prisoner of
> Warr misbehaving. . . .[15]

Samuel Woods was imprisoned until after the trial, and according to the Superior Court Record Book (1775–1780) he was released with the three state's witnesses, Sarah Stratton, Alexander Cummings, and Jeseniah (Jesse) Parker (the Spooner servants). It appears that Woods was a more-or-less innocent bystander to the drama building around him — though kept in jail, he was not apparently called as a witness. At the time in mid-February when Bathsheba conducted this flirtation, her desperation appears to be such that she was willing to enlist anyone who might listen to her murder scheme, utterly heedless of how she might be incriminating herself. By that time she would have missed her menses, thus confirming her condition and perhaps intensifying her sense of urgency.

The handkerchief episode also provides an insight into the Buchanan-Brooks relationship. Clearly, the sergeant pulled rank in ordering Brooks on a needless errand in the middle of a freezing-cold February night. Brooks's willingness to obey, at whatever inconvenience and discomfort to himself, suggests that his own motive for murdering Joshua might have been simply a matter of obeying the orders of his superior.

During the week following the handkerchief incident, the soldiers visited local taverns or stayed in the Spooner barn and dined on bread, cheese, and pork and beans brought to them by Cummings, Jesse Parker, or Bathsheba herself. When Joshua was asleep or gone from the house they would join Bathsheba and enjoy "the best the house afforded of meat and drink." At this point, the murder plotting began in earnest, involving Jesse Parker and Alexander Cummings as well as Buchanan and Brooks. According to "The Dying Declaration," Parker asked Brooks to meet Joshua as he returned from a trip he had taken to buy oats so that Brooks could murder him. With Bathsheba's encouragement, Cummings and Parker proposed to Brooks that they all three murder Joshua in his bed and then throw his body in the well, so it would appear that he had fallen in while getting himself a drink of water. "But Brooks's heart failed him," Buchanan wrote, "and Mrs. Spooner said she did not think he was so faint hearted."

The next plan was proposed by Bathsheba. Either Cummings or Parker was to tell Spooner a horse was sick in order to lure him to the barn, where Brooks was to kill him and put him among the horses' feet to make it appear he had been trampled. "But," Buchanan wrote, "Brooks told Parker not to tell him [Joshua], but to make her believe [Joshua] would not go over."

If Buchanan is to be believed here, the soldiers were no more interested in murdering Joshua than Ezra Ross was, but they kept up the appearance of interest perhaps to continue taking advantage of Bathsheba's hospitality and company. According to Buchanan, on Sunday, 22 February he told Bathsheba that he and Brooks planned to leave Brookfield the next morning. Prompted perhaps by some intimation of reason or conscience, the soldiers did indeed go, though Bathsheba tried to dissuade them. Buchanan worked for a smith in Western for two days, but because Brooks did not have the proper files to do his branch of smithing they "proposed to go to Worcester to get home," a route that took them by the Spooners' house once more.[16] Though Buchanan doesn't mention it in the "The Dying Declaration," a comment of Jesse Parker's from Justice Sargeant's notes suggests that Bathsheba went to Western herself to bring them back: "She said she had been to W. Parish to see the Regulars there & they were going to Worcester."

If only they'd had the good sense to follow their original inclination . . . but one suspects that Bathsheba was as irresistible to them as she was to Ezra Ross. Buchanan and Brooks stopped at the house on their way back from Western to tell her they were going to Worcester, and she told them she would meet them there on the following day. She had to borrow or rent a horse from a Captain Weldon. According to Jesse Parker's testimony as recorded in Foster's notes, "She asked Mr. Spooner for a horse, but he declined letting her have one."

On Thursday night, 26 February, Bathsheba called on Buchanan and Brooks at Mrs. Walker's tavern in Worcester. Mary Walker (daughter of Mrs. Sarah Walker, the innkeeper) testified that Bathsheba was very wet, suggesting that she had made the four-to-five-hour journey on horseback in freezing rain. According to Justice Foster's notes, she "gave [Buchanan] a letter which she said came from her grenadier — the contents of the letter was that he would meet him [Buchanan] to go to the hill. She came back from Doctor Greens [her brother-in-law] — very soon and said she forgot to give him a piece of cloth which was his — and said she would knit for her [Mary] because she could not sew for want of sight she staid there two hours."

This passage is interesting from several angles. It reveals that Bathsheba had in all likelihood been corresponding with Ezra Ross back in Linebrook and apparently had kept him abreast of the ongoing murder plans. Though Ross isn't positively identified as her grenadier, the existence of some other intimate living at a distance requiring correspondence seems highly unlikely. Ross did in fact return, as the letter writer said he would do, armed and prepared to do murder. "The hill" apparently refers to some location between Brookfield and Western (now Warren). From the letter's content it also appears that Ross was willing to join the conspiracy. One has to wonder whether Bathsheba, by writing to Ezra about the British soldiers and then showing Ezra's letter to Buchanan, meant to play them against each other in the hope of arousing one or the other sufficiently to get the job done.

The reference to knitting for Mary is explained further in Justice Sargeant's notes: "Soon after she came back and said she had forgot to leave the Cloath that Buchanan had left at her house and asked if he had not forgot it. He said yes, she got it out and asked me [Mary] to make Buchanan a shirt for she could not see, & offered to knit for me if I would." By this point on Thursday night, Bathsheba's desperation was great enough for her to be riding an unfamiliar horse for four hours on a dark and rainy winter night and bartering her knitting skills in order to bribe Buchanan with a new shirt.

According to the testimony of Prudence (who worked at Walker's), Mrs. Spooner stayed all Thursday evening but was often in and out: "Sergt Buchanan offered her his handkerchief. She said G——d D——n the handkerchief, I will not touch it. . . ."[17] Bathsheba left Walker's sometime later to sleep at her sister Mary Green's house.

On Friday, 27 February, Bathsheba returned to Walker's in the morning, staying there until night. Prudence testified that Brooks told Mrs. Spooner that Buchanan was sick and she went into his chamber with him. Prudence testified that she "went up there after a broom and see them together." That same day, Mary Walker testified, "Brooks often laid his head upon her neck and often times put his hands round her [waist] — she [Mary] observing it Mrs. Spooner said you must not wonder Billy meaning Brooks has lived at my house and is as fond of me as he would be of a mother."

Sometime during the day, Buchanan wrote in "The Dying Declaration," Bathsheba asked him to procure some poison. He bought one

dram of calomel, dividing it into twenty papers. Mary Walker overheard them talking about a sick child at Brookfield, which was most
likely a ruse to allay suspicions. Calomel is a mercurial compound that
induces salivation and violent purging. In the eighteenth century it
was commonly used for medical purposes, one of them to restore
"obstructed menses."[18] One dram divided into twenty papers would
have amounted to three grains per package, enough for a medicinal
dose — one to three grains — but not enough to be a poison. "I desired
her to give one in the morning," Buchanan wrote, but "she told me
she never gave him any." It is possible that Bathsheba intended to use
the calomel as an abortifacient rather than a poison; if she did, it
clearly didn't work.

On Saturday, 28 February, the day before the murder, Bathsheba
returned to Mrs. Walker's at about ten o'clock in the morning. Mary
Walker testified that Bathsheba "asked Buchanan when he would
go[;] she said she would send a letter by him and then said she would
write a letter at Mr. Nazro's. [I]t would not be any hurt to write to her
father. . . ." Prudence testified that on Saturday "when Mrs. Spooner
was going away [Prudence] asked her what Mrs. Green [Bathsheba's
sister Mary] said to her — [Bathsheba] said she told Mrs. Green she
dined at Mrs. Nazro's and dranked tea there and it was a pritty good
lye."[19]

In his confession Buchanan wrote that Bathsheba asked him to
meet her at Mr. Nazro's shop, where she would buy files for him and
Brooks. "I parted with her and sent Brooks up to the shop. But as he
came in sight he saw her ride from the door, and therefore did not go
there. . . ."

In these last three days before the murder, Bathsheba's behavior appears to have been frantic and more than a little deranged — trips
to and from Green's and the tavern, lying to her sister, visiting Buchanan's bedroom, allowing caresses from Brooks, promising to buy
files and then leaving Nazro's store before Brooks arrived to select
the files. Most interesting, on Saturday morning she asked Buchanan
"when he would go; [that] she would send a letter by him [and that] it
would not be any hurt to write her father" suggesting that even a day
before the murder she might have been considering joining her father in New York and/or sending Buchanan to her father with a letter

asking for help. Surely she hadn't intended to write to her father to tell him about the murder plans.

This reference to Timothy Ruggles calls to mind the enigmatic statement Bathsheba made to Obadiah Rice, when, after the discovery of Joshua's body, Rice brought her to Worcester for questioning. In both Foster's and Paine's roles Rice testified, "She said she had a great desire to see her Daddy and if it had not been for that this murder would have never been committed." The connection in Bathsheba's mind between her desire to see her father and the need to have Joshua murdered defies reason, but its inherent irrationality is characteristic of her thoughts and actions before and immediately after the murder. It is as though she evoked her father in the way a young child might call on her Daddy to rescue her magically from terrible trouble. The comment makes no sense except on the profoundest level, as a cry of the heart.

On Saturday afternoon just before she left Worcester to return home, Bathsheba stopped at Walker's for a brief conversation with Buchanan. Mary Walker overheard her say: "Tomorrow night at 11 clock remember Sargt." To which Buchanan replied, "Tomorrow night at 11 clock."[20] This testimony seems to imply that Bathsheba and Buchanan had finally agreed on a time and definite course of action. However, in Justice Sargeant's notes Mary Walker testified: "As she was going away she whispered with Sarjeant [i.e., Buchanan] & he said the time was eleven o'Clock tomorrow night & I asked what of that after some time he answered he was to meet with Grenadier," suggesting that the naming of a time did not refer to a murder plan per se, but to a meeting with Ross.

Given Bathsheba's intention on Saturday morning to send Buchanan off with a letter to her father, and given her erratic and aimless-seeming behavior up to her parting with Buchanan, it's hard to believe they had arrived at a logical, cold-blooded plan to commit murder. As defense lawyer Levi Lincoln noted during the trial, the fact that they had formed no plan to conceal the murder, no agreed-upon story and no means of escape argued against its ever having been a rational plan. Nevertheless, this particular testimony of Mary Walker's would seal Bathsheba's fate. Naming a time to meet Buchanan in Brookfield on Sunday would later establish her guilt as accessory to the murder.

[7]

"His Time Is Come"

BATHSHEBA had left Brookfield for Worcester on Thursday, 26 February 1778 and returned home Saturday, 28 February. Mrs. Stratton presumably had run the household and looked after the children in her absence. Joshua Jr., who was eight years old at that time, in all likelihood boarded away from home at a private grammar school in Ipswich or possibly Roxbury.[1] Elizabeth, the eldest Spooner child, was nearly eleven and might have attended a day school. She was considered old enough to assume many household duties, including looking after her little sister, Bathshua, who had just turned three. It's very possible that Elizabeth was often called upon to take on such duties as her mother's behavior became more erratic in the weeks before the murder.

Sometime on Saturday before Bathsheba returned from Worcester, Ezra Ross appeared at the Spooner house. According to Sarah Stratton's testimony in Foster's notes, "he had Mr. Spooner's horse a fortnight and hurt his back and was not willing he should see him." The author of the *Spy* account wrote that Ross spoke through the window to Sarah Stratton, who was ironing in the kitchen. He told her he was "exceeding cold but could not come in because he wanted to conceal himself from Mr. Spooner, whose horse . . . he had chafed."[2]

Ross had used Joshua's horse to ride from Princeton to Ipswich after he and Joshua had finished their business in Princeton early in February. We can only speculate as to why Joshua wanted Ezra to accompany him on that trip to the potash farm; perhaps it was simply for his company. In any case, Joshua's apparent good will and generosity in lending Ezra the horse contrasts poignantly with Ezra's carrying a bottle of poison for the purpose of murdering Joshua on the trip. That Ezra wasn't up to betraying Joshua's trust at that point, at least, illustrates the depth of conflict he must have been feeling.

However, something had instilled renewed purpose in Ezra during that fortnight spent back home in Linebrook village, Ipswich; in all likelihood it was the letter from Bathsheba telling him that Buchanan and Brooks were preparing to carry out her murder plans. The prospect of competition for her affections may well have prompted Ross to race back to Brookfield, prepared to commit murder himself. He had ridden the horse so hard that he'd hurt its back, and he came armed, according to "The Dying Declaration," with "a brace of pistols." These were very likely a pair of dueling pistols (paired pistols were not used otherwise), the arms of a gentleman. Perhaps Ezra had bought them with the intention of challenging Joshua to a duel—dueling with pistols was not illegal in Massachusetts at that period, and a duel would have presented an acceptable and lawful means of killing a man. From what we know of Joshua's timid disposition, however, it is doubtful that he would have accepted the challenge, especially from a boy who was not his social equal. In any case, the fact that Ross did not come armed with his soldier's musket suggests his intentions were not those of a cold-blooded killer.

After Ross appeared at the Spooner's house on Saturday, Mrs. Stratton hid him in the milk room. Bathsheba rode in soon afterward. She ordered Alexander Cummings to put up the horse she had obtained from Captain Weldon when Joshua had forbidden her to take one of his horses to ride to Worcester on Thursday. It is interesting that Cummings's testimony in Justice Sargeant's notes says "Mrs. Spooner & Ross told me to put the horses up," indicating that in Joshua's absence, Ezra assumed his authority with the servants as head of the household. The following day, Sunday, Ezra was concealed in an upstairs chamber for the entire day.

By Sunday evening, quite a number of people had assembled at the Spooner house. Paine's and Foster's trial notes say that Charles Cobbin, "Captain Weldon's negro," arrived at about sunset to retrieve Captain Weldon's horse. While there, he saw a man whom he identified as Ross. Ezra very likely felt it was safe to come out of hiding, because Joshua had left at dusk (about 5:30 P.M.) to spend the evening at his neighbor Ephraim Cooley's public house, about a quarter

mile west along the post road.[3] (According to the 7 May issue of the
Spy, it was Spooner's habit to spend an hour or two drinking with his
neighbors in the evenings, though on this evening he did so for over
three hours.) The two Spooner daughters, Elizabeth and Bathshua,
were somewhere in the house as well, according to Levi Lincoln's
defense notes, though their presence isn't mentioned in any other
account describing the events of Sunday night.

Charles Cobbin must not have stayed long, because Alexander
Cummings had already left with the horse to return it to Captain
Weldon. But Cobbin did see two other men at the Spooners' who, he
said, had come from Springfield. Sarah Stratton, in Paine's and Foster's notes, identified these two men as "Mr. Gray and his partner,"
travelers who had apparently stopped at Spooner's to lodge for the
night.

Next to appear were Sgt. James Buchanan and William Brooks. In
"The Dying Declaration," Buchanan states that he and Bathsheba
agreed to meet again on Monday night at eleven o'clock, but he later
wrote that he and Brooks arrived at the Spooner house on Sunday
evening, at about eight o'clock.[4] They saw Mrs. Stratton outside, at the
well. She told them there was company in the house, and she would let
Mrs. Spooner know they were there. The "company" was Ezra Ross
and the mysterious Mr. Gray and his partner.

Buchanan described his meeting with Ross in "The Dying
Declaration":

> Mrs. Spooner came out, and told us that one Mr. Ross was in
> the house, who had a brace of pistols loaded, and that he
> had promised her he would kill Mr. Spooner as he came
> home from the tavern, she desired us to come in, which we
> did, he shewed us a pistol, and said Mr. Spooner should die
> by that to night. Either Brooks or Buchanan said it would
> alarm the neighbours.

We can only speculate about Buchanan's reaction to another suitor
for Bathsheba's affection, and a boy at that. Ezra's age was seventeen
to Buchanan's thirty-six (or thirty, according to a quarto version of the
"Dying Declaration"). It is likely Buchanan quickly sized up the situation and overruled Ezra's romantic posturing.

Brooks said if Ross would help him he would knock him down, accordingly it was agreed on, and there was a look out kept at the sitting room door for his coming, in the mean time there was some supper brought by Mrs. Stratten to us; we had had some flip before, and there was now some rum brought, which we drank, each of us by turns giving a look out.

From the terse summary of this exchange in the men's confession, we are left to imagine the emotional content of their murderous bargain, the most critical moment in the entire drama. Though William Brooks proposed the actual plan to Ross, it is very likely that Sergeant Buchanan was pulling the strings. He outranked Brooks (Alexander Cummings heard him call Brooks "my man"), and he outranked Ezra Ross as well, since both Ross and Brooks were privates in their respective armies. It is interesting to note that Buchanan did not agree to help Brooks or Ross commit the murder but appears to have successfully delegated the dirty work.

From Sarah Stratton's testimony in Foster's and Paine's notes we know that she carried supper into the sitting room or "front room" (most likely the east room) for Ross and Buchanan, while Bathsheba ate supper with Mr. Gray and his partner in the kitchen. Just before the murder, then, Buchanan and Ross were eating in the sitting room, very likely getting drunk on the flip and rum freely supplied to them. According to Alexander Cummings, when he returned from taking the horse to Captain Weldon's stable, he found Bathsheba still in the kitchen, making chocolate. How out of place this homely little detail seems within the deadly progress of that night.

In "The Dying Declaration" Buchanan refers to a lookout— Brooks—posted at the sitting room door at the front of the house. Alexander Cummings said that upon returning he encountered Brooks "out by the Road," which would put him nearest to the front door. Paine's notes record that Brooks had told Cummings "he was watching for Mr. Spooner & he should not come home a living man that night." Cummings apparently wanted no part of the whole business and went upstairs to bed, sleeping for two-and-a-half hours, or so he testified.

"Mr. Spooner was at length seen coming," Buchanan related in

"The Dying Declaration." Brooks must have run in through the front door to notify Buchanan and Ross in the east sitting room. Ross then apparently asked Mrs. Stratton to summon Bathsheba from the kitchen. Brooks then went outside again, probably by the kitchen door, to await Joshua inside the small gate leading into the kitchen garden.

We can only wonder what happened to Gray and his partner, left to themselves in the kitchen after this puzzling flurry of activity. Gray's companion may have gone upstairs to bed at this point, for later on, after the murder was committed, Mrs. Stratton would light Gray to bed, where his partner was already asleep. However, Gray, at least, must have been aware that something strange was going on that night, with his hostess called by the mysterious occupants of the sitting room and abandoning him in the kitchen. The murder would take place within just a few feet of the kitchen door; surely Gray must have heard Joshua cry out. Yet neither Gray nor his companion appeared as trial witnesses, and as far as we know from the sources they were never heard from again. Yet that Bathsheba would allow the murder plan to proceed with two strangers as possible witness in the house (as well as her two children) further illustrates the irrationality underlying the "plan" and the surreal quality of the entire evening.

Nor do we know what Sarah Stratton was doing during the time immediately surrounding the murder, though the *Spy* account places her in the kitchen when it occurred.[5] Had she the courage to speak out she might have prevented it, for she certainly must have overheard the plans. "We are certain Mrs. Stratten could not but know what was going forward. That we leave the public to judge of," Buchanan wrote in "The Dying Declaration." However, she was very likely too intimidated by the British soldiers and by her modest station in life to utter a rebuke to those considered her betters.

And so William Brooks awaited Joshua Spooner by the kitchen garden gate, intent on murdering him. How had he come to rationalize the murder of a man in cold blood? He hardly knew Spooner and bore him no personal grudge. We can only guess what it was that overcame his initial reluctance to commit this act. A few days earlier, Bathsheba had chided Brooks when he was unwilling to go along with her murder plans, saying she did not think he was so faint-hearted. It may be that as a soldier he had become inured to impersonal killing and that the quantity of liquor he had drunk that night, as well as Bathsheba's offers of money, had eased his earlier compunction. Or perhaps it was Ross's assurance that he would help with the murder that had finally emboldened Brooks.

And why had Ezra Ross agreed to an act so villainous and so apparently out of character? Perhaps he was moved by a desire to prove himself a man before the two older enemy soldiers, or, more to the point, to prove his manhood before Bathsheba; he was, after all, only seventeen. However they each may have come to murder, on that moonless winter night William Brooks was no longer faint-hearted. When Joshua Spooner entered the kitchen garden, Brooks, "with his right Fist, the said Joshua Spooner to and against Ground did Strike down . . . on the Ground lying, he Wm. Brooks with both his Hands and feet . . . in and upon the back, Head, Stomach, Sides, and Throat . . . did Strike, beat and kick. giving to him . . . Several Mortal Bruizes. . . ."[6]

Death did not come as quickly to Joshua Spooner as the warrant represented. Brooks later admitted to the trial justices that when Mr. Spooner was first struck, he asked Brooks "what was the matter" and then he "cried murder," whereupon Brooks partly strangled him.[7]

Sergeant Buchanan confessed that he and Ezra Ross did not join Brooks until Joshua was unconscious or dead: "Ross took Mr. Spooner's watch out and gave it to Buchanan; Brooks and Ross took him [Spooner] up and put him into the well head first; before they carried him away, I, Buchanan, pulled off his shoes: I was instantly struck with horror of conscience, as well I might; I went into the house and met Mrs. Spooner in the sitting room; she seemed vastly confused."

According to Buchanan in "The Dying Declaration," Bathsheba immediately went to an upstairs chamber for Joshua's money box, where Mrs. Stratton saw her while lighting Mr. Gray's way to bed. Mrs. Stratton testified that Mrs. Spooner took her hand and said she hoped Mr. Spooner was in heaven.

Bathsheba brought the money box back down to the sitting room and had Buchanan break it open; she didn't have a key, which probably was on Joshua's body, in the well. According to "The Dying Declaration," "She gave two notes of 400 dollars each to Ross to change and give the money to Brooks; But there was found some paper money, which Brooks received (243 dollars) and the notes were returned. At the same time she gave Ross four notes, each of them ten pounds, to purchase camblet [camlet cloth] for a riding dress."

How odd that moments after her husband had been beaten to death, Bathsheba would be preoccupied with dressing Ross in the garb of a gentleman. And her behavior became still stranger. Brooks's clothes were covered with Joshua's blood, so she had him remove his waistcoat, breeches, and shirt. She had Ross give Brooks the clothing he was wearing and asked Mrs. Stratton to go up to the chamber and fetch a pair of Joshua's black knit breeches for Ezra to wear. Apparently either Alexander Cummings or Mrs. Stratton also brought down a waistcoast, shirt, and jacket belonging to Joshua for Ross to put on as well.

It would have been more logical and expedient for Bathsheba simply to give Joshua's clothing to Brooks, but she apparently thought gentleman's garb was more appropriate for Ross, who was instructed to give his more serviceable leather breeches to Brooks. Or perhaps she wanted Ezra to appear a gentleman in keeping with her earlier impulse to dress him in a riding habit. Buchanan received a ruffled shirt, which presumably was also Joshua's, and Brooks a shirt and handkerchief.

Alexander Cummings, who had gone upstairs to bed after seeing Brooks in the yard, was awakened by the smell of burning woolen and came downstairs to find Brooks, Buchanan, Ross, and Bathsheba burning Brooks's clothing in the parlor (which may have been the west sitting room, used for entertaining). "They asked him what made him look so sullen," Foster recorded. "They were then shifting cloaths Ross put on Mr. Spooners jacket and breeches."

After Bathsheba asked Cummings to go with Mrs. Stratton to the chamber to fetch Joshua's clothes, her next order illustrates what must have been a continuing state of dissociation, in that she appears to have completely forgotten what the soldiers had done with Joshua's body:

> Mrs Spooner bid him go and get some water to wash Spoon-
> ers buckles and he should have them he said he would not
> have them but he and Mrs. Stratton went to the well and
> could not dip the bucket. Mrs. Spooner asked him why he

did not get the water. He said he believed Mr. Spooner was in
the well. She said it was not true.

    Mrs. Stratton came in with him frighted and cried and ran
and got the Bible.[8]

Sarah Stratton wasn't the only one "frighted" that night; Cummings
asked her to go to the well with him, obviously suspecting that Joshua's
corpse was in it. In Justice Sargeant's notes he testified, "I put the
Bucket down & it catch'd in his cloaths which frightened me & we run
into the house, I said to Mrs. Spooner I am afraid your husband is in
the well; no says she that is not true — I sit in the Kitchen & Mrs.
Stratton fell a crying & took the book in her hand — I heard Mrs.
Spooner say if any person kills my husband — I will have him thrown
into the well."

In sending Cummings to the well when she certainly would have
been told by Buchanan where Joshua's body had been hidden (it had
been her idea to put him in the well from the beginning), Bathsheba
seems to have been both euphoric and almost wholly irrational immediately after the murder. Buchanan quickly pointed out the foolish-
ness of her request, saying "Should you [have] thought my man would
do the jobb for him,"[9] suggesting it would have been wiser to have
Brooks get the water.

The sources differ on exactly what it was that Bathsheba wanted
washed and given to Cummings: Justice Foster recorded "Spooners
buckles," but Paine and Sargeant agree that it was Brooks's breeches.
That Bathsheba would have offered Cummings Brooks's breeches
rather than Joshua's buckles makes more sense, in that the buckles were far more valuable and the murderer's due. Also, the buckles
could have been cleaned simply by wiping them with a rag, whereas
cold water would have been necessary to remove blood stains from
woolen breeches. However, in both Foster's and Sargeant's accounts,
Cummings testified that he saw Bathsheba throw Brooks's breeches
into the fire before she asked him to fetch the water from the well,
further illustrating her confused and dissociated state of mind.

After the clothes were exchanged and the men paid from Joshua's
money box, they prepared to depart. Bathsheba asked Buchanan
when she would see him again, to which he answered, in fourteen
days. It is impossible to guess whether she arranged another meeting

with romance in mind or to make a final payoff, though the two then shook hands, suggesting it was a business arrangement. Just before the three men departed, Mrs. Stratton asked Brooks what he had been about. Brooks answered her, "His time is come."[10]

Later that night Bathsheba asked Mrs. Stratton to sleep with her. Sarah Stratton testified that "She sighed and tumbled a good deal. . . . Often she said she hoped Mr. Spooner was in Heaven."

The reality of Joshua's murder had perhaps begun to set in, and Bathsheba could not bear to be alone with it. Though he was dead, she still could not escape him.

[8]

The Hands of Justice

JOSHUA SPOONER'S murderers bungled their escape, if escape was what they intended. Buchanan, Brooks, and Ross seemed almost to invite arrest. They left the Spooner house around eleven at night. One of them — apparently Ezra — was mounted on a Spooner horse, and all three wore clothes or possessed personal items belonging to the murdered man. They arrived together at Mrs. Walker's inn and tavern, nineteen miles away in Worcester, at four A.M.

Worcester was the county seat, chosen as such because of its central location despite the fact that Brookfield was wealthier and more populated.[1] Worcester's center consisted of a cluster of county offices, shops, taverns, two churches, and private homes lining either side of the post road and the town common.

The grimmest structure was the jail, or *gaol* as it was spelled then. Built in 1753, the 38-by-28-foot, two-storied building was constructed with six-inch square joists set five feet apart, plank walls inside and out filled with stone and mortar, and windows protected by iron gratings. The jail stood on the town common, on the south side of what is now Lincoln Square at the corner of Summer Street.[2] It shared a yard with the jailer's house and the Old South meeting house. Worcester's courthouse, built in 1751, sat just across the street from the jail, with stocks, pillory, and a whipping post in front. The courthouse would have been a familiar sight to Brig. Gen. Timothy Ruggles, Bathsheba's father, who from 1762 to 1774 sat as chief justice for the Court of Common Pleas, never dreaming that his favorite daughter would be brought to trial for a capital offense in Worcester's Superior Court.

Isaiah Thomas, publisher of the patriotic newspaper the *Massachusetts Spy (Or, American Oracle of Liberty "Undaunted by Tyrants we'll DIE or be FREE"),* set up his print shop in the center of Worcester.[3] In the same neighborhood were the county registry, a school house, various shops and storefronts advertising lawyers, doctors, mechanics, and traders, as well as two taverns.

It's highly likely that one of these taverns was Mrs. Sarah Walker's, where the three soldiers lodged the night of the murder, and the other tavern was Samuel Brown's, where all four murder suspects would be brought for questioning. Both taverns were located near Worcester's jail and court house.

According to Mary Walker's testimony in Foster's notes, Brooks, Buchanan, and Ross appeared at her mother's tavern early Monday morning, around 4:00 A.M. To explain their middle-of-the-night arrival they told her that "the Springfield guard were in pursuit of them and Brookfield was searched in every house — Mrs. Spooner met them at Leicester and told them of it. [Mary Walker] asked Ross if he had ever seen Mrs. Spooner and he said he did not know as he had but he had seen Mr. Spooner and rode to Lancaster with him." Buchanan asked Mary to rip the ruffles off a shirt for him (a dress shirt that had belonged to Joshua), and he bled himself on Monday, Mary testified. At that time bleeding was commonly performed to ease a hangover (as well as to relieve any number of other ailments).

Ezra Ross apparently went to bed, but James Buchanan and William Brooks began drinking, possibly as soon as they arrived at Walker's. According to "The Dying Declaration," "Brooks being in liquor went down to Mr. Brown's tavern; there showing Mr. Spooner's watch, and the people seeing him have silver Buckles, became suspicious of him."

Such carelessness wasn't in keeping with any logical plan of escape, a point that lawyer Levi Lincoln would later make in Ross's defense. Brooks showed off Spooner's watch and wore the murdered man's shoe buckles engraved with his initials, JS. The shoe buckles alone would (and did) attract attention by being far too aristocratic for a British foot soldier to wear. This reckless behavior suggests that Brooks was too drunk to care if he got caught or not, or perhaps on some level sought to expose his part in the crime.

Ezra Ross, who hadn't accompanied Brooks and Buchanan on their drinking spree, showed signs of a guilty conscience as soon as he arrived at Walker's. Foster records Mary Walker's testifying that Ross seemed "very dull" after he arrived. Mary asked him what made him so dull. He paced about the house and then leaned against a wall, answering, "reason enough." Sargeant's notes add that he would not tell Mary his name and sought to hide, because Prudence apparently showed him a place behind the chimney. Ross also hid a pistol there, which would be recovered later by Capt. Joshua Whitney, who found it loaded with two balls. The other pistol that Ross brought with him is not accounted for in any testimony.

By late Monday afternoon news of Joshua Spooner's murder reached Worcester, and Ephraim Curtis (Worcester's jailer), Captain Whitney, and Joseph Ball went to Walker's to question Buchanan, Brooks, and Ross.[4] Brooks was found with incriminating evidence (the watch and silver shoe buckles), and Buchanan tried to escape by jumping through a window. Joshua Whitney asked where "the other fellow" was and took a candle up to the loft in search of Ross, who had been sleeping. Whitney found Ross in the upper garret behind the chimney and described him as quivering and very scared. Ezra said at once that he was guilty of the crime and wanted a minister and that while he hadn't struck the first blow, he had aided and assisted the others. Ross was very penitent, Whitney said, and "full," perhaps meaning choked up. Ezra Ross clearly regretted grievously his part in the murder and had pondered his culpability as he remained alone in Walker's garret while his partners in crime were out and about drinking to assuage their own guilt. Ephraim Curtis, according to Sargeant's notes, testified that Buchanan "complained his arm was sore — I took of[f] the handkerchief . . . [which] was bloody & his shirt . . . [and] his arm . . . [were] very bad." Whether this wound occurred from his having botched the earlier blood-letting, from jumping out of the window, or as a result of his part in the murder is unknown. The three soldiers were arrested and brought to Samuel Brown's tavern for questioning Monday evening.

Bathsheba was the only one of the four accomplices who made any serious attempt to cover her tracks. According to Mrs. Stratton's testimony in Foster's notes, Bathsheba offered to give her "a good deal" to keep the murder a secret. And according to Alexander Cummings, "Next morning Mrs. Spooner went to the well and . . . told him to go and get a horse and go to the town and inquire for him [Spooner]. While they were at the well she said she wanted to have him put in the bottom of the well." Justice Sargeant's notes, however, quote Cummings as saying that Bathsheba "bid me take a horse & go out to enquire for him that it might be found out as soon as possible," indicating that she wanted the body discovered quickly, perhaps simply because the family had to use the well. Sinking his body to the bottom certainly defied common sense, as did the original plan of hiding his body in the well, thereby making the family's only source of water unusable.

Cummings rode one of Joshua's horses to Cooley's tavern between eight and nine in the morning, according to Ephraim Cooley. He told Cooley that Mr. Spooner had not come home the previous night. Cooley told him to go to Dr. King, but Cummings went only part of the way toward King's house and then turned back.

Ephraim Cooley was worried about Joshua's safety and took six men with him to the Spooner house, where he found Bathsheba eating her breakfast in the kitchen with Mrs. Stratton and the family. He asked her if Joshua was home, to which she answered no and cried. Cooley then went outside and found near the gate a heap of snow covering Joshua's hat, which he brought in to be identified by Bathsheba. Shortly the body was discovered in the well and blood stains were found on the well curb. Ephraim Cooley went immediately to fetch Brookfield's coroner, Thomas Gilbert, and when they returned Joshua's corpse had been taken from the well and laid out in the east sitting room on the table.

Dr. Jonathan King, a near neighbor of the Spooners, had been drinking with Joshua at Cooley's on Sunday night and testified that Spooner had left for home between eight and nine, sober and sociable. Given that Spooner was known to be "bad for his drink," King's attesting specifically to his sobriety that evening is telling. Next morning, Dr. King heard that Joshua's body had been found in the well — he was probably informed by Cooley — and he hastened to Spooner's in time to help remove the corpse. "We found one shoe in the Bucket," Sargeant recorded, "his watch & Buckles gone — found 5 or 6 Dollars in his Pocket — some blood on the Curb of the well — some Clods of Blood on the Cloak, cloak not tied on — with the tine of a fork drew up his Cloak, and then hooked him up from the bottom by hooking him under the left arm — he came up head first." This detail is at odds with the "The Dying Declaration," which states that the body was put into the well head-first. That one of Joshua's shoes (pulled off by Buchanan after the murder) ended up in the well bucket is also curious, given that Alexander Cummings attempted to dip the bucket into the well and couldn't, when he was accompanied by Sarah Stratton.

As to Spooner's wounds, King "observed a great bruise on his nose & the Bone broke all to pieces—face stripd.—his left temple much bruised with heavy blows—a gash on his head an Inch & ½ long—his throat very black & his breast much bruised."

No one in the family would enter the sitting room to look at the body, "except his little daughter," Dr. King testified. This, presumably, was little Bathshua. Even if eighteenth-century children were more accustomed to the sight of death than children are today, the view of her dead father had to be traumatic for the three-year-old child. His face had been battered and would have been purple with bruises where his skin was not gray and bloodless from submersion in the icy well water, his mouth likely open in the rictus of a scream. It was assuredly a recollection that the child would never outlive.

According to Dr. King, Bathsheba could not be persuaded to look at Joshua's body. She was eating her breakfast in the kitchen and "shut out & did not turn her Eyes," he said. After the coroner's jury had finished their inquiry, "at [Dr. King's] particular desire" Bathsheba put her hand on her husband's forehead.[5] According to an old superstition, "the medieval ordeal by touch," the skin of a slain corpse would show color at the murderer's touch.[6] It is clear from his testimony that Dr. King, and probably the other neighbors as well, suspected Bathsheba immediately. She did touch Joshua's forehead, though apparently without the desired effect, and said, "Poor little man."

Later that same day at Brown's tavern in Worcester, all three men quickly confessed to the murder and implicated Bathsheba. She was brought up for questioning from Brookfield, probably on Monday night, accompanied by Ephraim Cooley in Obadiah Rice's sleigh.[7] Sarah Stratton and Alexander Cummings, who were believed to have incriminating knowledge, were brought with her. All six apparently spent the night under guard at Brown's tavern.[8]

While on the road to Worcester, Obadiah Rice heard Bathsheba say, "This don't seem like Christmas day." Under the circumstances it might seem a callous remark, but it is in keeping with her ironic style of humor and she was probably trying to make light of the situation for her servants' sake, who at that point were in danger of being named as conspirators. She was anxious to protect them, saying "she would suffer ten deaths for Mrs. Stratton and Alex before they should suffer, for they were innocent." And she expressed remorse: "I would have given ten million of worlds the moment the breath was out of his Body, that it had been in again."[9] It was also on this trip to Worcester that she alluded to her desire to see her father.

Though Bathsheba would submit no formal confession, on the night of her arrest she appears to have been relieved to admit her involvement in the crime. Justice Foster recorded that Ephraim Cooley testified, "at Brown's in Worcester she spoke freely of the matter and said she was the whole means of this murder being committed She began the discourse herself," he said, and "wept when she talked about it."

Constable Elisha Hamilton testified about Bathsheba that "she told Cooley he had done no more than his duty it was her own doing. . . . [She] took on much and said if it was not for this thing I could meet my Judge. She said it happened by means of Ross's being sick at our house. . . . She said [that] Mrs. Stratton and Alek were innocent. She had bribed them to do and say what they had done." (Even a week later, after she'd had time to assess the gravity of her situation, she was still willing to admit to William Young that "she consented to the murder."[10]

On Tuesday the six prisoners were moved from Samuel Brown's tavern next door to Worcester jail.[11] The three soldiers were incarcerated on the first floor and were accessible to the heckling of passersby, who presumably talked to them through the grated window or were allowed within the prison building itself. According to Rev. Thaddeus Maccarty, the men spoke to young people who came by to vilify them, offering "the most serious, solemn and affectionate counsels," and they became a magnet for the curious. In an article in the 4 June issue the *Massachusetts Spy* stated:

> The prisoners complain very much of the multitudes that crowd in upon them, which tends greatly to confuse them,

and hinder them from reaping the benefit of the counsels and instructions of Ministers and good Christians that visit them, which they are very desirous of. They therefore desire that none would come to see them out of a vain curiosity, or merely to gaze at them, but leave them to enjoy their short time, in as profitable a manner, as it may be.

As a female prisoner, Bathsheba was probably spared this indignity and kept in more private accommodations on the second floor.

At the time of the Spooner murder, the Reverend Thaddeus Maccarty was minister of the Old South parish. He was greatly revered for his pastoral care of the sick and needy in his flock and admired for his eloquent prayers and preaching. As part of his pastoral duties Maccarty acted as confessor to condemned prisoners, and in this capacity he would become a frequent visitor to Bathsheba Spooner's prison cell. Ultimately, he would become her champion before the Massachusetts Council.

Back in Brookfield, Rev. Nathan Fiske presided over Joshua Spooner's interment on Friday, 6 March. He was buried in a cemetery plot next to the plots of Bathsheba's sister Martha and brother-in-law John Tufts. Brookfield cemetery records from that period were apparently burned in a later town hall fire, so we have no way of knowing if the plot was his or if it belonged to the Tufts family. Martha and John may have decided to make a public gesture, showing their loyalty to Joshua in order to placate a hostile community, or they may have buried him in their family plot simply out of affection. It is curious that none of the Spooner family claimed his body.

Rev. Nathan Fiske served Brookfield's Third Church for forty years and was well loved by his parishioners for his cheerfulness, kindness, and charity. Mr. Fiske had also socialized with the Spooners and frequently noted in his diaries that he "dined at" or "drank T. at Mr. Spooner's," or that "Mrs. Tufts & Mrs. Spooner [visited]."[12]

As treasurer of Brookfield's third precinct, Joshua Spooner paid the minister's salary. An undated receipt for an annual salary of £66.19.6 with Spooner's signature on it—written in a large, elegant, forward-slanting calligraphic hand—has survived among Fiske's voluminous papers. The salary receipt was most likely kept because it had been written over with what appears to be a fragment of a sermon extolling "a love and sacred regard for Chastity & purity, & a fixed Abhorrence of all lasciviousness, Immodesty . . . and incentive to carnality." Mr. Fiske, however, once nurtured a wayward incentive to carnality himself, as evidenced by the draft of a passionate love letter addressed to a married woman, written in a notebook from his student years at Harvard:

> To Mrs. Rebekah Phips
> My Charmer!
>   Nor heart can conceive nor Tongue of Men or Angels utter the Esteem & Regard I bear to your sacred & almost Divine Person. Ten thousand times ten thousand Graces adorn you: You are ye Beauty of Beauties, the Glory of Glories, the Perfection of Perfection, Splendor upon Splendor, by George Apples of gold or Pictures [*sic*] of Silver. A North American Helen & Massachusetts Venus, a Galascy a Milky-Way; A bright and glittering Combination of Excellencies and most sublime & unparalleled Delicacies. The Sun, that glorious luminary, stands still as in good father Joshua's day, blushing at & ashamed of his own inferior Lustre, hides his diminished head. I love you, I admire you. I am tortured to noncomposity when I think of you. O for the Kiss of Kisses, the canticle Kiss; the diphthong, matrimonial, consummate kiss; the sublime, profound Kiss of ardent & intense Charity. The Lord Bless you.[13]

Whether young Nathan Fiske delivered a copy of the letter to Mrs. Rebekah Phips or relegated his illicit passion to the privacy of his notebook will probably never be known; but he was no stranger to the power of desire.

Beyond the exercise of his pastoral responsibilities, Nathan Fiske's intelligence and interests ranged widely. His library contained Locke, Dante, Richardson, and Dryden alongside such works as *The Life of Cotton Mather*. His sermons were widely published in his own time, and he is still considered among the finest preachers of his age. Perhaps the best known of his surviving sermons is the one preached at Joshua Spooner's burial.[14] Pastor Fiske was preaching to a congregation of friends, neighbors, and relations of the victim and murderess, who were trying to comprehend a horrifying crime in their midst. He did not use the sort of hellfire and brimstone rhetoric employed by Reverend Parkman on the subject of the Spooner murder, though he condemned the act as barbarous and the cruelty of the murderers as damnable. Rather, he opened on a note of pity and sympathy for the friends and relations of the victim and interpreted the disastrous event as a parable of instruction. "What," he asked, "is the possession of wealth without domestic peace, and the sweets of conjugal affection and confidence? What are elegant apartments; what a house full of silver and gold to a man, if his house will not afford him a quiet retreat, nor a safe shelter, nor a single friend!" Toward the end of the sermon, Nathan Fiske asked that his congregation give their sympathy to, and never reproach, the innocent Spooner children, "so suddenly, so awfully bereft of their father . . . [and] of their mother too."

Though Fiske refused to indulge in inflammatory preaching about Joshua Spooner's murder, he apparently also refused to visit Bathsheba Spooner in prison. As her pastor, he had far more reason to visit her than did clerics such as Ebenezer Parkman or the others who hoped to extract a confession. He had a moral obligation to attend to the state of her soul. Though his own diary is missing for the year of the murder, if he had visited the prisoners in Worcester's jail it is highly likely that Ebenezer Parkman would have mentioned him in his own diary, where he made careful note of other clergymen who visited. It was an odd dereliction of duty in one who was known for his Christian charity and compassion.

The prosecution, headed by the attorney general, Robert Treat Paine, decided to use Sarah Stratton, Alexander Cummings, and Jesse Parker as state's witnesses, apparently in exchange for immunity from prosecution.[15] Levi Lincoln was assigned to defend the prisoners. At the time of the trial he was a young man only six years out of college, beginning his law practice in Worcester. He would later rise to prominence as U.S. attorney general under Thomas Jefferson, but in 1778 he was no match in experience to Robert Treat Paine.

At the next term of the Superior Court of Judicature after Joshua Spooner's murder (Tuesday, 21 April 1778), the grand jury found a true bill against Sgt. James Buchanan, age thirty; William Brooks, age twenty-seven; Ezra Ross, age seventeen; and Bathsheba Spooner, age thirty-two. The indictment charged that the three men, "not having God before their Eyes, but being moved and seduced by the instigation of the Devil . . . feloniously, willfully, and of their Malice aforethought in and upon Joshua Spooner . . . an assault did make." The bill further charged that William Brooks had struck Spooner down with his right fist, and with both hands and feet struck, beat, and kicked Spooner on the back, stomach, sides, and throat, giving him several mortal bruises from which he instantly died. And that James Buchanan and Ezra Ross were present aiding, assisting, abetting, comforting, and maintaining William Brooks in the murder; and that Bathsheba Spooner on February 28th incited, moved, abetted, counseled, and procured in the manner and form in which the murder was to be committed.[16]

The accused were arraigned and pleaded not guilty. Twelve male freeholders of Worcester were impaneled as jurors for the trial to be held on Friday, 24 April.[17] Chief Justice William Cushing headed the panel of five judges for the Massachusetts Superior Court, among them a Brookfield neighbor, Justice Jedediah Foster.[18] The other three judges were Nathaniel Peaslee Sargeant, David Sewall, and James Sullivan, who is believed to have written the 7 May account in the *Massachusetts Spy*.

On the day of the trial, the jury convened at 8:00 A.M. in the Old South meeting house, which was filled to overflowing with spectators. Rev. Ebenezer Parkman, who rode fourteen miles from Westborough to attend the trial, exclaimed in his diary, "A Great Throng!" He sat straight through from eight in the morning until midnight, when the testimony was finally finished, not daring to leave his seat for fear of losing it. In the eighteenth century, prisoners literally "stood before the bar" for the length of a trial, but since this trial lasted for sixteen hours, Bathsheba, at least, may have been allowed to sit.

The many witnesses for the prosecution presented a strong case against all four of the accused, and apparently no witnesses testified for the defense. Even though we have three separate, detailed transcriptions of the trial testimony available (see the appendix), the veracity of the witnesses for the prosecution is difficult to assess. We can only make assumptions by noting when individual testimony is substantiated by other testimony or documentation and by considering an individual's motivation to tell the truth. Mrs. Stratton, Jesse Parker, and Alexander Cummings were trading their testimony for immunity from prosecution, and so it would have behooved them to deflect guilt from themselves to Bathsheba and the three soldiers. Prosecutor Robert Treat Paine made this note under his transcription of points that Levi Lincoln apparently made in the prisoner's defense:

> The Credibility of Prue
> > Mary Walker
> > Mrs. Stratton
> > Alex

We can't know for certain if Lincoln questioned their credibility simply because of their low station — Prue was a black, Mary Walker the daughter of a tavern keeper, Mrs. Stratton a servant, and Alex a young boy and a British soldier — or for more concrete reasons that are lost to us. However, as far as we can tell, neither Prue nor Mary Walker had any reason to lie about what they had seen, and the level of concrete detail in their testimony suggests candidness. According to Rev. Thaddeus Maccarty, Bathsheba "often declared that the witnesses wronged her." She may very well have been right, but we have nothing to indicate which witnesses wronged her or in what way.[19]

Because the three male defendants had already signed a written confession, defense attorney Levi Lincoln faced a difficult task. He opened his defense by stressing the importance of the trial, the first capital trial since the establishment of American independent government. He asked that all prejudices and all indignation at the enormity of the offense be banished and that the prisoners be judged individually as innocent if they were not proven guilty by the evidence. He presented almost no defense for Brooks or Buchanan, except for an abstract discussion on perfect versus imperfect proofs and on the reliability of confessions, which may be dictated by fear or the hope of mercy.[20]

Lincoln was more eloquent on Ezra Ross's and Bathsheba's behalf, arguing that Ross had no design to hurt Spooner, that he was ignorant of the murder plan until a few hours before it was enacted, that he did not physically assist in the murder itself, and that he only wanted "to keep up an appearance of favoring the design to keep on terms." As for Bathsheba, Lincoln argued she was not of sound mind. "If it is said she could not live with her husband," he argued, "could she not have separated? Could [she] not have gone to her father, whose favorite she was? To her brother and her other friends? There with her address and engaging appearance she might have had any gallant she pleased. Not [such] as Ross. . . . There is the best evidence of a disordered mind that the nature of the thing will admit of." He also argued that her conduct was irrational in that there was no reasonable murder plan formed, no story agreed on, no place to flee to, and no hope of advantage or impunity. Neither defense effort prevailed.

On Saturday, 25 April the jury found all four prisoners guilty. "Upon which the awful and shocking sentence of death was pronounced," Ebenezer Parkman wrote in his diary. They were all four to be "hanged by the neck until their bodies be dead," on 4 June 1778.

In assessing the fairness of the trial, even some two hundred years later, one sees some glaring inequities.[21] After studying all the available sources, Vincent J. Fuller, a trial attorney with forty years experience in the practice of U.S. criminal law, made the following assessment of the legal proceedings:

> The procedures followed before and during the trial appear to be common to the English justice system. Our right against self-incrimination was not yet established, although the right to trial before a jury was generally recognized in England. (Significantly, at the first Provincial or 'Stamp Act' Congress of 1765, Brigadier Timothy Ruggles, Bathsheba's father, refused to sign a 'Declaration of Rights' dealing with the legality of taxation without representation and the right of the public to a trial by jury. These were rights not universally recognized at the time and became established after the adoption of the Constitution and Bill of Rights some twenty-five years later.)
>
> Nevertheless, the only records available show that there was an inquisition conducted by members of the Supreme Judicial Court of Massachusetts, which resulted in an indictment in April 1778, followed by the trial on 24 April. The

trial started at 8:00 A.M., and the taking of testimony concluded at midnight on the same day. The trial record is sparse, but from it one concludes that the trial lacked the most fundamental due process, which we so casually are afforded today in the United States.

First, and most important, it must be recognized that the four persons tried each had different, distinct, and conflicting defenses, which could only be presented by separate counsel for each accused. Bathsheba Spooner, alleged to be the instigator of the crime, was clearly an emotional, lonely woman of 32 years (probably middle aged in 1778) who was experiencing difficulties with her husband's habits. Her complaints eventually took the forms of fantasies bordering on delusions, which included schemes to do away with him. They may have been proposed with no serious intent. There were so many schemes proposed and not followed that perhaps the scheme eventually followed was not really intended. Separate counsel was imperative to pursue the possibility of insanity as well.

Ezra Ross was to poison Joshua when he accompanied him on a trip to Princeton in February 1778. He was carrying "Aqua Fortis," a form of nitric acid which, when ingested, tastes very bitter. Hardly a subtle lethal murder weapon. His separate counsel could have developed an explanation showing that the proposed scheme was not only absurd but also never attempted. Moreover, Ross does not appear to have been involved in the actual murder and only appeared after the fact. Separate counsel was imperative again.

Sergeant James Buchanan also was not present for the actual killing of Joshua. Properly represented, he might have isolated his involvement to events after the murder and not have to have been involved in the planning stages. Finally, William Brooks, the actual killer, might have argued that what he did was done under duress, or orders, or fear. He was, afterall, a lowly private, used to obeying orders.

Unfortunately for the defendants, they were all represented by the same inexperienced lawyer, Levi Lincoln, who could conduct no effective cross examination of the witnesses, because to do so would greatly damage the interests of his other clients.

Additionally, 'The Dying Declaration' of the three male participants in the murder is described as a statement in anticipation of their execution; it was not to have been used in that form as evidence at trial. But presumably, the substance of the document was offered at the trial in some form, because the existence of confessions is referred to in both attorney's notes and those of the presiding justices as well.

As these confessions were obtained subsequent to the apprehension of the participants, their use at trial would have been limited under today's standards, in such a manner that they would have had little probative value. More to the point, the statements of a coconspirator, after the crime and subsequent to arrest, are admissible only against the declarant and not his coconspirators, as they are not statements made in furtherance of the conspiracy. Such statements are admissible only against the person making them. Had this rule been in effect and followed in 1778, the prosecution would have had no choice but to immunize one of the accused in order to obtain the live testimony of one of the conspirators (participants) against the others. This is a common practice today in criminal prosecutions and is reported with great frequency in the press. Having an immunized witness testify and describe the role of each participant would have permitted trials of the other three defendants that would make no use whatsoever of the confessions.

If the prosecutor were to grant such immunity, which certainly existed in common law, I would venture a guess that only Ezra Ross would have been considered. He was the youngest and an experienced American veteran. The other two men had fought on behalf of the Crown. As for Mrs. Spooner, she would never have been considered, as the local attitude was demonstrably hostile to her, and the judges, themselves, appear to have been infected by the community ill feeling.

Of course, none of the accused was advised of the right to

counsel, as that right did not exist as we know it today. (Now it engages immediately when someone is charged, and frequently earlier.) In 1778 the right was nebulous at best, and it is unclear how these defendants obtained counsel.

The feelings against the defendants, especially Bathsheba, appear to have been very hostile, most likely transferred from the community's hatred of Brigadier Ruggles who had left Massachusetts in disgrace for his loyalty to the Crown. Today such strong, hostile community feeling would be dealt with if only by delaying the trial. Changing venue was probably not a viable option at that time in our history.

The legal system in eighteenth-century Massachusetts was nothing like it is today. Following their arraignment and one-day trial, the defendants were found guilty the next day, 25 April 1778. Each of the accused received swift justice, death sentences providing for their public hanging on 4 June 1778. Surprisingly, the right of a criminal to appeal did not exist in common law, and at the time there was no federal system to review the conviction and sentence. These faults were generally corrected in the nineteenth century, but not in all states.

Criminal justice in the difficult days of the American Revolution was nasty and brutish. This is best demonstrated by the conduct of the commonwealth when it became aware that there was a serious question about Bathsheba's pregnancy.

[9]

Petitions to the Council

I F THIS NARRATIVE can be said to have a hero, it would be the Reverend Thaddeus Maccarty, who in his role as confessor regularly visited the condemned prisoners in jail. At the time of the Spooner murder, he was fifty-seven years old and had served as minister of the Old South parish for thirty-one years. Described by a contemporary as a tall, slender man with black penetrating eyes, he was a man of compassion and conscience, qualities that were both called upon following the Spooner trial.

He had begun his ministry in 1742 as pastor of the church in Kingston, Massachusetts, at a time when New England churches were torn between quarreling "New-Lights" and "Old-Lights," "with . . . neither of whom was he in entire agreement," according to Clifford Shipton in *Sibley's Harvard Graduates*.[1] In 1745 Maccarty was accused by his parishioners of subscribing to New-Light Whitfieldism, an evangelical movement led by the English preacher George Whitfield, who was instrumental in the Great Awakening.

Rather than sign a confession to this effect, Maccarty asked to be dismissed. He was installed in Worcester's Old South parish in 1747, where he and his wife raised fifteen children and where he served until his death in 1784 at age sixty-three.

The notoriety of the Spooner trial prompted Maccarty to write an account of the prisoners "in their last stages," describing their states of mind and behavior during their commitment in the Worcester jail prior to their hanging. Accounts tracking prisoner's spiritual progress between sentencing and execution were a common part of the literary tradition associated with eighteenth-century executions, "identify[ing] the spiritual predicament of the condemned criminal with that of the larger community."[2] This account was appended to Maccarty's execution sermon and later published as "The appendix, giving some account of the prisoners in their last stage."[3]

The first part of this "Appendix" dealt with Buchanan, Brooks, and Ross: "When they were first committed, such was the horror of their consciences, that . . . they were resolved to lie at God's feet, to cast themselves upon him for mercy. . . . They gave themselves to prayer, they desired the prayer of others, and were eager to embrace all opportunities for religious counsels and instructions."

After their trial, Maccarty wrote, they didn't question their condemnation but "spent all their time, even till late at night, in reading the bible and many valuable books that were put into their hands, in praying and singing psalms and hymns. . . . They were persons of good, natural capacity: Buchanan and Ross in all their conversation, discovered a considerable extent of it [the significance of scriptural passages]; and Brooks had a good share of it. . . . There was all the external evidence of true penitence in them, that could be expected."

Though Maccarty had a vested interest in bringing the men to a state of true penitence, there seems no reason to doubt their remorse. In their own words from "The Dying Declaration," they affirmed it: "We, Buchanan, Brooks and Ross, are conscious to ourselves that we are indeed guilty of the above murder, and that hereby we have forfeited our lives into the hands of public justice. . . . We trust we have with deep penitence and contrition of soul consigned it to God, hoping an infinite mercy and compassion, through the atoning blood of his son Jesus that our scarlet and crimson guilt may be done away, that we may be saved from eternal damnation which we know we justly deserve, and obtain eternal life and salvation."

The three soldiers publicly consigned their souls to God and proclaimed their faith in the Christian doctrine of repentance and redemption, which was still, in 1778, a fundamental part of the public execution ritual. The emotional solace derived from resigning themselves to the greater will of the state and of God cannot be underestimated. Their behavior throughout suggests that all three were reluctant murderers, and public atonement represented perhaps the only honorable way through the awful catastrophe that had befallen them.

But what of the convicted "instigator" of this crime? In his "Account of the Behaviour of Mrs. Spooner . . ." within his "Appendix"

Maccarty states unequivocally, "Her guilt . . . appeared in most fla-
grant colors upon her trial as well as since. . . . [After the trial] she
declared that *though she had planned the matter, yet that she never thought
that it would be executed; that she relented when she found they were in earnest.*"[4] This last statement is italicized in the account and appears to
represent a direct quotation. To those with little sympathy for Bathsheba it perhaps sounded like a poor excuse and an evasion of respon-
sibility. Even Maccarty, whose sympathy for her is evident, adds, "She
doubtless could have given her husband notice of what was designed,
and so have prevented it, but she did not: nor did she make discovery
of it as soon as possible but sent the next morning to a neighbor's to
inquire after him, when at the same time she knew he was in the well."

His assessment is true enough. Yet her statement may in fact have
been credible, given her distracted behavior before and during the
time of the murder. Buchanan described her as "vastly confused"
when he came back in the house just after the murder was committed.
That she asked Alexander Cummings and Mrs. Stratton to get water
from the well — with Joshua's body in it — certainly illustrates a dissociated quality of mind.

In his account Maccarty characterizes her not as the fundamentally
depraved criminal whom Parkman denounced ("The Adultress! How
can we conceive of one who shall be so metamorphosed or changed
into such a monster!"),[5] but far more sympathetically as a victim of
unfortunate circumstances. "She was a person of uncommon fortitude of mind," he wrote, "[who] did not for the most part appear to
be affected with many circumstances in her case which were deeply
wont to affect others. She would indeed sometimes say, that she felt
more than she did or could express. Seldom a day passed but I visited
her, for which she expressed great gratitude. . . . Her behaviour to all
was very polite and compliant. From the frequent opportunities I had
with her, I was led to conceive of her as a person naturally of a kind,
obliging, generous disposition. But she was unhappy . . . in her first
setting out in the world, and so left to a fatal capital crime."

It is clear that Maccarty felt great compassion for her, though he
remained frustrated in his efforts to exact a confession of guilt. "It
seems she went upon the mistaken principle that she was not an
immediate actor. . . . I was wont to converse with her upon the main

point, and to endeavor to impress her mind with a sense of her guilt, hoping to observe upon her the symptoms of true penitence. Appearances of this were from time to time discouraging."

On 20 May 1778, a petition was presented to the Massachusetts Council requesting a stay of execution so that the prisoners might have more time to prepare themselves for their deaths. It was signed by James Buchanan, William Brooks (X his mark), Ezra Ross, and Bathshua Spooner. Her signature contains a curious misspelling: Spooer with the "n" added above the "oe" in a correction.

Maccarty appended a note to the petition supporting it, adding: "and as to the unhappy woman . . . she declares she is several months advanced in her pregnancy, for which reason she humbly desires, that her execution may be respited till she shall have brought forth." To which Bathsheba herself added: "The above application is made at my most earnest request."

Before the council acted on the petition, Ezra Ross was publicly baptized on 24 May, in anticipation of the original 4 June execution date. According to Maccarty, "He found it a good day, having had tokens of God's gracious preference with him." A temporary reprieve was granted, however, and on 28 May the council fixed the new date of execution as 2 July. Maccarty had apparently brought the petition personally to Boston and awaited the council's decision, because Rev. Ebenezer Parkman noted in his diary on 30 May: "Mr. Maccarty on his journey from Boston came and has Reprieve for the Criminals to July 2. He desires me to preach at Worcester tomorrow, but it was inconvenient. I wd. not be prepared, nor wd. my circumstances allow it."

Maccarty delivered the news of a reprieve to the prisoners himself and wrote in his account that the male prisoners "told me it was contrary to their expectations, trusted that they were in a state of readiness to leave the world . . . and set apart the 4th of June entirely for religious exercises." He also noted that the soldiers made good use of the extra time allotted them, affectionately counseling young people who came by the jail to vilify them.

Just before the council issued its official reprieve on 28 May, the more personal petition (dated 26 May) was presented to it by the parents of Ezra Ross, supported by their Linebrook pastor, Rev. George

Lesslie. The Rosses' plea for their son's life was heartfelt and eloquent: "Your memorialists are the unhappy parents of a most unfortunate son.... Of seventeen children [nine] alone survived to your aged and distressed petitioners, whose footsteps from that period have been marked with anxiety, and whose sorrows, from the melancholy fate of their youngest son, have received a tinge of the keenest kind."

The Rosses went on to describe Ezra's military service and how, at a young and impressionable age, he had fallen into Bathsheba's clutches. When he returned to the Spooners after his northern enlistment, "with a mind thus prepared, & thus irresistibly prepossessed, by her addresses, kindnesses, on his tender years" he was "seduced both from virtue, & prudence a child as he was, by a lewd artfull woman...."

They argued that his participation in the murder was accidental and that he was deeply penitent: "If an early confession of the whole matter and the suffering of a thousand deaths in the reflections of the mind; if the law, the Government, and the grave can be satisfied, and mercy displayed; in fine, if youth, if old age, the sorrows, the anguish of a father, the yearnings of a mother, the compassion & wishes of thousands can avail; if any or all of these considerations can arrest the hand of Justice . . . and thereby give him an opportunity of atoning to the public for the injury he has done it—restore him to his country, himself, his sympathizing friends, to his aged, drooping and distressed parents, this will console them under the weightiest afflictions, and turn the wormwood and the gall, into something tolerable...."

Ezra's life would not be spared, however, and no mention of any action regarding his parents' petition exists in the Massachusetts Council's records or in the records of the legislature for that term. It may have received no official hearing at all.

Along with the reprieve issued on 28 May, the council issued a Writ de Ventre Inspiciendo (Inspection of the Abdomen), directing William Greenleaf, the sheriff of Worcester, to take "two men midwives, and twelve discreet and lawful matrons of your County . . . to the said Bathsheba Spooner and cause her diligently to be searched by the said matrons, in the presence of the said men midwives, by the Breasts and Belly, and certify the truth whether she be quick with child or not, and if she be quick with child, how long she has so been . . . before the 25th day of June next. . . ." The phrase "quick with child" was critical. British common law, which was the basis for colonial, and then American law, did not recognize the existence of a fetus in criminal cases until it had quickened (the first perception of fetal movement by the pregnant woman).[6] Quickening generally occurs in the eighteenth or twentieth week after a woman's last menstruation, or early in the fourth month of gestation. If conception of Bathsheba's child had taken place sometime near the end of January, the fetus was likely to have quickened shortly before the first midwives' examination.

The twelve women examiners were chosen by Sheriff William Greenleaf, apparently from among prominent Worcester matrons. One of them, Mary Stearns (or Sternes) was the wife of William Stearns, Worcester's town clerk.[7] The two male midwives were Josiah Wilder, and Elijah Dix, who owned an apothecary shop in Worcester. On 11 June all twelve women and the two men signed a sworn statement testifying that upon examination they found Bathsheba Spooner not quick with child.

The midwives' jury finding, perhaps more than any other circumstance in the whole unhappy drama, illustrates poignantly the virulent hatred directed toward Bathsheba. The first soft stirrings of fetal life are so delicate and interior that they weren't likely to be felt by a hand laid on the pregnant belly. Nor could they have been discovered by a more intrusive manual examination of the vagina, which very likely also took place. A few days after the execution Ebenezer Parkman noted in his diary: "Mr. Stearns [who would have heard it from his wife, Mary, a member of the first jury] informed me of the method taken by the late Jury of Matrons &c. in the examination of the pregnancy of the late Mrs. Spooner, and by his account it was very indecent and cruel."

Whether quickening could have been discernible or not by the midwives, they surely would have recognized the undeniable swelling of belly and breasts evident late in the fourth month of pregnancy. Yet they refused to acknowledge what must have been obvious, and they found against her. Vindictiveness had to be at the root of such merciless and cruel treatment.

Sheriff Greenleaf returned the signed statement to the council, along with an affecting plea made by Bathsheba.

To the Honorable Council of the State of
Massachusetts Bay

May it please Your Honors

With unfeigned gratitude I acknowledge the favor you
lately granted me of a reprieve. I must beg leave, once more,
humbly to lie at your feet, and to represent to you that,
though the jury of matrons that were appointed to examine
into my case have not brought in my favor, yet that I am
absolutely certain of being in a pregnant state, and above
four months advanced in it, and the infant I bear was lawfully
begotten. I am earnestly desirous of being spared till I shall
be delivered of it. I must HUMBLY desire your honors, not
withstanding my great unworthiness, to take my deplorable
case into your compassionate consideration. What I bear,
and clearly perceive to be animated, is innocent of the faults
of her who bears it, and has, I beg leave to say, a right to the
existence which God has begun to give it. Your honors' humane *christian* principles, I am very certain, must lead you to
desire to preserve life, even in this its miniature state, rather
than destroy it. Suffer me, therefore, with all EARNESTNESS,
to beseech your honors to grant me such a further length of
time, at least, as that there may be the fairest and fullest
opportunity to have the matter fully ascertained; and as in
duty bound, shall, during my SHORT CONTINUANCE, pray,

Bathshua Spooner

Worcester Goal
June 16, 1778

While Bathsheba awaited the council's decision on her second petition, other lesser dramas were unfolding among the prisoners. Rev.
Ebenezer Parkman visited them several times, and according to Parkman other clergymen — Rev. Daniel Foster and the Reverend Mr.
Sumner from Shrewsbury — did, too, presumably to impart Christian
instruction. One can't help suspecting, however, that given the sensationalistic nature of the crime (and the beauty of Bathsheba), there
may have been less exalted motives behind these numerous clergy

visits. Parkman's diary shows a gossip's preoccupation with the particulars of Ezra Ross and Bathsheba's relationship, especially in one lengthy entry.

> June 25 . . . I went into the three men in the Jayle. Ross's Brother Timothy & Lucy McDonald (who was with child by Ezra) were there. The Criminals are very penitent and behave well, I questioned them concerning the woeful Proceedings? They said Mrs. Spooner began them—Each of them Affirmed it. but on visiting Mrs. Spooner I found her of no different mind from time past, unless it was in more avid denial of the Legality of her Condemnation. She was free & friendly in converse . . . But when I asked her who was foremost in the horrid & bloody acts, she laid this on Ross, which being contrary to what I had met with from the prisoners below, I inquired whether she would say this before them if they were together. She said she would be willing to with Ross, but did not want to have the other two present.—A paper was delivered me which Buchanan had drawn up from Ross' mouth, and Ross had signed it, while I was in the chamber. When we were together, Ross by my desire read the paper containing the First of her [Bathsheba's] promoting her Husband's death. The paper ran thus:
>
> I Ezra Ross do desire that Mrs. Spooner will take particular notice. The following is the first of her promoting her husband's Death. . . .

This extraordinary entry continues with Ross's confession as transcribed here in chapter 5, illustrating Parkman's peculiar personal involvement with the prisoners. He seemed bent on setting the men against Bathsheba and Bathsheba against Ross, at which he succeeded. And then there is the presence of the mysterious Lucy McDonald "with child by Ezra," who is mentioned in no other sources available to us. If Parkman is to be trusted (and there seems no motive for him to have lied blatantly about Lucy McDonald), we can only conjecture that she might have been Ezra's Linebrook sweetheart. But if she was, when (if he was indeed the father of her child) did he impregnate her? It would have to have been after Ezra had become romantically involved with Bathsheba, because he was gone from home for four months in the northern campaign prior to returning directly to the Spooner household in December.

Given Parkman's meddling tendencies, it is not amiss to suppose he might have informed Bathsheba about Lucy McDonald's pregnancy, which may well have moved Bathsheba to blame Ezra for beginning the talk of murder. Bathsheba would have been very vulnerable around the time of Parkman's diary entry (25 June), having undergone the brutal and humiliating midwives' examination, uncertain as to the fate of her second petition, and facing execution only a week away. And, thanks to Parkman's intercession, her lover, having apparently betrayed her with another woman, was making public the intimate details of their liaison.

The Massachusetts Council rejected Bathsheba's petition on 23 June, though a cryptic notation in the legislative records states that it was "debated thereupon," implying the decision was controversial. Nevertheless, another examination was arranged, most likely at Maccarty's behest. The second examination included the two midwives and two of the women who had participated in the first examination (Josiah Wilder, Elijah Dix, Elizabeth Rice, and Molly Tattman), a new female midwife named Hannah Mower, and Bathsheba's brother-in-law, the prominent Worcester physician John Green, who had just returned from sitting as Worcester's representative to the state legislature in Boston.

In the "Second Opinion" writ dated 27 June, John Green, Josiah Wilder, Elijah Dix, and Hannah Mower supported Bathsheba's claim of pregnancy. Wilder and Dix reversed their opinions from the first examination, but the two matrons of the 11 June jury, Elizabeth Rice and Molly Tattman, held to their original opinion that Bathsheba was not quick with child. This examination was also painful and injurious; according to Maccarty's account, Bathsheba was "greatly disordered" by it and could not attend the execution sermon a few days later.

We know that the second examination report was submitted to the council, because it is among the executive records. Maccarty wrote a letter to the council on 26 June that may have preceded the "Second Opinion" or accompanied it:

The news arrived last evening to Mrs. Spooner that her petition for a reprieve was not granted. People that are acquainted with her circumstances are exceedingly affected with it. I am myself fully satisfied of her being in a pregnant state, & have been so for a considerable time. And it is with deep regret that I think of her being cut off, till she shall have brought forth, which will eventually, tho' not intentionally be destroying innocent life. An experienced midwife belonging here, visited her this week & examined her, & found her quick with Child. Wherefore, tho' I think justice ought to take place upon her as well as the rest, yet I must beg leave earnestly to desire that she might be respited at least for such a time as that the matter may be fully cleared up. And I have no doubt it will be so satisfactorily to everyone.

I write this, may it please your honors, of my own accord, not at her desire, for I have not seen her since the news arrived.

I should be very sorry if your Honors, should consider me as over-officious in the matter. But principles of humanity, & of Christianity, a Desire that Righteousness may go forth as Brightness & Judgment as the noon-day, have powerfully prompted me to make this Application on her behalf.

I by leave with all dutiful respects, your Honors most obet. & most humble Servant—

Thaddeus Maccarty

Worcester, June 26th, 1778.

The council apparently took no action on the second examination report or Maccarty's letter, but remained intransigent. Ironically, after dispensing with Bathsheba's petition on 23 June it granted in the very next order of business a second reprieve to a male prisoner held in Boston who was also under sentence of death. Bathsheba received the council's final decision with great calmness, Maccarty recorded.

The council's inflexibility proved fateful, resulting in the state-sanctioned murder of an innocent child. In the post-execution autopsy that Bathsheba had requested, a five-month male fetus was, indeed, revealed.

Though Worcester's *Massachusetts Spy* failed to report the discovery of Bathsheba's unborn child, Maccarty himself revealed the results of the autopsy in his published account of the prisoners: "She was opened the evening after the execution, and a perfect male foetus of the growth of five months or near it, in the judgment of the operators, was taken from her."[8] The news surely spread quickly by word-of-mouth, but the grim result of the council's decision wasn't publicly acknowledged or decried until some sixty years later, by Peleg W. Chandler in his *American Criminal Trials*. Chandler noted that with the autopsy, "It was thus discovered ... that a great and humane principle, to be found in the laws of all civilized nations, had been violated in her death. . . . Under the circumstances of doubt with which the case was enveloped, the refusal of the council to grant a reprieve was certainly most extraordinary." Chandler concluded, "The whole subject is of a most distressing character, and to this day, when all the facts cannot be known, the only apology for these proceedings must be sought in the excitement of the public mind upon the subject, and the unsettled condition of the state governments during the war of the revolution."

Since the publication of Chandler's recapitulation of the case, the council's intransigence has been generally understood as politically motivated. It is reasonable to assume that the council feared that Bathsheba might somehow escape justice entirely by pleading her belly, which was not an uncommon ploy for women facing execution in England. Also, the nearly universal fear and hatred inspired by Brig. Gen. Timothy Ruggles would certainly have prompted vengeance on his daughter. But there is another, more personal and not generally known connection that very likely influenced the council's decision directly.

Massachusetts government was in some disarray during the years of the Revolution. After the British evacuated Boston in 1776, Massachusetts was without an acting governor. The patriot legislature appointed its own council, which became the highest state authority for the duration of the war.[9] The position of deputy secretary was second in authority to the council president. In 1778, when Bathsheba's petition came before the council, the president was Gen. Artemas Ward (known as "a personification of Puritanism in his generation"),[10] and the deputy secretary was John Avery Jr., whose signature authorized the final warrant of execution on 28 May.

Deputy Secretary John Avery Jr. was no disinterested official in this proceeding; he was the stepbrother of the murder victim. In 1765 his father, John Avery Sr. had married Sarah Bridges Spooner, who was the widow of John Spooner, Joshua Spooner's father. Sarah Spooner was, in fact, Joshua's stepmother, and she had raised him from the age of three. Joshua was twenty-four and John Avery Jr. twenty-six when Sarah Spooner and John Avery Sr. married, making their respective sons stepbrothers; Joshua married Bathsheba Ruggles the following year.

John Avery Jr.'s politics alone might have predisposed him to take an unfavorable view of Maccarty's and Bathsheba's petitions. Avery was a member of the Loyal Nine, the innermost circle of the Sons of Liberty who all nurtured a vendetta against Brig. Gen. Timothy Ruggles.[11] But even more telling, Avery's connection with his Spooner stepfamily was close. In December 1779 he cosigned a bond of guardianship with John Jones Spooner and William Spooner, for Bathsheba and Joshua's orphaned children.[12] Another indication of Avery's personal attention to the murder case may be found in the Superior Court record book, where the entry recording the indictment and sentence is followed by the statement, "Ordered that the Secretary be served with a copy of the Trial & Sentence."[13] No other trial record of that five-year period has such a notation. One can't help wondering if the council's brutal decision — in the face of serious questions about Bathsheba's condition — was influenced by personal vengeance on Deputy Secretary John Avery Jr.'s part.[14]

Rev. Thaddeus Maccarty may not have known about the Avery-Spooner connection, but whether he did or not his support of Bathsheba against the will of the community — among them his fellow clergymen, friends, neighbors, and parishioners — and especially his last-minute efforts to persuade the most powerful men in Massachusetts that they were about to commit a grievous moral wrong, were inestimably courageous. At that time he was fifty-seven, chronically ill, and the father of fifteen children. He risked the possible loss of his livelihood, and, given the violent mood of patriotic mobs in Massachusetts, he risked physical danger as well. He proved himself to be the very finest exemplar of the Christian faith he espoused.

For Bathsheba, who had lost everyone — her children, the affections of her lover, family, and friends — and who was about to lose her own life and that of her unborn child, Thaddeus Maccarty remained the only sympathetic presence. He would literally stay by her to the end.

Portrait of Brigadier General Timothy Ruggles, Chief Justice of Worcester's Court of Common Pleas, 1762–1774. This portrait is a copy of a contemporary portrait now missing, painted by Sante Graziani for the Worcester County Superior Courthouse. Photograph by Deborah Navas. *Courtesy Worcester County Law Library.*

(Following page) Homestead of General Timothy Ruggles by Winthrop Chandler. The painting of Bathsheba Ruggles Spooner's childhood home was first documented in 1799 as part of her brother-in-law Dr. John Green's estate. It was very likely commissioned for his wife, Mary Ruggles Green, whose childhood home it was as well. Because there is only one house foundation on the Ruggles house site, the presence of the second house has traditionally been attributed to artistic license. However, the neglected and abandoned state of the house to the left suggests that the painting may be a "before and after" portrait: the well-tended house full of people on the right may appear as Mary remembered it from childhood, and the same house painted on the left depicts it as it appeared at the time of the painting—after having been vandalized by a patriot mob when Ruggles left Hardwick in 1774 to join with the British in Boston. *Courtesy Worcester Art Museum, Worcester, Massachusetts. Lent by Julia T. Green*

Paul Revere's copper plate engraving entitled "A Warm Place—Hell" depicts Brigadier General Timothy Ruggles leading the Rescinders into the maw of Hell. The seventeen members of the Massachusetts Legislature, dubbed "Rescinders," voted against the proposed boycott of British manufactured goods on June 30, 1768. *Courtesy American Antiquarian Society*

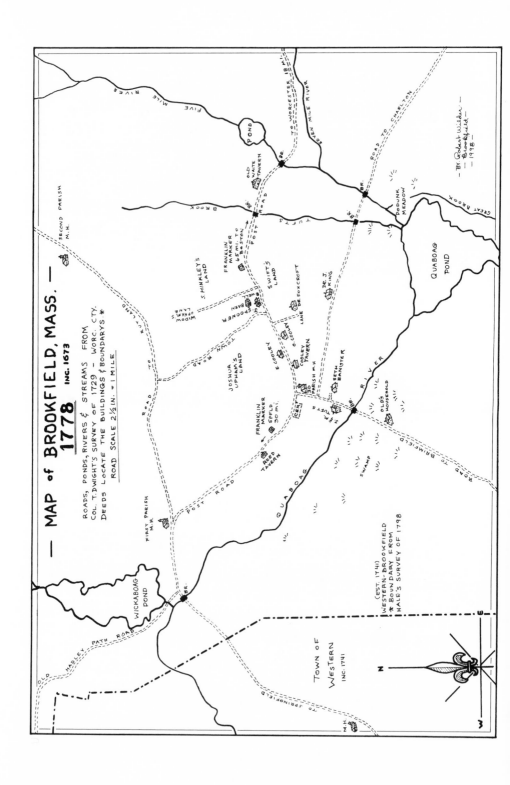

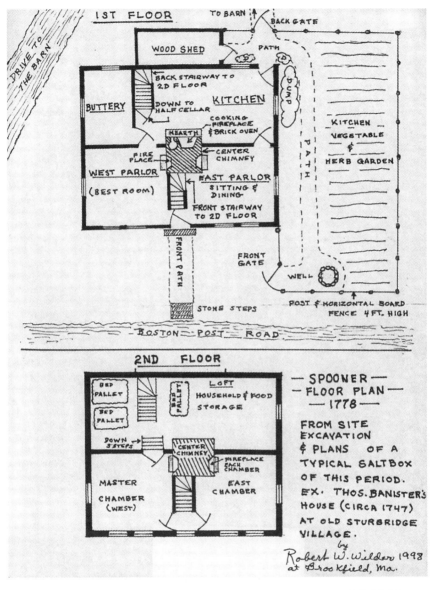

(Left) Map of Brookfield, ca. 1778, by Robert W. Wilder, Brookfield, Massachusetts. *Courtesy of the artist*

(Above) Floor plan of the Spooner house, believed to be a two-story saltbox, by Robert W. Wilder, Brookfield, Massachusetts, who excavated the house site. *Courtesy of the artist*

A mural of Bathsheba Spooner, commissioned by the Worcester County Law Library Association for the Bicentennial in 1976, decorates the Worcester Courthouse front stairway. The artist is Sante Graziani. *Published with permission of the Worcester County Library; photograph courtesy of the* Worcester Telegram and Gazette

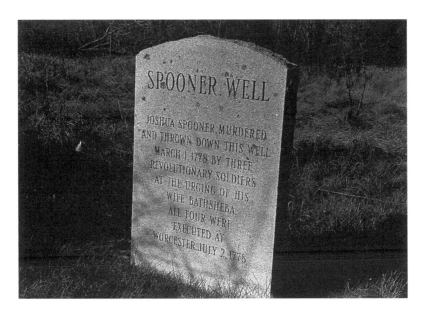

7. Marker identifying the Spooner house site and well, Brookfield, Massachusetts. *Courtesy of the* Worcester Telegram and Gazette

T H E   L A S T

WORDS and dying SPEECH

Of *James Buchanan*, *Ezra Ross* and *William Brooks*, who are executed this day at Worcester, for the Murder of Mr. *Joshua Spooner*.

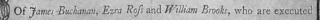

I JAMES BUCHANAN was a Sergeant in the Army under General Burgoyne born in Glasgow in Scotland, aged 36 years. I WILLIAM BROOKS was a private in said army, born in the parish of Wednesbury, in the county of Stafford, in England, aged 27. We together on February 8th 1778, left Worcester, with an intent to go to Springfield to work. In passing Mr. Spooner's, we were called in by Alexander Cummings, whom we thought was a British soldier. Having stood some time by the fire, he told us his master was gone from home, but he would go and call his mistress, for she had a great regard for the army, as her father was in it and one of her brothers. He called her, and she came down, and appeared glad to see us. She asked us, whether we came from the Hill? We told her, we had, and were going to Canada, as I Buchanan, had left my family there. She ordered breakfast for us, and as soon as it was ready we were desired to go into the sitting-room. We were very much surprized at this, for we should have thought ourselves well dealt by, to have received any favors she might see fit to bestow on us in the kitchen. However, we all breakfasted together. The weather being very bad, we were asked to stay till it cleared up. As we had but little money, we accordingly stayed. The weather continued very bad, we stayed there that day and night, I (Buchanan) am not positive whether it was the first or second day, she told me, when by ourselves, that she and her husband did not agree — that he was gone a journey to Princetown, and that he would not be at home soon, that we should not go from thence untill the weather was fair, there being a great fall of snow at this time. We very readily consented, and stayed from day to day, expecting Mr. Spooner home. Mrs Spooner getting very free in discourse with me (Buchanan) one day told me that she never expected Mr. Spooner to return, as there was one Mr. Ross gone with him, who had an ounce of poison, which he had promised her he would give it to Mr. Spooner, the first convenient opportunity. The reader must needs think this a very strange circumstance, that she should make such a discovery to an entire stranger. She said at the same time, we should stay, till we saw whether Mr. Spooner returned or not. Accordingly we stayed, and were never in better quarters, little thinking of the bait, the seducer of souls was laying for us, we were then in a disposition to catch at it, having no fear of God before our eyes, and entirely forsaken of him. Having tarried ten or eleven days, as near as can be recollected, he at length came home, and seeing us there, asked her who we were. She told him that I (Buchanan) was cousin to Alexander Cummings. He took no further notice of it; but going out among his neighbours, it is likely he was informed how long we had been there, and probably heard at the tavern of the quantity of liquor he had to pay for, since his going on his journey. Be that as it may, at night he came home, and seeing we were not gone, he desired us to go immediately. We begged he would let us stay 'till morning: He after some time consented, that we should stay by the fire all night. He was in the sitting room by himself, and Mrs Spooner went to bed. There was one Reuben Old, came upon some business with Mr. Spooner, and after some time came out and told us that Mr. Spooner told him he was affraid we should rob him, adding, that he had lost a silver spoon, and a great deal of pewter. This vexed us, as we were conscious we had no thought of stealing from him. Had we been so inclined, we had as much opportunity as we could have desired. The spoon, he found where he laid it, Cummings convinced him there was none of the pewter missing. Mr. Spooner went up stairs and brought down a box, which he had his money in, and laid down on the floor with it under his head. Every thing Mr. Spooner did or said, Old came and told us, and was out with us all the time he was asleep, and we were all merry together, sitting by the kitchen fire. Said Old declared in court, that I (Buchanan) said, if Mr. Spooner came out I would for two coppers put him in the well, which is false. In the morning, it not being convenient to see Mrs Spooner to take our leave of her, we, Buchanan, Brooks and Cummings, went to Mrs. Stratten's to pass the day, 'till we could get an opportunity to bid Mrs. Spooner farewell. We stayed at Mrs. Stratten's the best part of the day. Cummings having received five dollars from Mr Spooner, to treat his pretended cousin with, we went to Mr. Cooley's tavern and had some drink, from thence to Dr. Foxcroft's, stayed there until Cummings came and told us Mr. Spooner was in bed. We then went to the house, and had supper and liquor, retired to the barn, and tarried all night. In the morning had breakfast sent to the barn for us. And as Mrs. Berry and Mrs. Tufts had been there the day before, and wanted to see me, (Buchanan) I said I would go and see them. Mrs. Spooner said she would also go, which was agreed on. Buchanan and Brooks went there, and we all stayed at Mr Green's, drinking 'till late; some distance from thence, she said she had given a handkerchief to a British soldier that had some words in anger with me, Buchanan, upon which, Brooks went back on her horse, and she and I went home. Brooks missed his road on his return, but got to the house some time after us, but did not get the handkerchief, as the soldier would not deliver it, until he saw Mrs. Spooner. Buchanan and Brooks stayed that night in the barn, in the morning went to Mr. Gilbert's tavern, and stayed there some time, and on coming out from his house we saw Cummings coming on one of Mr. Spooner's horses, he told us his master was gone to the tavern, and that his mistress desired we would come there, which we did, and had supper, we went to the barn that night, and in the morning she sent us word that her husband was gone abroad into the country to get some oats. The boy Parker, had proposed to Brooks, if he would come and meet Mr. Spooner, and him on their return, he, said, Parker said he would help to take Mr. Spooner's life. We went over from the barn to the house, and found he was gone, and stayed there all day, and lived on the best the house afforded of meat and drink: Mr. Spooner came home in the dusk of the evening, so that we had like to have been seen; but we heard him come with the sley to the door, and Brooks ran into the cellar, and I went and stood on the back stairs, until he went into the sitting room. We then came out, and went to the barn, there stayed all next day, and at night when Mr. Spooner was in bed, we were sent for to the house, and received supper and liquor, to encourage another plan, which Cummings and Parker (who have for this time escaped punishment) proposed to poor Brooks, which was, they all three to go up stairs, and Brooks to take his life from him, for which he was to receive one thousand dollars, Mr. Spooner's watch, his buckles, and as much cloth as would make a suit of cloathes; but Brooks's heart failed him; and Mrs. Spooner said, she did not think he was so faint-hearted. Had this been done he was to be put into the well as he was taken out of bed; for she observed it would be thought he had fallen in, drawing water in the night; next day had breakfast brought us by Cummings. He informed us, there was another plan formed by her which was as to have been executed as follows. Either Cummings or Parker to tell Mr. Spooner one of the horses was sick, and as he came to the barn, [illegible] kill him, and put him amongst the horses feet, to make [illegible] believe when he was found in the horses had killed him. But Brooks told Parker not to tell him, but to make her believe he would not go over. The boy conducted accordingly. We stayed all that day and night. Next day, being Sunday, we stayed there; she came over at night; we told her we should go away the next morning; she desired we would not; but we would not stay. We set out to go to Springfield, as we went thro' Western on that road, we engaged to work with one Mr. Marks a smith; I Buchanan worked there two days; but as he had no files fit for the branch of trade, Brooks followed, we proposed to go to Worcester to get some, which was agreed to.

We set off on Wednesday about noon, and in going by Mr. Spooner's we called and told her where we were going; she said she would follow us down next day as she wanted to see her sister, saying she was glad we had got work so near; and further added, that she had two notes, one of 20 pounds, lawful, and another of 500 dollars, which she would endeavour to get changed, and let me, Buchanan have one hundred dollars, to purchase any thing I might want. We stay'd in the barn till morning, and then set out for Worcester, and she followed us the same day and called at Mr. Walker's for us, according to agreement; she came in and stay'd some time, and gave me, Buchanan, a note, as much cloth as made a shirt, and 6 or 7 dollars; observing to me, they came from one M'Donald, an acquaintance of mine; she then went to see her sister, and desired us to stay till she came back, which we did; she returned on Friday morning about 10 o'clock, and stayed till night; she told me, Buchanan, at parting, that she had no more paper money, but what she had given me: but begged I would procure her some poison to give Mr. Spooner; I accordingly that day got one drachm of C[illegible]mel, and made it into 20 papers. I desired her to give one in [illegible] morning; she told me she never gave him any; she went to her sister's late that night, and call'd on us in the morning, about ten o'clock, I went to the door; she would not come in, but desired me to come up to Mr. Nazro's shop; and she would get files for us, as we had not money sufficient to get what we wanted; she asked me, when we would come through Brookfield. I told her if she would set up, we would call on Monday night at eleven o'clock, she said she would; I parted with her, and sent Brooks up to the shop. But as he came in sight, he saw her ride from the door and therefore did not go there; we stayed at Walker's until Sunday afternoon, and then left Worcester, and about 11 o'clock at night got to Mr. Spooner's; we saw Mrs. Strattin at the well, I Buchanan spoke to her, she told me there was company in the house, but she would let Mrs. Spooner know we were there; Mrs Spooner came out, and told us that one Mr. Ross was in the house, who had a brace of pistols loaded, and that he had promised her he would kill Mr. Spooner as he came home from the tavern, she desired us to come in, which we did, he shewed us a pistol, and said Mr. Spooner should die by that to night. Either Brooks or Buchanan said it would alarm the neighbours.

Brooks said, if Ross would help him he would knock him down accordingly, it was agreed on, and there was a look out kept at the sitting room door for his coming. In the mean time there was some supper brought by Mrs. Stratten to us, we had some flip before, there was [illegible] some rum brought, which we drank, each of us by turns giving a look out. We are certain Mrs. Stratten could not but know what was going forward. That we leave to the judgement of the public. Mr. Spooner was at length seen coming, and then was the time for the Devil to show his power over sinners who had forsaken God.

An Account of the Murder as was committed.

William Brooks went out and stood within the small gate leading into the kitchen, and as Mr. Spooner came past him he knocked him down with his hand. He strove to speak when down, Brooks took him by the throat and partly strangled him. Ross and Buchanan came out; Ross took Mr. Spooner's watch out and gave it to Buchanan; Brooks and Ross took him up and put him into the well head first; before they carried him away, I, Buchanan, pulled off his shoes: I was instantly struck with horror of conscience, as well I might; I went into the house and met Mrs. Spooner in the sitting room; she seemed vastly confused: She immediately went up and brought the money which was in a box. She not having the key desired me to break it open which I did; At the same time Brooks and Ross came in: She gave two notes of 500 dollars each to Ross to change and give the money to Brooks; but there was found some paper money, which Brooks received (243 Dollars) and the notes were returned. At the same time she gave Ross four notes, each of them ten pounds, to purchase camblet for a riding dress. Ross gave Brooks his waistcoat, breeches and a shirt. She went and brought Ross a waistcoat, breeches and shirt of Mr. Spooner's. When they were shifted she gave me Buchanan, three eight dollar bills, and asked me when she should see me again. I told her in fourteen days, but it pleased God to order it sooner and in a dreadful situation. Had we all been immediately struck dead after the perpetrating so horrid a murder, and sent to Hell, God would have been justified and we justly condemned.

About 11 o'clock at night we set off for Worcester. About 4 o'clock in the morning we reached Mrs. Walker's house; Mary Walker and a Negro girl were within; we told them a parcel of lyes to excuse our sudden return; in the morning we went to drinking to endeavour to drown the horrid action we had been guilty of, we tarried there all day with a view to go off at night, but it pleased God to order it otherwise, for Brooks being in liquor, went down to Mr. Brown's tavern, there shewing Mr. Spooner's watch, and the people seeing him have silver Buckles, became suspicious of him, and one Ensign Clark going to Mr. Walker's and seeing what passed there gave information concerning us. The news of the murder had now reached the town, and we were all taken, and brought to trial before the Committee, examined and committed to goal. On the 24th of April last we were brought to tryal before the Superior Court, found guilty and received sentence of death.

JAMES BUCHANAN,
EZRA ROSS,*
his
WILLIAM + BROOKS,
mark

We, Buchanan, Brooks and Ross, are conscious to ourselves that we are indeed guilty of the above murder, and that hereby we have forfeited our lives into the hands of public justice, and exposed ourselves to have our part in the lake which burneth with fire and brimstone. We desire to give glory to God by a free and full confession of our heinous guilt. We trust we have with deep penitence and contrition of soul, confessed it to God hoping in his infinite mercy and compassion, through the attoning blood of [illegible] Jesus, that our scarlet and crimson guilt may be done [illegible] that we may be saved from eternal damnation, which we know we justly deserve, and obtain eternal life and salvation. We would as dying men, who have been made to feel what an evil and bitter thing sin is, earnestly warn all, especially young people, that they would avoid the vices we have been addicted to, and which prepared the way for our committing the heinous wickedness for which we are to suffer an immature and ignominious death: That they would avoid bad company, excessive drinking prophane cursing and swearing, shameful debaucheries, disobedience to parents, the profanation of the Lord's day, &c. That they would be pious, sober and virtuous, that so they may be in favor with God and man.

And now we commend our departing souls into the hands of a merciful God and Saviour, earnestly desiring that all who may be spectators or hearers of our tragical end, while we are the subjects of prayer, would lift up their hearts in fervent supplication for us, that God would receive us to his everlasting mercy.

* *A soldier in the continental army, born at Ipswich, in the parish of Lyndsbrook, (New-England,) aged 18.*

BOSTON: Printed and Sold by DRAPER and FOLSOM, at the Corner of Winter-Street.

(Facing page) One of at least six different broadside and quarto versions of "The Dying Declaration of James Buchanan, Ezra Ross and William Brooks, who are executed this day at Worcester, for the murder of Mr. Joshua Spooner." This broadside, decorated with a devil figure holding a noose in one hand and possibly the warrant of execution in the other, was published by Draper & Folsom of Boston, illustrating how widespread public interest was in the Spooner murder and execution. The broadside was very likely copied from Isaiah Thomas's original version of the confession which was published in Worcester and sold for two shillings on July 2, 1778, execution day. *With permission of the Princeton University Library.*

(Following page) This woodcut depicting Bathsheba's body about to be cut down from the gallows as well as the souls of the dead in the form of birds decorates a quarto version of the "Dying Declaration." It is assumed to have been printed in Worcester and probably was produced sometime after the execution, judging from its elaborate format and content, which includes the whole text of "The Cruel Murder: or a Mournful Poem." On execution day, Isaiah Thomas sold the confession and poem separately. *Courtesy American Antiquarian Society*

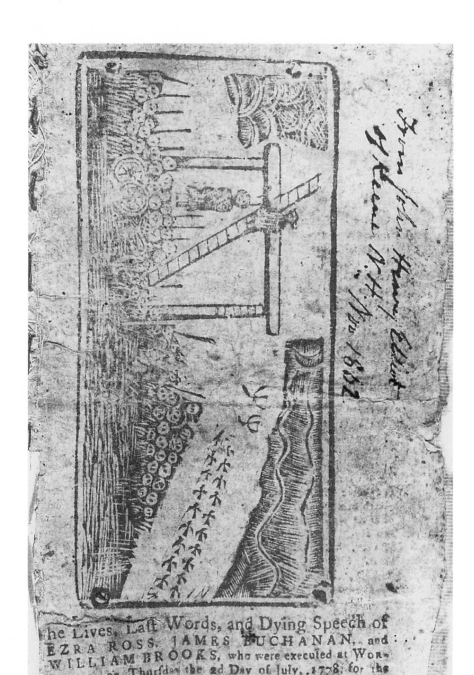

The Lives, Last Words, and Dying Speech of EZRA ROSS, JAMES BUCHANAN, and WILLIAM BROOKS, who were executed at Worcester, on Thursday the 2d Day of July, 1778, for the Murder of Mr. JOSHUA SPOONER, of Brookfield. BATHSHEBA SPOONER, who was convicted of being accessary to the Murder, was also executed at the same Time.

Portrait of the Reverend Thaddeus Maccarty, artist
unknown. *Courtesy American Antiquarian Society*

Bathsheba Spooner's petition written in her own hand to the Massachusetts Council, requesting a stay of execution until the birth of her child. *Courtesy Massachusetts State Archives, Boston, Executive Records,* Revolutionary Council Papers, 1777–1778

From a series of drawings believed to represent the execution of Joshua Spooner's murderers discovered on the attic walls of the Bigelow-Temple tavern, West Boylston, Massachusetts, now owned by the West Boylston Historical Society. This figure, originally drawn with chalk, depicts Bathsheba with a man who may be Ezra Ross caressing her, or he may be the hangman adjusting the halter. The bird very likely represents her soul departing. Tufts family tradition has it that she was hanged in her wedding dress, which appears to be substantiated by this drawing. Wedding dresses of the period were often high-waisted, as depicted here, and her choice may have been dictated by the need to accommodate her pregnancy as well as by a certain irony that would not have been lost on those who knew her well. *Photograph courtesy of Ed Whitcomb, president of the West Boylston Historical Society; enhanced by Robin Sloan.*

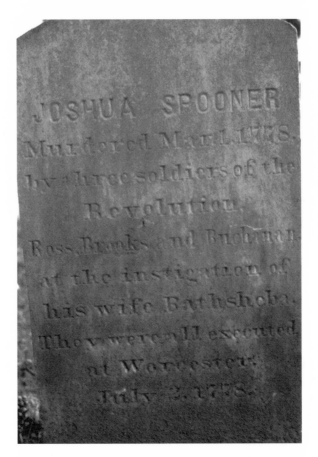

Joshua Spooner's gravestone stands in the Brookfield, Massachusetts, cemetery next to the graves of
his brother-in-law, John Tufts, and Bathsheba's sister, Martha Ruggles Tufts. The style and cutting of
Spooner's stone are characteristic of mid-nineteenth-
century gravestone art, though why it was erected
some thirty to fifty years after his death remains a
mystery. *Photograph by the author*

Dreadful Scene of Horror

THE TOWN of Worcester prepared itself for the execution and the massive crowds that were anticipated to attend it, later estimated by the *Massachusetts Spy* to be some five thousand. A notice in the 25 June issue of the *Spy* warned: "the selectmen of the town of Worcester, taking into their consideration the large concourse of people that will probably attend at the execution of the unhappy persons under sentence of death here, . . . DO, in behalf of the PUBLIC, caution and request all Physicians and Nurses, concerned in such [small pox] Hospitals, and persons having lately had the smallpox, not to appear in the assembly of spectators unless sufficiently CLEANSED. Otherwise their attendance may prove fatal to many, and render the execution, which is intended for the warning and benefit of ALL, a public detriment."

Execution day in the colonial and revolutionary era was entertainment as much as a civic and religious spectacle. Makeshift booths and tables were erected along the common and post road for the sale of spirits, cakes, pies, fruits, vegetables, and other eatables, as well as toys and memorabilia. Young boys were probably hawking copies of "The Dying Declaration" as well as an execution poem in doggerel entitled "A Mournful Poem." It was a type of generic occasional poem that might have applied to any execution of a murderer or murderers ("Behold the Murd'rers now in chains, / with sad and heavy Hearts, / Approaching low the Place where they / will have their just Deserts").[1] Anyone purchasing this poem for spiritual instruction, aesthetic pleasure, or for titillating details of the Spooner murder would have been sorely disappointed.

On execution day, Thursday, 2 July, the sun was very burning in Worcester, but the wind abated the heat, wrote Rev. Ebenezer Parkman in his diary. Early in the morning Mr. Maccarty visited the prisoners and found them prepared to meet their death. "I . . . found [the soldiers] calm and composed. One of them observed . . . that 'the sun would no more arise upon them here, but trusted before night they should be in glory!' " Maccarty would later visit Bathsheba in jail after his execution sermon because she was "greatly disordered" by the second examination and too ill to attend.

Worcester's Old South meeting house was packed for the execution sermon, which probably began at noon as was the custom, the service lasting about two hours. Buchanan, Brooks, and Ross were present.

Maccarty chose as text Deuteronomy 19:13: "Thine eye shall not pity him, but thou shall put away the guilt of innocent blood from Israel, that it may go well with thee." His stated purpose was to impress upon the prisoners and congregation the heinousness of the crime and justice of the sentence so "we may be all filled with an utter detestation [of the crime]."

Though Maccarty showed great sympathy for all four prisoners throughout their imprisonment, he in no way excused them. The sermon provided a detailed examination of the grievousness of the murder to God and man and an explanation of why public execution did not violate the law of God that forbids murder.

Maccarty stressed that the prisoners did not deserve pity — as one might pity them if their sentence were unjust — but the latter part of the sermon dwelled on the mercy of God and hope for their redemption. "As black a crime as murder is, it may be repented of, and in virtue of the great atonement by Jesus Christ, be pardoned by God." He asked the congregation to offer the prisoners compassion and to pray for their salvation. He spoke to the prisoners directly, praising the men for their free confession of guilt. "If God is yours, and Christ is yours, then attending angels will hover around the ignominious tree, to receive your departing spirits, and take them upon their wings, and bear them away safely to the regions of joy. . . ."

His address to Bathsheba, which he apparently did not deliver because of her absence, was nonetheless included in the published version of his sermon.

When we consider your sex, the respectable figure that in times past you made in life, your connections, and your many agreeable qualities, it is with a pungent grief that we behold you a prisoner of death, presently to be led forth to execution. Surely you must feel your circumstances this day.

It would have been very satisfactory, had you been free and ingenuous in acknowledging your guilt, and the justice of your sentence. But though you have not been disposed to do this to man, I hope you have done so upon your bended knees to the Omniscient God, who cannot be deceived. You are indeed looked upon by man, as guilty, yea, as the author and procurer of the bloody deed, but for whom it had never been perpetrated. The evidence in the case, was too glaring to lead anyone to a different sentiment. It is painful to me to say this, but I must be faithful to you in this matter, though this is not the first time by many. I say thus, to the intent that you may be led, now at the last, if you have never been so, to penitential grief and sorrow, before that holy, righteous God, at whose dread tribunal you must this day appear. . . . I would hope that under a deep sense of your guilt, you have been earnestly applying to God for pardoning mercy and grace: That from a sense of your unworthiness before him . . . that you have . . . seen there is a glorious and effectual remedy provided for you, the precious blood of Christ, . . . and have some comfortable evidences that God has received you to pardon and favour. Is it thus with you *poor dying woman*! Then the death before you, though shameful, will yet be late and joyful: And you shall ascend this day to be with God in glory. . . . This is what we all earnestly wish and pray on your behalf, and trust we shall continue to do so, till your soul shall take its flight into the eternal world. *And so we bid you a solemn and final farewell!*

If a little long-winded, Maccarty's goodbye to Bathsheba is heartfelt and affecting. It is clear that he anguished over her refusal to make a public confession, though, as she had explained to him, "It was a fixed principle with her, that confession of her faults was proper only to be made to her maker, not to men." Even to the end she graciously declined to expose her unhappy life to public view or attempt any kind of public justification despite what we can imagine was unremitting pressure from visiting clergymen and even from Maccarty himself.

After his sermon was delivered, Maccarty returned to the jail and visited Bathsheba, accompanied by a number of other clergymen.[2] He later wrote, "She appeared very calm, humble and penitent, professed her faith in the great Saviour and dependence upon him. Upon its being proposed to her, she readily consented to be baptized. She was so immediately, as but a few moments remained before she must go forth. The scene was very solemn and affecting; she was not at all daunted when the sheriff presented her with and put on the fatal cord. She told him she esteemed it as much as though he had put on a necklace of gold and diamonds."

According to the long-established ritual of public execution, criminals wore their nooses around their necks, and their hands were tied behind their backs. They walked to the place of execution between crowds of onlookers on either side, preceded by carts bearing their coffins.

Bathsheba was spared the indignity of the "execution walk" and may have been spared having her hands tied because of her feeble condition. She was "exceedingly unwell," according to the *Massachusetts Spy* account of the hanging, and allowed to ride in Maccarty's chaise from the jail (now Lincoln Square) to the gallows, erected in what is now Washington Square.[3] Though ill, she maintained her dignity and the elegance and manners befitting a lady of her class. One long-lived rumor has it that she wore an ostrich plume in her bonnet, and according to an anecdote passed down through the Tufts family, she wore her wedding dress to her hanging.[4]

When they came in sight of the gallows, Maccarty asked her "if the sight of it did not strike her? She answered not at all any more than any other object. Her constitutional politeness still remained, and she discovered it to numbers that were near her." The *Spy* reporter noted that "she heard the warrant read with as much calmness as she would the most indifferent matter; she was frequently seen to bow to many of the spectators with whom she had been acquainted."

Buchanan, Brooks, and Ross went on foot under a guard of about a hundred men, according to the *Spy* account. "The procession was regular and solemn. Just before they reached the place of execution a black thunder cloud arose and darkened the Heavens; here followed an awful half hour! The loud hallooings of the . . . officers, amidst a crowd of five thousand, to *Make way! Make way!* the horses pressing upon those on foot; the shrieks of women in the confusion; the male-factors slowly advancing to the fatal tree, preceded by their dismal urns; the fierce coruscations athwart the darkened horizon, quickly followed by loud peals of thunder, conspired together, and produced a dreadful compound scene of horror! It seemed as if the author of nature was determined to add such terrors to the punishment of the criminals as must stagger the stoutest heart of the most abandoned."

Parkman, too, noted the unusual weather. "After 4 P.M. arose a storm of thunder, lightening, and rain." Maccarty observed that the storm "seemed to add to the solemnity of the scene," and we can only wonder if he privately might have read it as a sign of heaven's dis-pleasure over the impending execution of an innocent life in utero.

The four prisoners were most likely hanged together on one oversized gallows constructed for the occasion. Hangings were not frequent in New England in the latter half of eighteenth-century, and gallows were most often erected for each execution and then dismantled. Occasionally onlookers either took, or were sold, gallows pieces as souvenirs of the event.

Gallows of the period were built high to accommodate public view-ing, with supports on either side of the scaffold and a heavy cross bar for attaching the rope or ropes. The scaffold was built with a hinged door or "stage" that dropped down, activated by metal weights and often a lever. Felons, the hangman, the sheriff, and whoever else might be involved ascended to the scaffold by a ladder. A ladder was also used by the hangman to reach the crossbar in order to tie on the nooses.

Prisoners on the scaffold were usually bound around the thighs and ankles (to restrain the jerking of limbs during the death throes), and black hoods were placed over their heads. Death, depending upon the weight of the prisoner and the skill of the hangman in devising the correct length of rope, could be almost instantaneous if the neck was broken, or considerably longer if death was caused by suffocation. The prevailing medical and ecclesiastical opinion was that death by hanging was painless, despite more than a few horrifying examples to the contrary.[5]

Published descriptions of hangings idealized and almost glorified the event, in keeping with public execution's religious justification. An exalted example of a "noble" death by hanging was the locally famous account (published by the *Massachusetts Spy* on 21 November 1777), of Dr. William Dodd. Dodd was an Anglican clergyman hanged at Tyburn, England, a year before the Spooner executions for forging the name of his patron to a bond for £4,000:

> As the most noble proof of dying well he took the cap from Jack Ketch's hand and put it on with a Christian fortitude. . . . Soon [he] was launched into eternity, with the tears and prayers of thousands as there never was an execution attended with such an naive concern and seriousness. He appeared not to suffer much in dying, though it was near two minutes before all motion ceased. . . . The serenity of mind which took place in Dr. Dodd the last two days gave great pleasure to his friends.

Just as it was the clergyman's duty to bring a condemned prisoner to confession and repentance, so it was the obligation of the felon to repent publicly and die well. If the accounts of their death can be trusted, James Buchanan, William Brooks, Ezra Ross, and Bathsheba Spooner all died well. On the scaffold, Ezra Ross "made an audible and very affectionate prayer, and the others went to their private devotions, and continued in them till they were turned off," Maccarty noted. "Buchanan in particular, upon the stage appeared with a pleasant aspect."

From all accounts, Bathsheba embraced her death. According to the *Massachusetts Spy*, "When called on to ascend the stage, with a gentle smile she stepped out of the chaise and crept up the ladder upon her hands and knees. The halters being fastened; the malefactors pinioned, and their faces covered, the sheriff informed them that he should drop the stage immediately; upon which Mrs. Spooner took him by the hand, and said, 'My dear sir! I'm ready! In a little time I expect to be in bliss: and but a few years must elapse when I hope I shall see you and my other friends again.' "[6]

And from Rev. Thaddeus Maccarty's account: "She presently mounted the scaffold, and while the sheriff was fixing her, she told him, with a serene countenance, *that it was the happiest day she ever saw, for she doubted not it would be well with her.* She acknowledged *that she justly died; that she hoped to see her christian friends she left behind her, in Heaven, but that none of them might go there in the ignominious manner that she did."*

Such presence! And such a loaded statement about her Christian friends, pointed, yet subtly witty. Maccarty apparently took it at face value, and he was very likely relieved to comment, "At the last, she did [confess] at least implicitly to the sheriff." It must have eased, to some degree, his personal concern that he had not been able to elicit a full confession from her in order to better assure her soul a place in paradise. He ended his account of her behavior as he had concluded his execution sermon:

> We know what are the infinite compassions of God, and that the blood of Jesus is of infinite value, cleansing from all unrighteousness. We may by no means limit the holy one of Israel. We read of the Servant that came in at the eleventh hour, who received the same wages as those who had borne the burden and heat of the day. We know what was done by our Saviour to the penitent thief upon the cross, just before he expired. This shows us what divine power and grace can do and may do. But secret things belong to God, and we ought to leave them with him.

*   *   *

We can only hope that Thaddeus Maccarty derived the spiritual comfort he deserved for his efforts throughout the wrenching drama in which he had become so deeply (and, it seems apparent, emotionally) involved. His courageous stand before the council was vindicated with the autopsy performed the night of the execution, and it may even have given him some small, grim satisfaction to publish the news of "the perfect male foetus of the growth of five months."

But for us looking on two centuries later, Bathsheba's acknowledgment that she died justly is not enough to grant a satisfying resolution to this tragic story. Mitigating circumstances show that the woman who was transformed from the "naturally kind, obliging, and generous" victim of an abhorrent marriage into a murderer deserves pity and sympathy. Also, the transformation of her confused, impulsive, and mortally foolish behavior into the courage and dignity with which she met, on her own terms, nearly universal hatred, cruelty, and her own humiliating death (as well as the murder of her unborn baby) deserves great admiration. Yet two fundamental questions underlying the documented facts remain only partly satisfied by historical recapitulation.

Why did she choose murder, that most radical and violent solution to her dilemma? A passage from the writing of a contemporary of Bathsheba's, Dr. Benjamin Rush, perhaps offers some more illumination. Rush was a signer of the Declaration of Independence, administrator of one of the first American hospitals for the insane, and a prominent Philadelphia physician who was instrumental in popularizing the practice of "heroic medicine," involving harsh purging and bleeding remedies. In his *Medical Inquiries and Observations Upon the Diseases of the Mind,* he discussed "Hypochondriasis," his term for a condition characterized by a terrible anguish of spirit and despair, which drives its sufferers to suicide, and, he wrote, "beyond a mere wish to die, . . . to precipitate the slow approaches of death with his own hand. . . . Sometimes horror is entertained by persons in this situation at the crime of suicide, but, in order to escape from life, they provoke death from the hands of government by committing murder; many instances of this kind are to be met with . . . in our public newspapers."[7]

For a man who attempted to cure mental illness by bloodletting, purges, emetics, doses of mercury, or the application of burning mustard plasters, it seems a surprisingly modern observation on depressive and suicidal behavior. Further, it offers an insight into Bathsheba's irrational compulsion to incite Joshua's murder with little thought of consequence. Two of her final statements to Sheriff Greenleaf show she welcomed her death: She esteemed the halter around her neck "as much as though he had put on a necklace of gold and diamonds," and upon the scaffold, she felt "that it was the happiest day she ever saw."

It is possible that Bathsheba turned to murder out of a combination of her utter loathing for Joshua and a sense of entrapment, obliquely fueled by her personal capacity for despair, anger, and self-loathing —

whatever it is that drives a person toward self-destruction. But then why murder and not a more easily accomplished "slow precipitation of death" by drink or some other self-destructive means at hand?

Murder is a more aggressive, masculine act (many more murders are committed by men than women). When women murder a spouse, the act is most often defensive — to escape cruel treatment — but it may also be retributive. Murder might logically represent a visceral response to a profound violation of one's inherent sense of who one is, one's spirit. Women were certainly not encouraged to harbor ideas of their individual value or worthiness in eighteenth-century New England, but Bathsheba — by virtue of her genes and upbringing — was an exception. She was, as Maccarty noted, "of uncommon fortitude of mind." She refused to be a passive victim of a marriage she detested, and she refused to be cajoled or threatened into making a public confession. She embodied a clear sense of who she was in facing her death: an American aristocrat, her father's daughter in her pride, courage, and dignity, coupled with her own graciousness and wit at the end. It is perhaps fair to characterize the murder as a crime of passion — dictated by loathing and entrapment, even though it involved some premeditation. Had she been a cold-blooded psychopath, she would surely have used her intelligence to insure her escape or she would have accomplished the deed herself.

The second fundamental question underlying this mystery is intimately related to the first; perhaps, in truth, it is the same question. How sorry was she? Because she was a private person ("She would indeed sometimes say that she felt more than she did or could express") her refusal to make a public confession did not necessarily imply lack of penitence. And, as noted before, she did express a kind of horrified remorse and confession of guilt to her neighbors on the day Joshua's body was discovered. Her assurance on the scaffold that she would see her Christian friends in heaven, however, suggests either that she had received divine assurances of forgiveness during her private devotions or that she believed what she had done wasn't nearly so evil as had been represented.

It is finally presumptuous to try to solve the mystery of individual personality, especially from such a distance of time and custom as this event presents. Yet, it is precisely that same desire to understand her that has made Bathsheba Spooner so compelling a subject of speculation for over two hundred years. Whatever her chances of everlasting life in paradise — the question so central to Reverend Maccarty and his peers — she has surely won immortality in her own all-too-human world of Worcester County, and beyond.

[11]

Remains

Drawings of the Execution

A NUMBER OF detailed drawings assumed to depict the Spooner execution were recently discovered on the attic walls of an eighteenth-century historic home now owned by the West Boylston Historical Society. The house is believed to have been an inn at the time of the Spooner execution. The drawings were originally made with chalk, though the images now are formed where the wood beneath the original chalk markings retained a lighter color as the surrounding unmarked boards darkened with age.

These drawings include two representations of the gallows, with hanging bodies, numerous onlookers, and carts holding the coffins below the scaffold; four portraits of male heads in profile, and two smaller drawings of male faces; and a detailed drawing of Bathsheba with a male figure touching her neck. They most likely were made by someone who viewed the hanging. There are also some eighty chalk marks crossed off by fives, as if someone were counting off days. If this is so, counting back from the execution date would place the artist in the house somewhere at the beginning of April, before the trial. The name "Lucy W. Gervis" (or possibly Graves, Gervais, or Jarvis) is written in large script on one wall, probably identifying the artist. But who Lucy was, and why she was moved to record the hanging in meticulous detail, is a mystery. Frank A. Brown, who wrote a booklet to accompany the drawings reproduced by April Whitcomb Gustafson (published by the West Boylston Historical Society), speculates that the mysterious Lucy might possibly be the Lucy McDonald "with child by Ezra" who was mentioned in Parkman's diary (using an assumed name), or she might be Ezra Ross's sister Lucy (using her married name). Ross's brother Timothy was in the Worcester area after the trial and it is very possible that he, Lucy McDonald, and other members of the family were present during most or all of Ezra's imprisonment.

Women Hanged in Massachusetts

Several accounts of the Spooner murder conclude with the sentiment that the state's citizens were so horrified by the execution of Bathsheba's unborn child that no woman was executed in Massachusetts afterward. This assumption dates back to an 1899 *New York World* article by Elizabeth Cady Stanton, "The Fatal Mistake that Stopped the Hanging of Women in Massachusetts," which was probably the first published recapitulation of the Spooner murder that was sympathetic to Bathsheba and her unborn child. Stanton researched and wrote the article in order to incite the public and prevail upon Gov. Theodore Roosevelt to grant a pardon in the case of another woman sentenced to death in New York.

However, the article's premise was not true; at least two women were hanged later: Abiah Converse, for infanticide, at Northampton, 6 July 1788; and Rachel Wall, for highway robbery, at Boston, 8 October 1789.[1]

Bathsheba's Family

Joshua and Bathsheba's children, Elizabeth, Joshua, and Bathshua were moved to Roxbury to live in the household of their guardian and older cousin, John Jones Spooner, who was the son of Joshua's older brother, John, and his first wife, Hannah Jones Spooner. Not a great deal is known about John Jones Spooner, except that he was twenty-four when he took in the Spooner children and he appeared to be a poor businessman. In 1783 he married Salley (Sarah) Heath, who was the only daughter of Gen. William Heath. They built a large house in Roxbury (which still stands on the corner of Blanchard Street, called the Spooner-Lambert mansion), but John Jones was soon forced to sell it to Capt. William Lambert. According to his father-in-law, his business failed and he left Massachusetts in 1789 without the Spooner children. He became rector of Martins Church in Hampton, Virginia, and died in 1799. In 1789, Bathsheba's cousin Nathaniel Ruggles Jr.

(the son of Brig. Gen. Timothy Ruggles's brother Nathaniel) was granted guardianship of Bathshua, age fourteen at her request.

The older sister of Joshua Jr. and Bathshua, Elizabeth Spooner, was eleven in the year of her parents' death. Shortly after John Jones Spooner and his wife, Salley, left the state in 1789, Elizabeth married William Heath Jr., Salley's brother. Elizabeth was twenty-two, a marriageable age, and one hopes — given all her childhood suffering — that it was a marriage of love and not of convenience. She bore two children, Sarah and William, and she died at age fifty-two. William Heath was appointed administrator of Joshua Spooner's still unsettled estate in 1792. He sold the Brookfield and Middleborough properties and cleared a balance of $1,860.

Joshua Spooner Jr. was eight in the year of his parent's death. Little is known about his adult life except (from a letter of General Heath's) that "he went to sea [in 1789 or 1790] and has not since been certainly heard of."[2] Some confusion surrounds the identity of Joshua Jr., because another Joshua Spooner lived in Brookfield and married a Dolly Harwood in 1797. But a will filed with Worcester Probate in 1801 by this Joshua Spooner listing bequests to family members with unfamiliar names suggests that this Spooner family is no relation. The Spooner genealogy recorded Joshua Jr.'s death as occurring 18 September 1801.

Little Bathsheba Spooner, her mother's namesake — or Bathshua, as she signed herself — was perhaps most affected by the tragedy. She married twice: Peter Trott of Boston, with whom she had two children, and Thomas Crocker, also of Boston. She died, according to the Spooner genealogy, at age eighty-three, "hopelessly insane for many years before her death."

Mary Ruggles Green, Bathsheba Ruggles Spooner's older sister by five years, died at age seventy-four in 1814. She was said to have suffered insanity during the time of Bathsheba's trial and hanging, but she apparently recovered and had three more children (ten, in all). It was very likely Mary who commissioned Winthrop Chandler's painting of the Ruggles Homestead that now hangs in the Worcester Museum, lent by a member of the Green family. First documented as a part of John Green's estate, the painting depicts two houses; one is clearly run-down and abandoned, while the other facing it is well cared for and inhabited by a large family. The painting might well represent a "before and after" portrait of the same house.

Mary's husband, Dr. John Green, served two terms as Worcester's representative to the General Court and built a large medical practice. According to William Lincoln's *History of Worcester,* Dr. Green worked to bring about the change of public sentiment toward expelled adherents to the crown."

Martha Ruggles Tufts, Bathsheba's oldest sister, was widowed nine years after the hanging. She raised her five children and lived in Brookfield until her death in 1813, with her daughter Patty, who never married.

Timothy Ruggles Jr., Bathsheba's oldest brother and namesake of the Brigadier, was listed on the Continental rolls as a captain. In 1779 and 1780 he joined the Continental army as a guard at the prison camp at Rutland. It is apparent he opposed his father politically, and he stayed with his mother in Brookfield when the family divided. Yet the son did finally follow his father to Nova Scotia. He was named executor of his father's estate and brought his family from Brookfield to settle in Nova Scotia in 1795, where he became a prominent citizen.

Bathsheba Bourne Newcomb Ruggles, Bathsheba's mother, was eighty-three when she died in 1787, at the home of her eldest son Timothy, in Hardwick.

Brig. Gen. Timothy Ruggles's friends and family, according to Gov. Thomas Hutchinson's diary, kept the news of his daughter's murder conviction and execution from him by persuading the New York papers to refrain from printing any accounts until after her execution. He retired from active duty near the end of the war in 1780 and in 1782 was one of forty thousand Loyalists to resettle in Canada, his "fourth banishment" he called it. Parliament granted him ten thousand acres in Wilmot, Annapolis County, on the Bay of Fundy in Nova Scotia, £4,994 in compensation for his losses, and an annual pension of £150 for services rendered. His sons John and Richard, who had followed him to New York in 1774, were each given eight hundred acres. The land and climate pleased him, and, at age seventy-two, he immediately began clearing his acres for cultivation.

In 1784 a visitor, Benjamin Marston, remarked in his diary: "Spent two days with that brave, worthy old man, who at three score and ten is beginning the world anew with as much activity as if he were but one score and ten."[3] Ruggles built his home on a hilltop with a view of the Annapolis valley, using granite imported from Quincy for foundation stones. He sent to the old Hardwick farm for cuttings of apple trees and other fruits, which he planted in deep, south-facing ravines. He grew peaches, quinces, black walnuts, and varieties of grapes not seen before in that latitude, and he is considered the father of the apple industry in the area. A Ruggles descendant, Mrs. Melville Rood, visited the house site on North Mountain in 1954 and learned that the walnut trees he planted flourished for over a century. They were later cut down and manufactured into furniture, which is still in use within the county.

In August 1795, Ruggles was showing friends his grape vines and peach trees and slipped on a steep slope, reopening an old hernia. He died 4 August, at eighty-three. He was buried in the Pine Grove Church cemetery in Wilmot, near the modern village of Middleton.

Burial of the Principals

The exact location of Bathsheba Spooner's burial place, shared with her unborn infant, is a mystery, though it is somewhere on a hillside in Worcester's Green Hill Park. After the post-execution autopsy, her brother-in-law Dr. John Green buried her body with her unborn son on his property, which was sold to the city by the Green family in 1905. One tradition has it that the exact location was kept a family secret lest angry citizens dig up her body, and the secret was passed down through the generations from father to son until one Green postponed revealing the spot until it was too late, and the chain was broken. But, in fact, her grave was marked for a time. According to a history of Worcester written in 1879, Bathsheba's grave site was often visited in former times, "and there are still some who are drawn thither by the fascination which intense human passion lends to person and to place."[4]

Sometime before 1910 (according to a librarian from the American Antiquarian Society, who saw it) the simple stone that marked her grave was enclosed by a rail fence, but the notoriety occasioned by a sensationalistic newspaper article (probably Elizabeth Cady Stanton's article in the 1899 *New York World*) prompted a groundskeeper to take down the fence and eradicate any evidence of the grave site.

The site of Ezra Ross's burial has not been clearly documented. The original Linebrook meeting house stood one quarter mile on the Rowley side of the Ipswich-Rowley line during Ezra Ross's short life. It was moved in 1828 to Linebrook Road where it is still in use today as a Baptist church. A marker commemorates the original site in a wooded area off Leslie Road, listing a number of names of those church members who were buried in the original churchyard; neither Ezra Ross nor any of his family are listed. But he very well may be among the others buried there who are "about 100 nameless dead" as the marker says. According to church records, the Linebrook church members who were Ezra Ross's family and friends united in "a day of fasting, humiliation, and prayer, which was solemnly kept" on his execution day, and they would have surely admitted his body to their consecrated burial ground. Ezra's brother Timothy and the Reverend George Lesslie, who attended him at his death, would very likely have brought his body home so that his final rest might be among those who loved him so dearly.

No documentation has yet come to light about the burial of the two British soldiers, Sergeant James Buchanan and Private William Brooks.

In the old section of the Brookfield cemetery, Joshua Spooner's grave is marked with a light gray headstone, contrasting with the older, dark slate of the Tufts family and other surrounding gravestones. It is of a style used some twenty-five or more years after Joshua's death, suggesting that someone other than the Tufts commissioned the stone, considerably later. However, no cemetery records exist from that time, so the donor of the gravestone remains a mystery.

The grave, itself, is shady and moss covered. Harvey Bennett, who has been the Brookfield cemetery superintendent for over a decade, said that he has spent a lot of money on grass seed and fertilizer, but grass won't grow on the grave because of the shade and visitors trampling it down. Others in Brookfield believe that no grass has ever grown on Joshua Spooner's grave.

APPENDIX A

THE
DYING DECLARATION
of
JAMES BUCHANAN, EZRA ROSS,
AND WILLIAM BROOKS,

Who were executed at Worcester, July 2, 1778,

FOR THE MURDER OF

Mr. Joshua Spooner.

Several versions of "The Dying Declaration" were produced around the time of the hanging, apparently by different printers. The texts of the broadside editions are almost identical but vary somewhat from the text of the quarto edition, reproduced here with notations where the broadsides differ significantly. The "Last Words" broadside begins: "I James Buchanan, was a sergeant in the Army under General Burgoyne, born in Glasgow in Scotland, age 36 years. I William Brooks, was a private in said army, born in the parish of Wednesbury, in the county of Statford, in England, age 27. We together on February 8th 1778 left Worcester . . ."

ON February 8th, 1778, We, *James Buchanan* and *William Brooks* left Worcester with an intent to go to Springfield to work. In passing Mr. Spooner's we were called in by *Alexander Cummings*, who we thought was a British soldier. Having stood some time by the fire, he told us his master was gone from home, but he would go and call his mistress, for she had a great regard for the army, as her father was in it and one of her brothers. He called her, and she came down, and appeared glad to see us. She asked us whether we came from the Hill? We told her we did, and were going to *Canada,* as I, *Buchanan,* had left my family there. She ordered Breakfast for us, and as soon as it was ready we were desired to go into the sitting-room. We were very much surprised at this, for we should have thought soldiers* well dealt by to have received any favors she might see fit to bestow on us in the kitchen. However, we all breakfasted together. The weather looking very bad, we were asked to stay till it cleared up. As we had but little money, we accordingly stayed. The weather continuing very bad, we stayed there that day and night. I (Buchanan) am not positive whether it was the first or second day, she told me, when by ourselves, that she and her husband did not agree — that he was gone a journey to Princetown, and that he would not be home soon — that we should not go from thence until the weather was fair, there being a great fall of snow at this time.

We very readily consented, and stayed from day to day, expecting Mr. Spooner home. Mrs. Spooner getting very free in discourse with me (Buchanan) one day told me that she never expected Mr. Spooner to return, as there was one Mr. Ross gone with him, who had an ounce of Poison, which he had promised her he would give to Mr. Spooner the first convenient opportunity.

The reader must needs think this is a very strange circumstance, that she should make such a discovery to an entire stranger. She said at the same time, we should stay till we saw whether Mr. Spooner returned or not. Accordingly we stayed, and were never in better quarters, little thinking of the bait the seducer of souls was laying for us; we were then in a disposition to catch at it, having no fear of God before our eyes, and being entirely forsaken of him.

Having tarried ten or eleven days as nearly as can be recollected, her husband came home, and seeing us there asked her who we were. She told him that I (Buchanan) was cousin to Alexander Cummings. He took no further notice of it, but going out among his neighbours, it is likely he was informed how long we had been there, and probably

---

*"ourselves" in the broadside versions

heard at the tavern, of the quantity of liquor he had to pay for, since his going on his journey. Be that as it may, at night he came home, and seeing we were not gone, he desired us to go immediately. We begg'd he would let us stay till morning. He after some time consented that we should stay by the fire all night. He was in the sitting-room by himself, and Mrs. Spooner went to bed. There was one *Reuben Old* came upon some business with Mr. Spooner, and after some time came out and told us that Mr. Spooner told him he was afraid we should rob him, adding that he had lost a silver spoon, and a great deal of pewter. This vexed us, as we were conscious we had no thought of stealing from him. Had we been so inclined, we had as much opportunity as we could have desired. The spoon he found where he laid it, and Cummings convinced him there was none of the pewter missing.

Mr. Spooner went up stairs and brought down a box, which he had his money in, and laid down on the floor with it under his head. Every thing Mr. Spooner did or said, *Old* came and told us, and was with us all the time he was asleep, and we were all merry together, sitting by the kitchen fire. Said *Old* declared in court, that I, *Buchanan,* said if Mr. Spooner came out, I would for two coppers put him into the Well, which is false. In the morning, it not being convenient to see Mrs. Spooner, to take our leave of her, we, *Buchanan, Brooks,* and *Cummings* went to Mrs. Stratten's to pass the day, till we could get an opportunity to bid Mrs. Spooner farewell. We stayed at Mrs. Stratten's the best part of the day, Cummings having received five dollars from Mr. Spooner, to treat his pretended cousin with, we went to Mr. Cooley's tavern and had some drink, from thence to Dr. Foxcroft's, stayed there until Cummings came and told us Mr. Spooner was in bed. We then went to the house, and had supper and liquor, retired to the barn and tarried all night. In the morning had breakfast sent to the barn for us. And as Mrs. Berry and Mrs. Tufts had been there the day before and wanted to see me, (Buchanan) I said I would go and see them. Mrs. Spooner said she would also go, which was agreed on. Buchanan and Brooks went there, and we all stayed at Mr. Green's, drinking until late; some distance from thence, she said she had given a handkerchief to a British soldier that had some words in anger with me, Buchanan, upon which Brooks went back on the horse, and she and I went home. Brooks missed his road on his return, but got to the house sometime after us; but he did not get the handkerchief, as the soldier would not deliver it, until he saw Mrs. Spooner. Buchanan and Brooks stayed that night in the barn; in the morning went to Mr. Gilbert's tavern and stayed there some time, and on coming out from his house we saw Cummings approaching on one of Mr. Spooner's horses; he told us his master was going to the tavern, and that his mistress desired we would come there, which we did, and had supper; we went to the barn that night, and in the morning she sent us word that her husband was gone abroad into the country to get some oats.

The boy Parker had proposed to Brooks, if he would come and meet Mr. Spooner and himself, on their return, he, said Parker, said he would help to take Mr. Spooner's life. We went over from the barn to the house, and found he was gone, and stayed there all day, and lived on the best the house afforded of meat and drink.

Mr. Spooner came home in the dusk of the evening, so that we had like to have been seen; but we heard him come with the sleigh to the door and Brooks ran into the cellar, and I went and stood on the back stairs, until he went into the sitting-room. We then came out, and went to the barn, there stayed all next day, and at night when Mr. Spooner was in bed, we were sent for to the house and received supper and some liquor to encourage another plan, which Cummings and Parker (who have for this time escaped punishment,) proposed to poor Brooks, which was, they all three to go up stairs, and Brooks to take his life from him; for which he was to receive one thousand dollars, Mr. Spooner's watch, buckles, and as much cloth as would make a suit of cloathes; but Brooks's heart failed him; and Mrs. Spooner said she did not think he was so faint hearted. Had this been done he was to be put into the Well as he was taken out of bed; for she observed it would be thought he had fallen in, while drawing water in the night; next day we had breakfast brought us by Cummings. He informed us there was another plan formed by her, which was as follows. Either Cummings or Parker were to tell Mr. Spooner one of the horses was sick; and as he came to the barn to kill him, and put him amongst the horses' feet, to make people believe when he was found that the horses had killed him. But Brooks told Parker not to tell him, but to make her believe he would not go over. The boy conducted accordingly. We stayed all that day and night. The next day being Sunday, we stayed there; she came over at night; we told her we should go away the next morning; she desired we would not; but we would not stay. We set out to go to

Springfield, as we went through Western on that road, we engaged to work with one Mr. Marks, a smith; I Buchanan worked there two days; but as he had no files fit for the branch of trade Brooks followed, we proposed to go to Worcester to get home, which we agreed to.

We set off on Wednesday about noon, and in going by Mr. Spooner's we called and told her where we were going; she said she would follow us down the next day as she wanted to see her sister, saying she was glad we had got work so near; and further added, that she had got two notes one of 20 pounds, lawful, and another of 300 dollars, which she would endeavour to get changed, and let me, Buchanan, have one hundred dollars, to purchase any thing I might want.

We stayed in the barn till morning, and then set out for Worcester, and she followed us the same day and called at Mrs. Walker's for us, according to agreement; she came in and stayed some time, and gave me, Buchanan, a note, as much cloth as made a shirt, and 6 or 7 dollars, observing that they came from one M'Donald, an acquaintance of hers;* she then went to see her sister, and desired us to stay until she came back, which we did; she returned on Friday morning about 10 o'clock, and stayed till night; she told me, Buchanan, at parting, that she had no more paper money, but what she had given me; but begged I would procure her some poison to give *Mr. Spooner;* I accordingly that day got one drachm of Calomel, and made it into 20 papers. I desired her to give one in the morning; she told me she never gave him any; she went to her sister's late that night and called on us in the morning, about ten o'clock. I went to the door; she would not come in, but desired me to come up to Mr. Nazro's shop, and she would get files for us, as we had not money sufficient to get what we wanted; she asked me, when we would come through Brookfield. I told her if she would set up, we would call on Monday night at eleven o'clock, she said she would; I parted with her and sent Brooks up to the shop. But as he came in sight he saw her ride from the door, and therefore did not go there; we stayed at Walker's until Sunday afternoon, and then left Worcester, and about 8 o'clock at night got to Mr. Spooner's; we saw Mrs. Stratten at the Well, Buchanan spoke to her, she told me there was company in the house, but she would let Mrs.

---

*"acquaintance of mine" in all broadside versions

Spooner know we were there; Mrs. Spooner came out, and told us that one Mr. Ross was in the house, who had a brace of pistols loaded, and that he had promised her he would kill Mr. Spooner as he came home from the tavern, she desired us to come in, which we did, he shewed us a pistol, and said Mr. Spooner should die by that to night. Either Brooks or Buchanan said it would alarm the neighbours.

Brooks said if Ross would help him he would knock him down, accordingly it was agreed on, and there was a look out kept at the sitting room door for his coming, in the mean time there was some supper brought by Mrs. Stratten to us, we had had some flip before, and there was now some rum brought, which we drank, each of us by turns giving a look out. We are certain Mrs. Stratten could not but know what was going forward. That we leave the public to judge of. Mr. Spooner was at length seen coming, and then was the time for the Devil to show his power over them* who had forsaken God.

An account of the murder as it was committed.

William Brooks went out and stood within the small gate leading into the kitchen, and as Mr. Spooner came past him he knocked him down with his hand. He strove to speak when down, Brooks took him by the throat and partly strangled him. Ross and Buchanan came out; Ross took Mr. Spooner's watch out and gave it to Buchanan; Brooks and Ross took him up and put him into the well head first; before they carried him away, I, Buchanan, pulled off his shoes: I was instantly struck with horror of conscience, as well I might; I went into the house and met Mrs. Spooner in the sitting room; she seemed vastly confused: She immediately went up and brought the money which was in a box. She not having the key desired me to break it open which I did: At the same time Brooks and Ross came in: She gave two notes of 400 dollars each to Ross to change and give the money to Brooks; But there was found some paper money, which Brooks received (243 dollars) and the notes were returned. At the same time she gave Ross four notes, each of them ten pounds, to purchase camblet for a riding dress. Ross gave Brooks his waistcoat, breeches, and a shirt. She went and brought Ross a waistcoat breeches and shirt of Mr. Spooner's when they were shifted she gave me, Buchanan, three eight dollar

---

*"sinners" in broadside versions

bills, and asked me when she should see me again, I told her in four-teen days, but it pleased God to order it sooner, and in a dreadful situation. Had we all been immediately struck dead after the perpetra-tion of so horrid a murder, and sent to Hell, God would have been justified and we justly condemned.

About 11 o'clock at night, we set off for Worcester. About 4 o'clock in the morning we reached Mrs. Walker's house; Mary Walker and a Negro girl were within; we told them a parcel of lies to excuse our sudden return; in the morning we went to drinking to endeavour to drown the thoughts of the horrid action we had been guilty of; we stayed there all day with a view to go off at night, but it pleased God to order it otherwise; for Brooks being in liquor went down to Mr. Brown's tavern; there showing Mr. Spooner's watch, and the people seeing him have silver Buckles, became suspicious of him, and one Ensign Clark going to Mrs. Walker's and seeing what passed there gave information concerning us. The news of the murder had now reached the town, and we were all taken, and brought before the Committee, examined, and committed to goal. On the 24th of April last we were brought to trial before the Superior Court, found guilty and received sentence of death.

JAMES BUCHANAN.

EZRA ROSS,

his

WILLIAM X BROOKS.

mark.

James Buchanan was a Sergeant in the army under Gen. Burgoyne born in Glasgow in Scotland aged 30 years. William Brooks, a private in said army, born in the parish of Wednesbury in the county of Statford, in England, aged 22. Ezra Ross a soldier in the continental army, born in Ipswich in the parish of Lyndebrook, New-England, aged 18.

We, Buchanan, Brooks and Ross, are conscious to ourselves that we are indeed guilty of the above murder, and that hereby we have for-feited our lives into the hands of public justice, and exposed ourselves to have our part in the lake which burneth with fire and brimstone. We desire to give glory to God by free and full confession of our heinous guilt. We trust we have with deep penitence and contrition of soul consigned it to God, hoping an infinite mercy and compassion, through the atoning blood of his son Jesus that our scarlet and crimson guilt may be done away, that we may be saved from eternal damnation which we know we justly deserve, and obtain eternal life and salvation. We would as dying men, who have been made to feel what an evil and bitter thing sin is, earnestly warn all, especially young people, that they would avoid the vices we have been addicted to, and which prepared the way for our committing the heinous wickedness for which we are to suffer a premature and ignominious death: That they would avoid bad company, excessive drinking, profane cursing and swearing, shameful debaucheries, disobedience to parents, the prophanation of the Lord's day &c. That they would be pious, sober and virtuous, that so they may be in favour with God and man.

And now we commend our departing souls into the hands of a merciful God and Saviour, earnestly desiring that all who may be spectators or hearers of our tragical end, while we are the subjects of prayer, would lift up their hearts in fervent supplications for us, that God would receive us to his everlasting mercy.*

---

*One broadside version notes beneath the bottom right column: "Mrs. Spooner said nothing at the Gallows."

APPENDIX B

Notes on the Trial of Bathsheba Spooner 1778
Associate Justice Jedediah Foster

William Brooks, James Buchanan, Ezra Ross as principals
Bathsheba Spooner as accomplice
Indicted for the murder of Joshua Spooner at Brookfield on the
　first day of March 1778 arraigned
Severally plead not Guilty.
Witnesses on the part of the gov. & People
Jury of Inquisition that the said Joshua was murdered at the hands
　of persons unknown taken on the third day of March 1778.

Dr. Jonathan King that he spent Sunday Evening with Mr. Spooner
Mr. Cooley a tavern about a quarter of a mile from Spooners House.
That Spooner went home between 8 & 9 o clock and the next morning hearing that Mr. Spooner was in the well he road there with all
speed and they having found his body in the well took it out found the
face above his nose and his temple very much bruised the scalp was
cut an inch and half long Carried the body into the east room They
could not perswade Mrs. Spooner to look at him and the family declined going to look at it except his little daughter. After the Jury had
finished their inquest Mrs. Spooner at his particular desire went to the
body and put her hand on his forehead and said poor little man.
There was blood on the curb of the well.

Ephraim Cooley
That Mr. Spooner was at his house on Sunday Evening was pleasant,
& sociable and he went away when Doctor King and his wife went
away — was well. The next morning Alexander Cummings one of the
family Came and inquired if Mr. Spooner was there — he was anxious
from some apprehensions for his safety he went to Spooner's House
and six more with him and they asked if Mr. Spooner was at home.
Mrs. Spooner said no and cried — he went to look among the neigh-

bours and near the gate he found the snow in a heap and kicking of it found his hat. Carried it in said this is Mr. Spooner's hat what do you think. Mrs. Spooner said it is his hat—and after he had got about 30 rods, they called him back the body was in the well—he saw blood in the curb in two spots. he went immediately for the coroner and officer the next he saw of the body was in the house and the bruises—were as Doctor King relates he came down with Mrs. Spooner to Worcester and at Brown's in Worcester she spoke freely of the matter and said she was the whole means of this murder being committed. She began the discourse herself Wept when she talked about it.

Ephraim Curtiss that hearing that the persons were at Walkers he went there and found them there on Monday Evening he stood at the door until they were taken They were carried to Mr. Brown's to be examined a few days after he was committed he found a ring which is now in court in possession of Buchanan he had a wound on his arm.

Joshua Whitney that on the second of March he was at Browns and Mr. Curtiss came in said he heard Mr. Spooner was murdered and three fellows were at Walkers who were suspected He went there and found two them and Brooks had a watch in his pocket and a pair of silver buckles in his shoes he asked where the other fellow was he looked on high and went into an upper loft and found Ross who trembled and appeared to be surprised and when he came down found Buchanan gone: he see Brooks turned round to the negro girl who shew him the watch and said Brooks gave it to her the watch is now in court he had a pair of buckles in his shoes with the initial letters of Mr. Spooner's name—upon the watch being shown to him he said it was the same which he had in his pocket he watched to keep the prisoners Ross said he wished he could see a minister for he was Really guilty of the crime but he did not strike the first blow. but he was aiding and assisting they were then talking about the killing of Mr. Spooner said he would confess the whole when the minister came he said he had got Spooners jacket and breeches had let Brooks have his because his were bloody — he found in his pocketbook 4 ten pound notes which Mrs. Spooner gave him and three 8 dollar bills— he said the rest was his own he said he had Spooner's knife, shirt, and saddle baggs.

Joseph Ball that on the 2nd of March in the Evening he went to Walkers and found Brooks and by Capt. Whitney ordered him to lead him down to Mr Browns, and when they were there Ross was committed to his care, he had on a pair of black knit breeches and had a cloth jacket with metal buttons. The horse that was there was one that he saw Spooner and his wife ride on heretofore. he had seen Buchanan at Walkers some weeks before he was a blacksmith he heard Ross say he labored under a good deal of concern he wished a minister was sent for.

Samuel Bridge that he went to Mr. Brouns and went from thence to Walkers and when they came back to Brown's Doctor Green's son said the buckles were his unkel Spooners The jacket Ross had on was brown cloth with yellow mettle buttons. talked with Mrs. Spooner when she came down and heard her say if she could see the persons face to face she could give satisfaction Said this is the effects of bad company — She had been in Worcester the Friday and Saturday next preceding the time of her being brot.

Mary Walker on Thursday Evening Brooks and Buchanan came to her mother's. and after they had been there a little while Mrs. Spooner and a young man came to the door and Mrs. Spooner asked if Sergeant Buchanan was there and gave him a letter which she said came from her grenadier — the contents of the letter was that he would meet him to go to the hill. She came back from Doctor Greens — very soon and said she forgot to give him a piece of cloth which was his — and said she would knit for her because she could not sew for want of sight she staid there two hours Buchanan & Brooks were there all the time and they staid there until Sunday forenoon Mrs. Spooner was often with them. Sergeant Buchanan wrote sundry letters he said was to her servant Brooks often laid his head upon her neck and often times put his hands round her waste — she observing it Mrs. Spooner said you must not wonder Billy meaning Brooks has lived at my house and is as fond of me as he would be of a mother. She see Buchanan divide powder into eighteen papers they talked about a sick child up at Brookfield She asked Buchanan when he would go she said she would send a letter by him and then said she would write a letter at Mr Nazro's. it would not be any hurt to write to her father Buchanan was very sorry that Mrs. Spooner did not come on Saturday afternoon she came and they having been in the chamber together a few minutes she went away on Saturday in the afternoon Mrs. Spooner upon her going away said tomorrow night at 11 clock remember Sargt. he said tomorrow night at 11 o'clock.

On the next Sunday night Brooks Buchanan and Ross came back and in the morning early they told her the Springfield guard were in pursuit of them and Brookfield was searched in every house — Mrs. Spooner met them at Leicester and told them of it She asked Ross if he had ever seen Mrs. Spooner and he said he did not know as he had but he had seen Mr. Spooner and rode to Lancaster with him. Ross seemed to be very dull all Sunday She asked him what made him so dull he had walked about the room and leaned against the side of the house and said reason enough Sargt. Buchanan desired her to rip of the ruffles from a shirt She riped the ruffells of the sleeves — Brooks told her Mrs. Spooner gave him a shirt and pair of stockings. Buchanan bled himself on Monday morning.

<u>Negro Woman Prudence</u> Sergt Buchanan came to Mrs. Walkers with Brooks on Thursday and talked about going to Mrs. Jones — and Mrs. Spooner came there and soon went away and soon after came back again with Doctor Green's two sons and staid all the evening and was often in and out Mrs. Spooner told John Green he had better go and see if his mother was at home Sergt Buchanan offered her his handkerchief She said G——d D——m the handkerchief I will not touch it — on friday morning Buchanan had some powders which he did up in papers — Mrs. Spooner came in Brooks told her Buchanan was sick and she went into the chamber to him and she (the witness) went up there after a broom and see them together on Saturday when Mrs. Spooner was going away she asked her what Mrs. Green said to her — she said she told Mrs. Green she dined at Mrs. Nazros and dranked tea there and it was a pritty good lye — on Sunday Brooks and Buchanan went away and on Sunday night came back and said they should have been taken if it had been for a friend there dress was altered she asked what became of Brooks silk they answered they sold it for want of money they met with Ross two miles from Leicester tavern.

<u>Thomas Green</u> the buckles he know to be Mr. Spooner's they were marked J.S. He saw them in his uncles shoes the next time he saw them with Esq. Young.

Charles Simson he altered the jacket for Spooner which Brooks has on.

John Hibbard he lived with Mr Spooner has seen Ross, Buchanan and Brooks there above a week Before Mr. Spooner was murdered he believes the saddle baggs were Mr. Spooners.

Reuben Olds that he has been frequently at Mr. Spooners the winter past, and about a fortnight before the murder Buchanan & Brooks were there one evening Mr. Spooner desired him to tarry with him that night. He did tarry there and he bid Olds go out and see what they were doing in the kitchen he went out and Buchanan say what is the old fellow about (meaning Spooner) he said he will not come to say much to me it won't be healthy for him for I would put him in the well for two coppers. The next morning Mrs. Spooner told him she would go through with her plan he supposed it was to go to her father.

Loved Lincoln that about the first of February he was at Spooners and Spooner wanted to know when he went to Oakham and he and Spooner and Ross set out and he went with them as far as Chadwicks in Oakham and the Tuesday following he went to Spooners to see if he had done some business for him and then saw Brooks & Buchanan there afterwards he was there and somebody looked into the window and presently he heard Sergt Buchanan speak Spooner says how came you here they said to warm them — he said you may stay by my fire till morning but you must not let me see you afterwards. Soon after he heard Buchanan say if Spooner turns me out of doors tonight I will have his life before morning.

The night after the murder Mrs. Spooner said she did not know how he came by his Death (meaning Mr. Spooner). She said the Regulars went away the day before yesterday and Ross took Spooner's jacket and breeches. Mrs. Spooner said Ross was concealed there because he hurt the horse's back. She said the Regulars and Ross went away together.

Charles Capt. Weldon's Negro he was at Mr. Spooners the night ~~before~~ he was murdered and he see Ross there — it was about dusk of evening.

<u>Mrs. Wilson</u> that about three weeks before the murder she was at Mr. Spooners. Buchanan and Brooks were there and a Doctor was there and Alexander Cummings was whispering with Mrs. Spooner — She saw Ross there a little before thanksgiving last fall.

<u>Alexander Cummings</u> he has lived with Spooners from the time Burgoins Troops came down about a fortnight before the murder Brooks & Buchanan came there Spooner was gone She was at home They staid all day & dined there with Mrs. Spooner lodged there and Buchanan breakfasted with her Mrs. Spooner had ordered him to call in all the British troops who passed along — he heard Mrs. Spooner tell Buchanan she wished Mr. Spooner was out of the way. She could not live with him. Buchanan said he wished he was out of the way — they staid there backwards & forwards all the time Mr. Spooner was gone to Princeton. Ross went with him. That time when Spooner came home on Monday night Brooks and Buchanan were there. Heard Brooks & Buchanan say they would try to get Spooner out of the way — he sat up with Spooner at his request, who said he did not love to have Brooks in the house he did [not] like the looks of the man. He desired his wife to get them off. He said if she did not he would send for the committee next morning he saw them in the barn they lay there two days and two nights Mrs. Spooner carried them victuals once he carried them victualls one time by her order on Thursday morning they went to Worcester on the Saturday night following Mrs. Spooner came home and Ross was in the milk room Said he did not want Mr. Spooner should know he was there all day on Sunday Ross was kept concealed in the chamber.

On Sunday night he was sent to Capt. Weldons to take his horse home and then he came back. He saw Buchanan and Brooks there Mr. Spooner was then gone to Cooleys. He went out of doors and see Brooks there and he asked if that was Mrs. Spooner and he said no he then told him to ask Mrs. Spooner to come out to him he said I will not. Brooks had told him just before that Spooner should not come home a living man tonight — he the witness went in and Mrs. Spooner was in the kitchen he then went to bed and slept he believes about two hours and an half and waked smelt the burning of woolen and got up went down and see Brooks, Buchanan, Ross and Mrs. Spooner in the Parlour they were burning cloaths they asked him what made him look so sullen they were then shifting cloaths Ross put on Mr. Spoon-ers jacket and breeches. Mrs. Spooner bid him go with Mrs. Stratton into the chamber to bring down Mr Spooners clothes. Mrs. Stratton got the black breeches and brot them he knous. Buchanan had on a shirt of Mr. Spooners he heard Mrs. Spooner say she gave Brooks a shirt and handkerchief he saw Brooks' breeches thrown into the fire all bloody — he saw Mrs. Spooner take Mr Spooners money from the tin box, which was kept in a mahogany chest. Mrs. Spooner bid him go and get some water to wash Spooners buckles and he should have them he said he would not have them but he and Mrs. Stratton went to the well and could not dip the bucket. Mrs. Spooner asked him why he did not get the water. He said he believed Mr. Spooner was in the well. She said it was not true.

Mrs. Stratton came in with him frighted and cried and ran and got the Bible.

Buchanan said to Mrs. Spooner should you thought my man would do the jobb for him. Mrs. Spooner about a month before had desired him — the witness — to kill Spooner and she would make a man of him — he asked Mrs. Spooner if they cut Mr. Spooners throat. She said no they knocked him down. The night before they went to Prince-ton Ross dropped some aqua fortis into some toddy to poison him. Spooner said if he had any enemies in the house he should think they intended to poison him. Ross said to Mrs. Spooner when he came that he had no opportunity to give him the aqua fortis while they were gone Mrs. said he carried half a bottle full.

When they went away after the murder Buchanan shook hands with Mrs. Spooner and told her she might expect to see him in about a fortnight. Next morning Mrs. Spooner went to the well and said she hoped he was in heaven and told him to go and get a horse and go to the town and inquire for him. While they were at the well she said she wanted to have him put in the bottom of the well.

Asa Bigelow that the foreman of the Jury of Inquest told Mrs. Spooner she must go to goal. She confessed that she hired the people to commit the murder, was to give them one thousand dollars and had paid them two hundred. She mentioned the names of Brooks and the Sergeant. She said they were all three together.

Sarah Stratton She lived at Mr. Spooners at several times. The first time she saw Ross there was in the fall of the year between the two thanksgivings. Spooner came from Boston after they were in bed. Mrs. Spooner got up and let him in. About three weeks before Spooner was killed Buchanan and Brooks were there — and the night he was murdered one Gray and another man lodged there. She carried some supper into the room where Ross & Buchanan were. Mrs. Spooner supped with Mr. Gray and his partner — She did not see Mr. Spooner killed but when she went to light Mr. Gray to bed she saw Mrs. Spooner showing a money box. She took her by the hand and said she hoped Mr. Spooner was in Heaven. When she went to light Gray to bed his partner was in bed and asleep as it appeared to her.

She brot. down the box and soon after Mrs. Spooner asked her to go up chamber and get a pair of black knit breeches but she could not find them. Mrs. Spooner was paying some money, and Buchanan had a great deal of paper money in his hand. She heard Mrs. Spooner tell Alexander to go and get some water and he asked her to go out with him — She went out and Alek said Mr. Spooner was in the well. They came in without any water. They brought down Mr. Spooner's jacket & she had seen Mr.* Spooner ware a ring very much like the one in Court. She lodged with Mrs. Spooner part of the night. She sighed and tumbled a good deal. She told Mrs. Spooner she would go and tell the neighbors. Mrs. Spooner said if she would keep it secret she would give her a good deal. Often said she hoped Mr. Spooner was in Heaven. When they went away she gave them money. [illegible word] The witness asked Brooks what he had been about. He made answer his time is come. The Saturday night before Spooner was murdered Ross came in — said he had Mr. Spooner's horse a fortnight and hurt his back and was not willing he should see him. Mrs. Spooner came in soon after Ross came.

---

*In Chandler's transcription of Foster's notes in "The Trial of Mrs. Spooner and Others," the word here is *Mr.* However, in the copy of the original manuscript the last part of the word is obscured where the book pages are bound together, and it could as easily be "Mrs." Sarah Stratton's testimony from Robert Treat Paine's notes, "I have seen her ware a ring like this," suggests that the ring in Buchanan's possession was Bathsheba's, not Joshua's.

<u>Jesse Parker</u> He lived at Mr. Spooner at times. Has seen Buchanan and Brooks there in the barn about a fortnight before Mr. Spooner was killed they lay there two or three nights. Mrs. Spooner, Alek, and he carried victuals to them. Mrs. Spooner told him to ask Mr. Spooner to go to the barn to look at the horses and take care of the doors but he did not because the Regulars were about. When Mr. Spooner came from Princeton Mrs. Spooner said she never was so stumped in her life. He heard Mrs. Spooner say she had been to the west Parish and the Regulars were gone to Worcester and she wanted to go there after her sister — She asked Mr. Spooner for a horse but he declined letting her have one, and she sent to Captain Weldon's and got his. He went from the house on it Sunday and Ross was there.

<u>Obediah Rice</u> That sometime before the murder heard Mrs. Spooner say she wished Old Bogus was in heaven. When Mrs. Spooner, Alex and Mrs. Stratton were brought to goal the came in his slay and when they were on the road Mrs. Spooner said this don't seem like Christmas day. She said she had a great desire to see her Daddy and if it had not been for that this murder would never have been committed. He heard Mrs. Spooner say she would suffer ten deaths for Mrs. Stratton and Alex before they should suffer, for they were innocent.

<u>Elisha Hamilton</u> that he was the constable, Mrs. Spooner took on much and said if it was not for this thing I could meet my Judge — She said it happened by means of Ross's being sick at our house. She told Cooley she did not blame any body for this was all her own doing, she said the Mrs. Stratton and Alek were innocent. She had bribed them to do and say what they had done.

<u>William Young, Esq.</u> That the confessions of the prisoners were made freely and of their own accord. Mrs. Spooner confessed since her commitment that she had consented to the murder.

<u>Mr. Cunningham</u> That Brooks since he made the confession before Justice Young said that he gave the blow.

William Brooks ——
Confession that &c ——

James Buchanan
Confession

Ezra Ross
Confession

Joseph Wheeler Esq. That he was present with Justice. Said when he committed Jesse Parker, Brooks said he should be glad to alter his confession for he struck the first blow— This was the beginning of April.

APPENDIX C

Minutes of Trial and Law Cases, 1777–1782
Robert Treat Paine

Worcester. Sup'r Court. April 1778
State vs. William Brooks, James Buchannon, Ezra Ross, for Murder of
Joshua Spooner, & vs. Bathsheba Spooner as an Accomplice before
the fact.

Sally Bragg a fortnight before then Jesse Parker was saying how bad a
man Mr. Spooner was, bad to his Wife. had just got him drunk, that
Mrs. Spooner had send for Brooks to have their frolic; Mr. Spooner
will not get drunk many times more he is a short lived man, he was
directing him Brooks & Cummings, Cumming said yes I am sure he is

Hannah Walker Mrs. Stratton sd. Mrs. Spooner told me what I durst
not tell for my life, this was last fall, in Worcester She went to live at
Spooners, she said she was going to live at Mrs. Spooners and was like
to do well, last fall the week before she went to live there, she lodged
with Mrs. Spooner & he came home she sd. she hated him

Mary Parks Mrs. Spooner never wished her Hus dead or intimated she
would put him out of the way, she said she did not love her hus:

Dr. Jona. King I spent Evng wth Decd. at Mr. Cooleys, between 8 & 9
he went from there I went there abt. dusk & found him there, we
came away together & parted at the Door. he sd. good night. he was
sober & sociable. blood lay within 8 ft. of the corner of the house, on
the Gate, curb of the well & on his Cloak none of the house went out
to look at the Corpse; wn. we carried Corpse into the Room, Mrs.
Spooner shut out & did not turn her Eyes, the bruises, Mrs. Spooner
eating her breakfast.

Ephm. Cooley Came to my house between Sun down & Dark tarried
till between 8 & 9. & went away, was very pleasant next morning Alex.
came riding on Spooner's horse between 8. & 9. & enquired for Mr.

Spooner, he was told to go to Dr. Kings & he went part of the way & turned back; I went to Mrs. Spooners they ate Breakfast. talked with her wept & took it hard for such reflections went out found his Hat under Snow

Charles Cobbin a Negro Master Weldon sent me to Mrs. Spooners after his horse she had to Worcester saw a man there, I took it to be Mr. Ross wm. I had seen before, in the kitchen, he went into the Parlour, Saw two men come in from Springfield

Reuben Old I lived at Mr. Spooners last Fall, abt. fortnight before murder he asked me to stay with him he fetched down a Trunck & we sat up at night, Brooks was up Stairs a bed, Sergt. there Spooner sd. he was afraid they were agoing to rob him, I went into other Room to Buchannon & he said he wd. put him into the Well for a copper & if he comes out & says a word he would put him into the Well, Mrs. Spooner opened the Window & sd. people may call it a negro frolic I'm determined to go through with my design

Obadiah Rice Last Fall I heard her say she wish'd Old Bogus in Heaven, in Coming down, she sd. if it had not been I had a great desire to see my Daddy this murther had never been committed & also the moment the breath of life left his Body I would have given 10,000,000 of World it had been in again that she wd. suffer 10 deaths before Mrs. Stratton & Alex shd. suffer.

Susannah Wilson I saw Sergt. & Brooks, there a fortnight abt. three weeks before murder She asked one of them to go into the other Room She & Alex. were whispering together. Saw Ross at Mr. Spooners last Thanksgiving.

Thos. Green Swears to the buckels

Dr. Jona. King

Ephm. Cooley at Mr. Brown. She told me she had been the whole cause of the murder she mentioned an old grudge & began the Discourse

Ephrm. Curtis I was at the taking & Walkers & stood Guard, Buch. jump'd out of the Window, he let himself blood on Wednesday. bled much, found an Ring on him.

Capt. Josha. Whitney 2nd March at Mrs. Walkers Saw Brooks with a watch in his pocket and Buckles in his Shoes; Standing by the fire & Buchan. was sitting on the bed. I asked for the others took a light & went up Stairs, found Ross in upper Garret he quivered & was much scared, Buchannon jump'd out of window, Brooks gave the negro Girl the Watch in Examn. he owned that to be the watch he had in his pocket, Ross told me he was guilty of this crime, was very full & wanted a minister Did not strike the first blow, but was aiding & assisting. very penitent.

Ross sd. he had on Mr. Spooners jacket & Breeches & had given his own to Brooks who had bled his own in taking up the body. & Brooks afterward owned he took up the body, Ross, said his Pistol was at Mrs. Walkers. & I went & found it there, & his Pocket book with 10£ notes & 8 Doll. bills, given him by Mrs. Spooner & other money his own, Mr. Spooners horse was in Mrs. ~~Spooners~~ Walkers barn, the baggs & shirts in it, he sd. the marks burn't out

Saml Bridge the buckles in Brooks shoes. Mr. Spooners, the jacket was on Ross. Mrs. Spooner sd. If she cd. see the persons face to face she cd. give Satisf; & this is the Effect of bad Company

John Green abt. buckles & watch

Charles Simpson the Jacket, Brooks has on, I altered for Mr. Spooner

John Hibbard The Jacket Mr. Spooners, abt. 9 mos before murder. while, Decd. gone to Springfield, Serjt & Brooks at Mrs. Spooners, afterwards saw Brooks there I think the Baggs Mr. Spooners

Alex Cummings I came to Mr. S the day the troops came to town, fortn. [fortnight] before murder. S & B came to Mr. Spooners house, no Rel. [Relation] to Serjt. I knew him in Canada Mrs. Spooner ordered me to call all British Troops in that went along, she asked 'em how they did Gentlemen, she said she wished she had Mr. Spooner was out of the way they could enjoy one another, he sd. he wished he was out of the way, they staid while Mr. Spooner was absent at Princeton, Wn. he came home Sergt. & Brooks sd. they wd. put him out of the way after they were ordered away they tarried two days & nights in the Barn, & I carried 'em victuals by her orders & she carried some Ross came there Saturday night then Mrs. Spooner came home. Mrs. Spooner ordered the horse put up. Ross was kept concealed all day. The Sergt. & Brooks came there Sunday Evening while I was gone to carry home horse. I found Ser. & Ross in Parlour & Brooks was out by the Road, I step't out with a blanket coat on & Brooks took me for Mrs. Spooner & bid me ask Mrs. Spooner to step out. I said I would not, Brooks told me he was watching for Mr. Spooner & he should not come home a living man that night I went to Bed & got to sleep, & was waked by their coming up stairs & smelt woolen burning. I went down, & saw the pris. all in the Parlour sitting & Brooks wn. he came to the house had white woolen Jacket & Breeches & they were burning Cloathes. Mr. Ross put on a pair of blk breeches of Mr. Spooners. I fetched down Jacket & Mrs. Stratton the Breeches. Buchannon had on a Ruffled Shirt.

Mrs. Spooner took Mr. Spooner's Money and carried it into the Setting Room, but I did not see her give 'em any money, She told me to get water to wash Brooks breeches & I should have 'em, She had told me if ever Mr. Spooner was killed she would have him thrown into the well. Sergt. sd. did you think this man of mine could have done the Jobb. abt. a month before She asked me if I would kill Mr. Spooner for her & she wd. make a man of me, She sd. had not cut his throat but pushed him down. the night before he went to Princetown he spit out Grog, Ross sd. he had put aqua fortis he told Mrs. Spooner he had carried poison to Princeton, but had no opportunity to give it him, Buch. when he went away shook hands with her & said she might expect to see him again in a fortnight, next morning she went with me to the Well & she sd. she hoped he was in heaven & desired me to take the horse & go & enquire for him, she sd. she wanted him to be put to the bottom of the Well

Sarah Stratton Ross at Mr. Spooners between thanksgiving, the Sunday all there in Front Room & Ross asked me to call Mrs. Spooner in, she went in: Gray & al. came there & Sup'd in the kitchen, & the Pris: sup't in Sitting Room; I went to light Mr. Gray to bed & coming down saw Mrs. Spooner taking the money Box. She took hold of my hand & said she hoped Mr. Spooner in Heaven, she carried the box into the sitting room, She sent me for Breeches & I came down & saw 'em all standing round Table in sitting room & the box open & money in Buchns hand She bid Alex get water & wash Breeches that were

bloody & he should have 'em we went to well & could not get water they had some Buckels: I have seen her wear a ring like this. She
sighed & turn'd all night, in the morning she desired me not to tell of
it & I should not want anything, they all came into the Kitchen & bid
'em good night & Bucc. sd. to Mrs. Spooner you Shall see me in a
fortnight: Brooks sd. his time was come. Ross when he came there
secreted himself from Mr. Spooner.

Jesse Parker Buc. &. Brooks there she used to be in setting room with
Serg'nt, they kept in the barn She & I & Alex. carried victuals to them.
She asked me to get Mr. Spooner to the barn, wn. he came from
Princeton she said she was never so stump'd in her life, she sd. she was
going to Worcester the regulars were going there.

Obadiah Rice some time ago she wished old Bogus was in Heaven; I
came down with Mrs. Spooner, Mrs. Stratton, & Alexr.

Elisha Hamilton She sd. if it was not for this thing I cd. meet my
Judge, she told Cooley he had done no more than his duty it was her
own doing.

Asa Biggelow before the Inquest, she sd. she was the cause of it tho she
did not lay hands on him. She had hired Sergt. & Brooks to do it &
gave 1000 dollsr & had given 200

Wm Young, Esq. abt. a week after the Examn. I went into the Goal to
converse, Ross sd. a good part of his Exmn. was lying he said he took
him by the feet & Brooks by the shoulders & put him into the well
Brooks acknowledged he gave the blow.
Mrs. Spooner sd. she must confess she consented to the Murder

John Cunningham Brooks sd. to me I made a mistake in my Confession, for he struck the blow.

Joseph Wheeler, Esq Brooks desired some alterations to be made, for
he struck the first blow. Ross sd. he wanted to make some alteration

    Mr. Sprague
  The Evid: vs Ross, only makes him an access. after fact.
  The Pris: suffer by being tryed all together because they charge
    one another

Mr. Lincoln
Confessions sometimes prove false.

Ross's good Character
if he had engaged to comit the crime why did he not do it before
 he was obliged to conceal himself on acc't of the horse

Marq. of Beccaria*
Presumptive evidence dangerous
the case of the Uncle & niece
   of the stolen horse

the Credibility of Prue
    Mary Walker
    Mrs. Stratton
    Alex.

Mrs. Spooner must be <u>out of her head</u> to comit this crime & or-
 phanize her Children hus. a Cloak
Could she expect impunity.
Would they not have agreed upon a plan of escape

---

*Cesare Bonesana, Marchese di Beccaria, was an Italian criminologist, econo-
mist, and jurist, whose *Essay on Crimes and Punishments* (1764) arguing against
capital punishment and cruel treatment of criminals became a tenet of En-
lightenment thinking.

APPENDIX D

Indictment of William Brooks, James Buchanan & Ezra Ross

Associate Justice Nathaniel Peaslee Sargeant

Indictment of Wm. Brooks, James Buchannan & Ezra Ross for the
Murder of Joshua Spooner on the 1st day of March last at Brookfield & Bathsheba Spooner as accessory before the fact.

Prisonrs pleaded not Guilty

A motion made that two of the Prisoners were Aliens, therefore
the trial ought to be per Medictm. Linguce — The court unani-
mous that by our Law we could not have a Jury called per Medic-
tatem Linguce —

Inquisition made 3rd March, 1778.

Jona. King — I spent the even. with Mr. Spooner at Mr. Cooleys — was
pleasant, drank but little, went away between 8 and 9 o'clock. I told
him I feared his negro woman would hurt him — he said he did not
fear her. Sun half an hour high I heard Mr. Spooner was drowned in
the well. I rode there & they had found his hat & his cloak, was insp.
the Jury. found Blood on the Ground near the Gate not more than
6 or 7 feet from the house. I saw a Club which was found standing
up, & supposed to be wt. they knocked him down with, I helped get
him out of the well. I observed the family. They were in the Kitchen
eating their Breakfast & none went out to look on him while they were
getting him out, Alexr. Cummings passed by but did not turn his face
toward the well. I observed a great bruise on his nose & the Bone
broke all to pieces — face stripd. — his left temple much bruised with
heavy blows — a Gash on his head an Inch & ½ long — his throat very
black & his breast much bruised. none of the family went to him 'till
the Jury finished, then she went & touched him on being bid, &
said — Poor little man — we found one shoe in the Bucket, his watch &
Buckles gone — found 5 or 6 Dollars in his Pocket — some blood on

the Curb of the well—some Clods of Blood on the Cloak, cloak not tied on—with the tine of a fork drew up his Cloak, and then hooked him up from the bottom by hooking him under the left arm—he came up head first—

The family agreed that Ross had been there & secreted before, once or twice—

Mr. Cooley—Spooner came to my house between sunset & dark—was Chearful—went of with Doctr. King—next morning I see Alexr. between 8 & 9 riding up to my house on Mr. Spooner's horse—when we came to the house six of us went in & Mrs. Spooner & Stratton were at Breakfast, & we asked if Mr. Spooner was at home, she said no indeed he was not at home & she wept & said Mr. Dor I don't like such reflections. I then proposed going to the neighbours for him, she said he did not come home last evening. I went out and seeing a rising in the snow & gave it a kick & found his hat. I shew it to Mrs. Spooner— she said that is his hat—saw the Cloak in the well & blood on the Curb in 2 blotches—while gone for the Coroner, I saw no more, till I saw him on the Table—Doctor King has related about the wounds exactly—Mrs. Spooner passed the room 2 or 3 times don't recollect she said anything then—at Worcester at Mr. Browns she said she was the whole means of this Murder being committed—I cannot recollect the whole we had been at Variance—I had been the means of bringing her out in some misdemeanors—she owned I had done no more than my Duty—Mr. Rice was present & Hamilton & many People—I cannot recollect the discourse—she began the discourse of her own accord— she did not appear affected till she got to Mr. Browns there she seemed much affected & wept a good Deal—I heard his son call his father old Bogus. I don't recollect seeing any tracts—the snow blew very much—

Ephr. Curtis—I went to Mrs. Walkers & there found there three persons, we had heard of the Murder of Mr. Spooner—I stood on the outside while others went in, a little before day light, brou't them away & had an examina. before Mr. Cunningham & Esq. Young—found a Watch & pair of Buckles—after locking them up I found a pocket Book & some Small things—he complained his arm was sore—I took of the handkerchief & found the ring—his handkerchief was bloody & his shirt—the ring was found on Buchannon—his arm, Buchannans was very bad—

Joshua Whitney — 2d. March at Mr. Browns — upon the informa. of Mr. Curtis we went to Mrs. Walkers & went in & found those three persons there & Brooks had the Buckles in his Shoes & the watch chain hang out of his pocket. I told the men to take Care of Brooks & Buchannan — I looked in the Chamber and could not find the other — I looked behind the chimney and there I found Ross, I bid him come out & he shook & quivered very much — when I came down, I found Buchannan was gone out of the window — when I reprimanded the negro for showing Buchannan away — Brooks sliped the Watch into the negros hand & she gave it to me — the watch produced is the same with what I took with Buckles when taken out had the two first Letters of Mr. Spooners name — upon examina. he owned this was the watch he gave the negro Girl —

I talked with the prisonrs. a good deal, & afore morning he repented very much & said he was really guilty of this Crime & want a minister to be sent for, he said he did not strike the first blow — he said he was aiding & assisting — he said he would confess the whole when the minister came — Ross owned he had got on Mr. Spooners Jacket & Breeches — he was obliged to let Brooks have his for he had blooded his own in taking up Mr. Spooner oXo*

Joseph Ball — went to Mrs. Walkers 2nd. March, in the house I heard one had broke out of the window & I took the care of Brooks & led him to Mr. Browns — there Whitney put Ross into my Care, & took Brooks away Ross had on a pair of knit breetches black — a cloth Jacket & metal buttons — I knew the horse to be Mr. Spooners have seen Buchannan about Walkers a little before this happened — near a month before Ross said he was under concern, & had asked to talk with a minister.

oXo Mr. Whitney — we understood that they had a pistol & asked Brooks & Buchann. who had the pistol, they said Ross had it. Ross said he had left it in Mrs. Walker's Garret, when morning we went with Ross to Mrs. Walkers & he went to the Garret & found the Pistol & said he brou't it from home — I found it loaded with 2 balls & he had the Pocket book, we found 3 8 dollar bills & 4 10 £ notes & some other

---

*This symbol appears to be Sargeant's private notation reminding himself that Whitney's testimony continues later on.

Money which Ross said was his own, he said Mrs. Spooner gave him the Money—I found the horse which was Mr. Spooners and saddle bags & Shirts in them where the name was burnt out—he said it was the horse that was Spooners—all these things were in Mrs. Walkers Barn—I think he said

Mr. Bridge—after they were at Browns, Brooks had Buckles which appeared by the letters to be Mr. Spooners & enquiry was made after the watch & found it as Mr. Whitney has said—the Jacket & Breetches on Ross I examined & found the Cloath good, the Breeches knit—I said to Mrs. Spooner, I was sorry to see her so Soon in town again for I had seen her the Saturday and Friday before—she said it was sorrowful indeed but if she could see them face to face she could give him Satisfaction, this was the affects of bad company—

Mary Walker—Thursday Eveng. Buchanan & Brooks came to our house and asked if her Mother was at home, she said no but she would be at home on Friday Buchanan said he wanted to see as soon as she came for he had worked there as a Blacksmith & should want to live there again—she told him he might stay till her Mother came—he said he must go to Jones—for they were to be there in ½ an hour after they came into town. Thursday night Mrs. Spooner came to our house & asked for Sarg't Buchannan & he came to her & asked her to go in for she was very wet & she refused to come in because she would go to her Sisters Greens soon after she ~~came back and~~ gave him a letter and said it was from her Grenadier, I read the letter which was that they were to meet him somewhere to go to the hills—soon after she came back and said she had forgot to leave the Cloath that Buchanan had left at her house and asked if he had not forgot it. he said yes, she got it out and asked me to make Buchanan a shirt for she could not see, & offered to knit for me if I would—

Friday forenoon she came to our house & would knit for me & spent almost the whole time with Buchanan & Brooks—Buchanan was writing Letters & gave 'em to her & told her to read 'em. she put 'em into her Pockit & said she could trust him & would not. Brooks appeared fond, & she excused it—Saturday morning Buchanan ~~gave out~~ maker up six papers under pretence of getting Powders for a neighbours child sick—she asked him when he would go—he said, Sunday noon—

Buchanan was uneasy because she did not come earlier Saturday for it was after noon when she came. as she was going away she whispered with Sarjeant & he said the time was eleven o'Clock tomorrow night & I asked what of that after some time he answered he was to meet with Grenadier — Buchanan & she were in the chamber alone just before they parted —

Brooks & Buchanan were alone the chief of the forenoon, dressing, & one told the other they must get some files at Nazros. they went away about noon —

Monday morning they were come in with Ross & I asked them they said they could not stay in Brookfield, for all Springfield was in alarm & they had Searched every house in Brookfield & Mrs. Spooner had sent a man to Leicester who met them & told it — Ross was with them & would not tell his name — Ross said he did not know Mrs. Spooner but knew him — Buchanan gave her a shirt to rip the Ruffels of. it was a full Ruffle & would not have them Ripd. off the Bosom — Brooks said he went to Mrs. Spooner & she gave him a shirt & pair of stockings & said Buchanan did not go further than Leicester —

1g. Powders 3 Rows — I tasted of all: one white two reddish — one he said was Cream of Tartar

Monday forenoon — Buchanan was bleading & he had bled himself —

Prudence a Negro — near the same in substance with My. Walker — Brooks hand was swelled all up — Ross with him & their dress was so altered that I did not know him — they said Brooks had sold his coat & Jacket to get them Money — I told Ross where to hide himself — Brooks jogg'd me on the knee & gave me the watch which I took & gave to Mr. Whitney —

Jno. Green — suppose the Buckles Mr. Spooners because he had seen the same patterned Buckles for two of Mr. Spooner's Daughters — I saw the Buckles in Brooks shoes —

Thos. Green — I knew the Buckles and saw them in my Uncles shoes at Brookfield, when next time I saw them in Whitneys hands I knew the Watch & he described it —

Charles Simpson — I see the Breetches but so much worn that I can't swear to them the Buttons I know for I let Mr. Spooner have when I altered the Jacket I know the alterations—I altered two at the same time—

John Hibberd—I think I know the Jacket but every like is not the same. I think I know the saddle bags there was a Button gone—now a Button has lately been set on—about 4 weeks when Mr. Spooner was gone to Princeton I saw Buchanan & Brooks there & I asked where Buchanan was going he gave an account. after Spooner came home I saw Brooks behind the barn putting up nails, but did not think any harm—

Reuben Olds—sometime this winter I went to borrow Mr. Spooners Collar about a fortnight before he was murdered—Buchanan & Brooks were about. I tarried all night. Mr. Spooner in sitting room, B. & B. in Kitchen & Mrs. Spooner abed—I went into the Kitchen & asked what they were about, they asked what the old man was about, & said Damn him he won't come out to us for if he does, I will for 2 coppers put him into the well—the next morning as I was going a way Mrs. Spooner said, I will go thro my Plan now. I thou't she meant to go to her father for she asked me sometime before to carry away some things for her—

Lovid Lincoln—about 1 Feby. was at Mr. Spooners there see Ross there, Tuesday after he went to Princeton I saw three Regulars there as I took them to be—two of them were the prisoners—I saw the men passing back & forwards in the sitting Room—the Tuesday following in the dark he was Sitting & drinking & I saw somebody look into the window, & in the Kitchen I saw the two prisonrs. there & he bid them go out, but gave them leave to stay all night if they would go off next morning & never come again—as I was going out Buchanan said if Spooner him out of Doors he would have his life before morning Monday night Mrs. Spooner spoke & asked what was doing, he said guarding the house, the talk with Mrs. Spooner—

Charles Cobbin—a Negro—I was at Mr. Spooners the evening before he was killed, I saw Ross there & he went out into another Room, & I saw him no more—then I saw two other men come after me he they were I did not know—it was just after day I overtook Mr. Cooley a going—

<u>Susanna Wilson</u> — I saw B&B about 3 weeks before this happened & Mrs. Spooner asked one of them into the other room — & he went. Alexr. & Mrs. Spooner were whispering, & I asked what it was about, she said they were often whispering & she thought about her & she was mad & had a good mind to go-off — I saw Ross last fall before thanksgiving at Mr. Spooners —

<u>Alexr. Cummings</u> — I came to Mr. Spooners when the troops came into town — I saw on Sunday about a fortnight before this happened B. & B. at Mr. Spooners — She was at home. he not — I am not related to Buchanan but knowed him in Canada — they stayed all day and got their dinners they dined with Mrs. Spooner & the next morning breakfasted with her — she told me to call all the British Troops in that went by — I called them in. I heard Mrs. Spooner say she wished Mr. Spooner out of the way that they might enjoy one another. Buchanan said he wished he was out of the way. They stayed there backwards & forwards a fortnight while Mr. Spooner was at Princeton — Ross was at Princeton — did not return with Mr. Spooner — they were both in the house when Mr. Spooner came home — I heard Buchanan say they would contrive to get Mr. Spooner put out of the way — I heard Brooks say the same — & sat up all night. Mr. Spooner bid me. They went away in the morning, I returned in the afternoon they lay in the barn that night. I saw them next morning in the barn, they lay there next night. Mrs. Spooner carried them Victuals Bread & Cheese — I carried them Pork & Beans —

Mr. Spooner came home Monday night Saturday following Ross came there, Mrs. Spooner came home late in the Evening, I was abed, & got up & Mrs. Spooner & Ross told me to put the horses up, but not Ross's horse in the Stable for he said he would not have Mr. Spooner know how he had been used, or that he was there at all — Ross was kept concealed in the Chamber all day — when I went to carry Weldens horse returned, I found Ross & Buchanan in the fore room — & Brooks watching the Yard — when I came home I set down by the fire having hurt myself & then got up & went out to the door to take a little Air & go to bed & Brooks asked if it was Mrs. Spooner, I said no. he asked me to call Mrs. Spooner out, I said I would not & asked what he did there, he said by God Mr. Spooner should not come home a living Man that night — I went in and she making chocolate in the

Kitchen — I went to bed & lay about 2½ hours waked up & heard them going up & down & smelt the burning of Woollen — I got up & went down & found all the prisoners in the parlour — Brooks & Ross were had a Blanket Jacket & Breeches white when he came. & I see cloaths burning but almost all burnt up —

Ross put on a pair of black Breeches of Mr. Spooners & gave Brooks his leather ones — Mrs. Spooner desired me and Mrs. Stratton to fetch down a pair of Breeches and a Jacket & we went & I brou't the Jacket & she got the black Breeches — Mrs. Spooner said she gave Brooks a shirt & handkerchief — after I came into the Room Brooks Breeches were thrown into the fire, I saw all them all Bloody — I saw Mrs. Spooner get a Box where Mr. Spooner kept his Money, & carried it on to the table in the room where they were & I was in the Kitchen with Mrs. Stratton, I suppose it was 11 o'Clock when they went away — she told me to get some Water out of the Well to wash Brooks Breeches — I was afraid & asked for Mrs. Stratton to go with me, & she went & I put the Bucket down & it catch'd in his cloaths which frightened me & we run into the house, I said to Mrs. Spooner I am afraid your husband is in the well; no says she that is not true — I sit in the Kitchen & Mrs. Stratton fell a crying & took the book in her hand — I heard Mrs. Spooner say if any person kills my husband — I will have him thrown into the well — Mrs. Stratton made some pies against she came home & Saturday some Company was there and they brout out some pies & Mrs. Spooner said one must be kept whole for she expected some Company the next night — Buchanan said who would have thou't I had got such a Man with me to do the Jobb — Mrs. Spooner several times said to me if I would Kill her Husband she would make a man of me — I asked when I saw Brooks Breeches I asked if they had cut Mr. Spooners throat, she said no. but they had cut his throat — Ross the night before Mr. Spooner went to Princeton, Mr. Spooner came out with some Grog & spit it into the fire & said if he had any Enemies he could have swore they had put aqua fortis in it — Ross went out. & I asked him & he said he had — that Saturday night he said he carried Aqua fortis to Princeton but had no opportunity to give it this he said to Mrs. Spooner — when they went away Mrs. Spooner shook hands, & Buchanan said he would see her that night fortnight — the next morning she went out with me to the well & we see his cloak, she said she hoped her husband was in heaven & bid me take a horse & go out to enquire for him that it might be found out as soon as possible — she said she wanted to have him put to the bottom of the well —

Sarah Stratton — I saw Mr. Ross there between the two thanksgivings —

Jesse Parker — had been at Mr. Spooners by times before Mr. Spooner was killed — Mrs. Spooner used to be in the Sitting room along with Buchanan. Brooks & B. went to the barn & kept there & Alex & I & Mrs. Spooner carried victuals to the barn — Mrs. Spooner told him to ask Mr. Spooner to go to the barn — I told Alexr. of it & told him I would not — I did not see them for a week before he was killed — I was there when Mr. Spooner came from Princeton, & Mrs. Spooner said she never was so stump? in her life as she was at his coming home —

They lodg'd one night. I think it was the next day or day but one she asked me to get him to the barn, but did not say whether by day or night, she said it was because the doors were broke down — she said she had been to W. Parish to see the Regulars there & they were going to Worcester & she said she was going to Worcester to see her sister sick & asked her husband for a horse, but he would not do it. & she got Mr.   Horse.

Obadiah Rice — some months before this happened I heard her say she wished Old Bogus well in Heaven. This I heard Sundry times — Mrs. Spooner, Mrs. Stratton, & Alexr. coming down in a Slay. Mrs. Spooner said this don't seem like Christmas Day. she said if I had not had a great Desire to see my Daddy, the Murder would never have been committed. afterwards I would have given ten million of worlds the moment the breath was out of his Body, that it had been in again — she said she would suffer ten Deaths before Mrs. Stratton & Alexr. should suffer for they were innocent —

Elisha Hamilton — constable — while attending on Mrs. Spooner, she said if it was not for this thing I should not be afraid to meet my Judge. she said Mrs. Stratton & Alexr. were innocent for she had bribed them to do what they had done or say what they said, he did not know which — speaking to Mr. Cooley she said he had done no more than his Duty — this is all my own doing or Jobb or to that effect —

Asa Bigelow — the foreman told Mrs. Spooner he did not want to see her any more, for she must go to Goal, after she had been gone a little

while she returned & seeming full of trouble, she said she did not lay
hands on him herself, yet she was the cause of all this & twas her
doings or to that effect, she said she had hired it to be done & was to
give 1000 dollars & had paid 200 — she said she had hired Buchanan
& Brooks. I don't know that Ross was mentioned — but she said they
were there all three — Mrs. Stratton Differed Alexr. near the same —

Mr. Cunningham —

Esq. Young — Brooks Examina. was begun when I came in — have examined since —

Esq. Wheeler —
  with respect to Brooks —
  with respect to Buchanan —
  with respect to Ross.
  with respect to Bathsheba Spooner an accessory before the fact —

  witnesses of his spending The Sunday night — Mr. King, & Mr.
Cooley —
  with finding him and the blood — Mr. King & Mr. Cooley —
  the apprehending the Prisrs. & finding Mr. Spooner's Goods — Mr.
Curtis, Mr. Whitney, Mr. Ball, Mr. Bridge —
  that the Goods were Mr. Spooners. John Green, Thos. Green, Mr.
Simpson, Mr. Hibberd
  there Behaviour at Mrs. Walkers — Mary Walker, Prudence a
Negro —
  Witnesses of the Prisrs. being at Mr. Spooners — Mr. Olds, Mr. Lin-
coln — Cobbin & Wilson.
  Threatening — Mr. Cooley Olds Lincoln — Alex. Parker Rice
  Confessions Mr. Cooley. Whitney, Alec. Mrs. Stratton Rice Hamil-
ton, Bigelow,
  Examina. Esq. Young, Esq. Wheeler & Mr. Cunningham — all defts.
found Guilty & recd. Sentence of Death —

APPENDIX E

Minutes in the Case of the Murder of Mr. Spooner

Levi Lincoln

1. Introduction — bbs on the nature and importance of the case, its expectation with the public —

2. It is the first case of bloodshed, the first capital trial since the establishment of government —

3. It is equally remarkable in its nature if you consider the number, and the persons concerned, the manner of doing it, its rise, progress, and consequences, perhaps a more important, and a more difficult case was never committed to the charge of an American Jury — Four persons are indicted — Here give a History of them —

4. It is my duty to suggest to you such principles of law, with such observations on the evidence, as will enable you to determine the quality of each ones conduct in this matter on which you are to form a judgment —

5. You are apprised of that important duty you are called upon to discharge in this trial — you are to consider it as the trial of A&B, banishing all prejudices, contracted by reports — all indignation [illegible word] the enormity of the offense — all opinions from here-say — from their country — profession, connexions, political sentiments in conduct — You are to attend to, decide by, and give your verdict according to the fair result of the evidence — you are to suppose them innocent so far as they are not proved guilty by the evidence that has been given in the trial —

6. Murder is when a person of sound memory and discretion unlawfully kills and reasonable creatures in the peace, of government, with malice aforethought, either expressed, or implied.

7. Accessory before the fact is he who being absent at the time, doth yet procure, counsel, commend &c — For if present — aiding & a. and one only doth the act, they are all principles of Burn 3 —

8. In order therefore to determine whether the prisoners have been

guilty of the crimes respectively charged in the indictment or not, it will be necessary that you keep in your minds the evidence against each one separate and distinct. It is necessary that you be convinced that each one was, designedly influential of his death, both of which facts must be proved by such evidence as to leave not even the shadow of doubt in your minds — for if you are doubtful you must acquit —

9. It is an invincible rule of law, that in proportion as an offense rises in guilt in the same proportion ought to be the evidence against the offenders in order to his conviction.

10. The fact of killing is not denied, that it was murder in some body, is confessed, but it does not necessarily follow from that, that A B & C are the murderers, which must be proved beyond all doubt before you can convict them, for you can't infer, from the murder itself, which did the murder, where it might be one of three, one must do it —

11. Could not all the facts take place as testified, and yet it not be concerned to that degree which this indictment supposes — if the proof is of a less degree of guilt than this indictment supposes — then with respect to this indt it is no proof at all —

12. It is not my business to defend either of the prisoners against the imputation of guilt — all have been wicked, have been guilty in degree — I can't deny I trust I may safely admit that A was privy to, and concealed his death, and perhaps consented to it, or did not try to prevent it and was guilty of misprison of felony — and yet firmly stand upon the only ground, which it behooves me to maintain, principal or accessory is the gist of your inquiry, and the proof of nothing else is to the purpose. Every thing that is proved respecting R[oss] is perfectly innocent in reference to the crime charged in the indictment. I am sure the circumstances taken all together don't afford proof presumption probability or even suspicion of there being a design in R to hurt Mr. Spooner if they don't go to the enclusion of suspicion —

13. Is there any thing in the nature of things that R doing so & so — necessarily implies the existence of all those circumstances that constitutes murder — is not innocency in the sense of the indictment, perfectly consistent with those facts proved —

14. And it is a rule that no mans guilt can be proved by any evidence that is compatible with his innocence.

15. The proof of a crime may be divided into two classes, perfect & imperfect, those are perfect which exclude the possibility of guilt

innocence — Imperfect those which do not exclude this possibility. Of the first one only is sufficient for condemnation — of the second as many are required as form a perfect proof, that is if each, taken separately, does not exclude this possibility, yet if they do by their union, it is perfect proof which is allway requisite — but separate, independent prooffs, that not connect in time, so as at last to connect with the fact to be proved, don't amount to perfect prooff —

16. The confession of a criminal can rarely be turned against him without obviating the end for which he must be supposed to have given it — Its uncertain, there have been instances of murder avowed that have not been committed, and confession of goods stolen that were never out of the possession of the owner —

13. It is unjust and dangerous to suffer confessions dictated by the distractions of fear, or the misdirected hopes of mercy to have much weight — Besides the evidence of words ought to be received with great caution and distrust which are spoken in unsuspicious confidence, or in the hurry and perturbation of a mind anxious and pressed by leading questions — The words may be very innocent when spoken and criminal when related — much depends on the time and concomitant circumstances.

14. If one come casually not of the confederacy, tho' he hindered not the felony he is neither principal nor accessory Who has apprehend not the felon — If Rosses going to Brookfield was ignorant as to what took place — he knew nothing of the appointment at Walkers — or of Brooks & Buchannon going there —

15. What makes an accessory is ones commanding, counseling, abetting and procuring another to commit a felony. And therefore words that sound in bear permission make not an accessory — so if A. says he will kill J.S. and B. says you may act your pleasure for me this makes not B accessory — Cunningh. tit. sucp 2d Art. 1 Burn 3 — does the evidence about Ross amount to more than this?

16. He who barely conceals a felony which he knows to be intended is guilty only of misprision of felony — and shall not be adjudged an accessory for this is not abetting, procuring &C — 1 Burn 4

If A. sees to commit a felony and consents not in this and we (:) to apprehend him is not accessory — Bost. 350.

17. No bear omission can make a person accessory either before or after the fact. Dem 6 —

18 But it may be misprision of felony, and the person may be proceeded against as such if the state pleases   2 Burn 172

19. If A counsels or commands another to kill a person and before he hath killed him, A repents, and countermands it, charging him not to kill him and yet he doth, it shall not be adjudged accessory—For the law judgeth no man accessory before the fact but such as continues in that mind at the time the felony is done and enlisted—1 Burn 4 Obs. Is there not as much evid. of his repenting & countermanding as there is of commanding or unto the influence of that command extend to the completion of the fact when he ran away—&c

20. Principal, as if several set out on one common felonious design and each taketh the part assigned him—Some to commit the fact, others to watch at proper distances and stations to prevent surprise or to favor the shape of those engaged (if need be) in the eye of the law are present—For each one operated at the same instant with design and to the same end—Q.C.I. Burn3

21. Or if one present, did nothing yet came to assist the party if needfull—idim

22. For it gives countenance, encouragement and protection to the whole[illegible word] and to assure success of their common enterprise—idim now here is the reason why he is accessory—if it does not encourage them he is not accessory

23. Obs.—If principal he must be present with design to assist if needful, and this design the Jury must be convinced of by proof beyond all doubt—There must be an evil design with respect to the crime committed—For merely being in company with others, being present, without a design to have anything to do with it, altho he did not endeavor to prevent it is no doubt punishable but not as murder—he might be present for many reasons without designing to assist in the murder—It might be difficult to leave them without danger—considering how he was connected—it might be dangerous to attempt to prevent it by a discovery.

24. If he had a design against Mr. S. life had he not frequent opportunities at his own house, at Princeton, and on the road by poison, by strangling, & by weapons—The matter had been long in agitation and his not doing it shows he had no real design—But only to keep up an appearance of favoring the design to keep on terms—Nay it goes further and proves he had not such a design, that he was deter-

mined not to do it — Or why did he not do it, when in so many instances, place opportunity and means favored it — and solicitations were pressing — why did he not do it — the omission proves not only the absence of a design to do it, but a determination against it — For every opportunity omitted, every solicitation rejected, was in the nature of things [illegible word] many against it — Now if you are convinced of that can you say he was with a design to help —

25. Rosses interest in procuring the poison It was countermanded by taking it back — besides the murder did not take place in consequence of it — and therefore tho a crime has nothing to do with the crime in the indt. — You are to consider him there only in that point of [illegible word] view in which he is placed by the evidence — and if the facts proved would not convict any other man — who was innocent of and a stranger to all the previous transactions, it ought to convict him they are different crimes — for which I hope he will be punished if he is acquitted here —

26. Tho Ross did not attempt to conceal it afterwards — his riding the horse, his cloaths, & c — and continuing one day in Worcester when he might have made his escape, was discovering of it & it might be with design —

27. Spooner was dead when Ross went to him and took him by the leg therefore, that don't prove Ross guilty of murder

The Jury must be convinced that Mrs. Spooner — was of a sound mind & c —

1. This collected from the nature of the facts & c —

2ndly   If the conduct is irrational — If it is what could not be directed by a person in the exercise of reason — Then there is the best evidence of a disordered mind that the nature of the thing will admit of —

3dly — Conduct is only evidence of the state of a persons mind —

4th — Disorders of the brain operate variously

5thly   The difference between a fool and a ~~mad man~~ distracted person —

6 — Instance the woman preacher Now survey her conduct — Mrs. S is either fool or a distracted person —

7 — What end could it [illegible word] — were there any reason, any advantage arising from this death —

8 — The consequence — orphan children to maintain, widowhood and a third instead of the whole of the estate —

9 What hope of impunity? It is a well known principle, that the source of wickedness — the incentive to guilt, is the hope of impunity & what hope here?

10 — The number of persons knowing to it — Their character, their situation, and their profession —

11. No plan formed, no story agreed on, no place to flee to — strangers no evidence of their fidelity — seen in company with them the night before — procure calomel, agrees on the time, reminds them of it before company — why the calomel if he is to be assassinated —

12. Gives the murderers Mr. S cloaths, watch buckels, waistcoat & C — which were well known — Is this the conduct of a person in the exercise of reason

13. Is it possible that she would ever intrust such an affair to strangers, diserters and foreigners — to women and boys — that she not have had some motive some means, some place fixed on, some confident, some hope of impunity before she would have engaged if she had been in her senses —

14. Thrown into the well, strangers lodging in the house — Her life and & all at stake — her composure afterward — she again suffers [illegible word] — Their confession — if one is admitted as evidence of truth — then may another which is inconsistent with the first — If the first is taken for truth, merely because it is confessed. Why not the second, if both then a confession is admitted as evidence of truth, which is necessarily untrue — Besides he is not to be regarded against others and why against himself, seeing he won't be believed on his own veracity — For if veracity is the foundation of believe it is as good against another, as himself — and if any other reason can be assigned besides its being true, then it is no evidence of truth.

Minutes & Observation in Mrs. Spooner case of Murder & c —

What end could it serve? Was there any reason persuading, hopes inviting, or advantages arising from the death of Mr Spooner to Mrs. S—— By his death at best she orphanised the children by depriving them of a father, bewidowed herself, subjected herself to burdens of supporting herself and children, and instead of enjoying the whole, could enjoy but one third of an Estate — could she then have success-

fully have projected this matter, with a design of having it enacted —
and if she did could she have been in the exercise of her reason —

If it is said she could not live with her husband, could she not have
separated, could have not gone to Home to her father whose favorite
she was, to her brother and her other friends — There with her address, and engaging appearance she might have had any gallant she
pleased, not as Ross, if she was capable of murdering her husband, she
was sufficiently advanced to have imbraced this or any course of life —
But what was the necessary consequence —

It is a well known principle founded in nature, that the source of
wickedness, the incentive to guilt, is the hope of impunity. But what
hopes of being undetected, what presumption of impunity could she
have — Was it possible to conceal the matter, considering the number
of persons employed. Their character, their situation, & their profession no plan formed to conceal it, no story agreed on, no place to flee
to, strangers, no evidence of their fidelity, could therefore have no
confidence in them — Is seen in company with them the night before,
at Walkers, procures Collumel, agrees on the time, reminded them of
it before company, at eleven o clock says she — why the columel if he is
to be assasinated its ridiculous — she previously tells that Mr. Spooner
is going a long journey — and inquires if any body wants to hire his
farm — after the murder, she gives the murderers his watch buckels
waistcoat breeches & shirts, and even puts them on, to be worn in the
eye of the world, where they were well known to be Spooner cloaths —
and from their goodness and fashion must be known not to belong to
the persons wearing them being low & vulgar. Is this the conduct of
a person in the exercise of reason — Would it have been less rational
to have wrote on their foreheads in capitals The murderers of Mr.
Spooner — If the conduct is irrational, if it is what could not be directed by a person in the exercise of Reason, then there is all the best
evidence of a disordered mind, that the nature of the thing will admit of —

For there is no knowing the state of the mind, but by a persons conduct. The distinction, the disorder of the mind operates variously —
The difference between a fool & a man disorded — the fool draws
wrong conclusion from right principles — the disordered mind, ar-
gues right from wrong principles — Instance the woman preacher that
pretends she has rose from the dead.

As to their own confession it is not evidence any further than from the nature of the things and circumstances it can be supposed to be true. If one's confession is taken as conclusive evidence of the truth, than may another, which is different and inconsistent, but if the first is taken for true, merely because he confessed, why not the second, if both are taken for true, then a confession is admitted as evidence of truth, which is necessarily untrue — Besides a person confessing his own turpitude is not to be regarded against others and why against himself, seeing it must be believed on the veracity of the witness, for if that is the foundation of believe, it is as good against another person, as himself — If the grounds is because it is against his interest then if any reason can be assigned for his doing it besides it being true it can be no evidence of truth — Then, why should he not make a wrong confession as well as a true one — a man that has murder cant feel an obligation to speak the truth —

It is incredible, that it should ever enter into the head of a person of so much capacity, & so much cunning to intrust and affair so heinously criminal to strangers, deserters & foreigners who had they escape a detection here would probably have boasted of their feats after they got off to the enemy and if she was affraid they would not disclose it, to intrust it with other women and boys — Must she not have had some motive, some proper means, some plan fixed, some chosen trusty confident, or some reason to hope either to accomplish or conceal the crime of so detestable an action before she would have engaged in it if she had been in her senses. It was perpetrated in the heart of a populous town, near neighbors where it must at farthest be discovered by the morning — liable to be heard in the time of it — by the people abroad, by the two travelers who lodged there that night, by the children, and other of the family —

X [mark in margin] Is it possible she would commit so atrocious a crime & run so great a hazard from no motive. It is said she was upon ill terms with her husband, this is to trump up one crime, that there may seem to have been a motive to have perpetrated another from. But to whom did she commit the execution of it, whom did she make use of as her accomplices, whom as her confident, whom did she trust with the management of a villainy that so nearly affected her reputation, her safety, her life, her children, the lives of others and the happiness of her friends — The answer is prostitutes, boys, regulars, deserters, strangers, and foreigners. But was a woman who is admitted to have sense, so stupid, if in the exercise of her reason, as to trust all that was valuable to her & hers, in the hands of such persons. Would she if rational have given them so much money when she knew it was known how much Mr. Spooner had, and would she have given them such large notes, who did empart to own [illegible words]

[Pages with concluding arguments are missing.]

APPENDIX F

Notes of Cases decided in the Superiour and Supreme Judicial Courts of Massachusetts from 1772 to 1789

Chief Justice William Cushing

Indictment v. W. Brooks, Buchanan, & Ross for murder of Joshua Spooner & against Bathsheba Spooner, his wife, as accesary before the fact.

After the arraignment of the prisoners the counsel for the principals (they being british soldiers), moved for a moiety of the jury of aliens—which was overruled by the Court. The Chief Justice stated that he had never heard of such a motion being granted in this Province—except in the instance of an indian who was indicted under the old charter government—and was allowed a jury de medictate linguae—viz—6 English & 6 Indians. —

APPENDIX G

Account of the Murder, Trial, and Execution from the Massachusetts Spy

5 March 1778. On Sunday night a most horrid murder was committed in Brookfield, on the person of Mr. Joshua Spooner. From the long premeditation of this murder, the number of persons concerned (there being no less than seven capitally concerned) and the methods made use of to accomplish their designs, it is supposed to be the most extraordinary crime ever perpetrated in New-England.

Monday evening three of the villains concerned in the murder of Mr. Spooner were taken up in this town. On examination they impeached their accomplices, in consequence of which Mrs. Spooner, (the inventor of the murder) and the rest of her associates were seized, and on Tuesday evening brought to this town and confined in goal.

7 May 1778. The following is a particular account of the trial of the persons mentioned in our last. *William Brooks, James Buchanan,* and *Ezra Ross,* were indicted for the murder of Mr. Joshua Spooner of Brookfield, and *Bathsheba,* his late wife, was indicted as an accessary thereto, by causing, procuring, aiding, and abetting the same. They were set at the bar, and severally pleaded, not guilty; having council assigned them the trial came on, and lasted 16 hours, wherein every legal indulgence were granted them. They were all found guilty and received sentence of death accordingly.

It appeared by the course of the evidence, that Mrs. Spooner had, for some time, conceived a great aversion to her husband, with whom she had lived about 14 years: His only fault appears to be his not supporting a manly importance as head of his family, and not regulating the government of it. It is very uncertain what this aversion in Mrs. Spooner's mind at first arose from, but from the general tenor of her conduct, it is probable that she cherished a criminal regard for some other persons, until, having followed the blind impulses of wicked and unchaste desires, she left all moral sensibility, discarded reason and conscience from her breast, and gave herself up to infamous prostitutions, and finally became determined to destroy the life of her husband, who seemed to check her wanton career in no other way then by preventing her wasting his whole estate as she pleased, in pursuance of this horrid design, she at various times, procured poison, but never gave it to him; and sometime before the commission of this cruel fact, she became acquainted with Ross, to whom she made some amorous overtures, and told him, that if he would kill her husband, she would become his lawful wife: It appears, by the examination of Ross, before the Justices, that his conscience at first started at the appearance of so much guilt; but upon her persuasions and the fancied happiness of marrying a woman so much above his rank in life, and the allurements of wallowing in Mr. Spooner's wealth he fatally consented. Previous to this, Ross had been sick at Spooner's house, and was kindly treated there, and that after these guilty overtures, tarried there some time, with freedom as one of the family, when Mr. Spooner treated him with great civilities, and many marks of particular friendship; that while he was there, he put poison in his drink, which was discovered; and that he rode with him to Oakum and Leicester, and had engaged to poison him on the road; that he bought arsenic to effect his death, but never gave it to him.

Mrs. Spooner tired with the delays of Ross, made like overtures to Sergeant Buchanan of the convention troops, whom she directed to be called in, as he was passing on the road. Buchanan and she engaged one William Brooks, of the same troops; to commit the murder, promising him the deceased's watch, buckles, and a thousand dollars. Buchanan and Brooks came to Spooner's about a fortnight before his death, and stayed in his kitchen all night: He then being afraid they would rob him, brought his money from the chamber and procured one of his neighbours to stay with him, and sat up all night, but on his ordering them to go away in the morning, they went to the barn, and layed concealed there two days and two nights, in which time Mrs. Spooner sustained them with victuals and drink. That on the Tuesday next before the first day of March, which was the day her husband was murdered, she met them at one Widow Walker's in Worcester, where, although she was a stranger in the house, she tarried with them the greater part of that and the two following days, was often alone with

them, treated them very familiarly, and suffered them to use great fa-
miliarities with her, to the astonishment of Walker's family, who knew
her rank in life. On Saturday, when she went away from Walker's,
some words passed between her and Buchanan, at parting, which
leaves no doubt of their having agreed to meet at Brookfield, the next
day, to effect the death of Mr. Spooner.

While she was absent on Saturday, Ross came into the house, and
concealed himself till evening, when he looked through a window and
spoke to one Widow Stratton, who was ironing in the kitchen, and told
her that he was exceeding cold but could not come in because he
wanted to conceal himself from Mr. Spooner, whose horse he had
borrowed to go to Ipswich, to see his father, and which he had chafed.

This woman concealed him in the buttery until Mrs. Spooner came
home, who was received pleasantly by her husband: She concealed
Ross all the next day, being the Sabbath on the evening whereof the
deceased went out and spent an hour or two with one of his neighbours as he usually did. While he was gone, Buchanan and Brooks
came to his house, and, after a great deal of conversation on the
killing Mr. Spooner, she stimulated them to the murder, (sometimes
by promises of reward and others by upbraidings of cowardice, until it
was agreed upon that the three men should stand sentry by turns to
watch his returning to his own house. About nine o'clock he left his
company, in a cheerful humour, and great calmness of mind, without
the least suspicion of the villainy. As he came near to his own door,
Brooks met him and knocked him down; he asked what was the matter, and cried murder (as appears by the examination of Brooks, before the Justices) but they all three fell upon, and presently dispatched him, with repeated blows, and unparalleled cruelty, and then
threw him into the well. After this they came into the house to Mrs.
Spooner, with the clothes of Brooks wet with the blood of her innocent husband. She went up to his bed chamber to get his money to
pay Brooks, according to her promise, and to distribute his wealth
amongst his murderers; but while she was there, she told the Widow
Stratton who was in the kitchen when the murder was done (and
whose conscience must witness whether she was before, privy to this
hostile design against the life of a man who found her bread), that she
hoped Mr. Spooner was in Heaven, and seemed much affected. She
however, came down, brought the money, and distributed it amongst

the ruffians. She then sent a second servant, whom she had often invited to kill her husband, to the well to get water to wash the bloody cloaths; he knowing of the murder was afraid to go alone, and Stratton went with him; but, when he put the bucket down into the well, he felt his master, dropped the pale and they both ran into the house, where Stratton took down the bible, went to reading, and cried. They then agreed to burn the bloody cloaths; Ross gave Brooks his breeches and put on Spooner's. She gave Brooks 200 dollars, the watch and buckles; and the three murderers set off in the dead of night for Worcester, with Mr. Spooner's horse and goods. They were there overtaken on Monday and apprehended. The next morning after the murder, Mrs. Spooner and the Scotch servant went to the well, and saw her husband there, and, after some proposals of sinking him, she sent the servant on horse back, to inquire for him, that she might not be suspected; when the neighbours were collected they observed the strongest marks of guilt in the whole family.

She appeared to be but little affected either on trial or when sentence of death was passed upon her, and it is to be wished, that there may be in the other convicts, more signs of repentance, before their execution than has yet been observed in her.*

August 6, 1778. On the 2d ult. were executed in this town, James Buchanan, Ezra Ross, William Brooks, and Bathshua Spooner, for the murder of Mr. Joshua Spooner, late of Brookfield. At about half past two in the afternoon, the criminals were brought out of prison, and conducted to the place of execution, under a guard of about an hundred men. The three male prisoners went on foot, Mrs. Spooner was carried in a chaise, being, as she had been for a number of days,

---

*According to a note written by Esther Forbes on a transcript of this article, it is almost the same word for word as an article that appeared in the *Independent Chronicle,* 30 April 1778. Forbes wrote that according to a letter written by Dwight Foster (Jedediah Foster's son), "The circumstantial account of the murder &c. as published in Powers and Willis' *Independent Chronicle* of last Thursday was made up by Judge [James] Sullivan from the evidence in Court and is very correct." Both the article and the letter were located in the archives of the American Antiquarian Society, Worcester, Mass., although they appear now to be missing.

exceedingly unwell. The procession was regular and solemn. Just before they reached the place of execution a black thunder cloud arose and darkened the Heavens; here followed an awful half hour! The loud hallooings of the officers, amidst a crowd of five thousand, to *Make way! Make way!* the horses pressing upon those on foot; the shrieks of women in the confusion; the malefactors slowly advancing to the fatal tree, preceded by their dismal urns; the fierce coruscations athwart the darkened horizon, quickly followed by loud peals of thunder, conspired together, and produced a dreadful compound scene of horror! It seemed as if the author of nature was determined to add such terrors to the punishment of the criminals as must stagger the stoutest heart of the most abandoned. While the sheriff was reading the Death Warrant, Buchanan, Brooks, and Ross were on the stage; Mrs. Spooner, being excessively feeble, was permitted to sit in the chaise; she heard the warrant read with as much calmness as she would the most indifferent matter; she was frequently seen to bow to many of the spectators with whom she had been acquainted. When called on to ascend the stage, with a gentle smile she stepped out of the chaise and crept up the ladder upon her hands and knees. The halters being fastened; the malefactors pinioned, and their faces covered, the sheriff informed them that he should drop the stage immediately; upon which Mrs. Spooner took him by the hand and said, "My dear sir! I'm ready! in a little time I expect to be in bliss: and but a few years must elapse when I hope I shall see you and my other friends again." They all were calm and almost smiled at the approach of death, considering the king of terrors but as a kind messenger to introduce them to the regions of eternal joys.†

---

†On the same page, Thaddeus Maccarty's published execution sermon with appendix (an account of the prisoners in their last stages) was advertised for six shillings.

APPENDIX H

Petition of Jabez and Johana Ross

To the Hon. Council of the said State now setting at Boston:

The Memorial and petition of Jabez Ross, and Johana Ross of Ipswich in the County of Essex, humbly sheweth that your memorialists, are the unhappy parents of a most unfortunate son now under sentence of death for the murder of Mr. Spooner—a murder the most shocking in its kind, and in circumstances not to be paralleled—that out of the public troubles of the day, your memorialists have been called by providence, to suffer a large and uncommon share. That at the commencement of hostilities, of seventeen children, six sons, and three daughters alone survived to your aged and distressed petitioners, whose footsteps from that period have been marked with anxiety, and whose sorrows, from the melancholy fate of their youngest son, have received a tinge of the keenest kind.

At the first instance of bloodshed, five of the six sons entered the public service; four fought on Bunker Hill, three marched to the southward with General Washington, of which number was the unhappy convict, who engaged for one, the other two for three years. A fourth mingled at the northward his bones with the dust of the earth.

On his return, from the first year's campaign, he was by the lot of Providence, cast upon Mrs. Spooner, in a severe fit for sickness from whom he received every kind office and mark of tenderness, that could endear and make gratefull a child of sixteen, sick, destitute, in a strange place, at a distance from friend and acquaintance. After the evacuation of Ticonderoga, in his march to reinforce the Northern Army, gratitude for past favors led him to call on his old benefactress, who then added to the number of her kindnesses, and engaged a visit on his return—with a mind thus prepared, & thus irresistibly prepossessed, by her addresses, kindnesses, on his tender years, he for the first time heard the horrid proposals, tempted by promises flattering to his situation, and seduced both from virtue, & prudence a child as

[160]

he was, by a lewd artfull woman, he but too readily acceded to her measures, black as they were—but never attempted an execution of the detestable crime, notwithstanding repeated solicitations, and as frequent opportunities, untill on an accidental meeting, he became a party with those ruffians, who, without his privity, had fixed on the time and place for that horrid transaction, of which he now stands justly convicted.

Your petitioners, by no means attempt an extenuation of guilt, or measures inconsistent with the safety of the community, and the preservation of individuals. But if it is consistent, if the criminal, who is thoroughly possessed with a sense of what is past, present, or to come, can be spared, and his guilt condemned; if he has been a valuable member of society and fought in her cause, altho from the inexperience peculiar to youth, the strength of some momentary impulses, and alluring seducements, he gradually <u>erred</u> until he arrived to the violent act of wickedness; if upon recollection he has found repentance, confessed his life a forfeiture to the law, looking up to heaven for that forgiveness which none can find on earth; if an early confession of the whole matter and the suffering of a thousand deaths in the reflections of the mind; if the law, the Government, and the grave can be satisfied, and mercy displayed; in fine, if youth, if old age, the sorrows, the anguish of a father, the yearnings of a mother, the compassion & wishes of thousands can avail; if any or all of these considerations can arrest the hand of justice, plead effectually for mercy, and induce your honors to extend that pardon towards one of the poor unhappy victims destined to a most awful execution, and thereby give him an opportunity of atoning to the public for the injury he has done it—restore him to his country, to himself, his sympathizing friends, to his aging, drooping, distressed parents. It will console them under the weightiest afflictions, and turn the wormwood and the gall into something tolerable; and your petitioners, in duty bound, will ever pray.

Jabez Ross
Johana Ross
Ipswich, May 26th, 1778
At the earnest desire of the above named Jabez Ross & Wife, the distressed parents of the above said unhappy convict, I the subscriber, minister of the gospel in the parish of Linebrook, of which the said

petitioners are inhabitants, join with them in their request for the life of their son, provided the Honourable Council, in their wisdom and governess, judges it may be granted consistent with a due regard for publick justice & the safety of the community. George Lesslie, Pastor of the Church at Linebrook.

May 26th, 1778

APPENDIX I

Documents from the Executive Records, Revolutionary Council Papers, 1777–1778

Death Warrant

The Government and People of the State of Massachusetts Bay

To the Sheriff of our County of Worcester, Greeting,

Whereas William Brooks resident at Charlestown in the County of Middlesex laborour, James Buchannon of the same Charlestown laborour and Ezra Ross of Ipswich in the County of Essex laborour now Prisoners in our Goal in said Worcester were by the Jurors for us for the Body of our said County at the Superior Court of Judicature, Court of Assize and General Goal delivery held at Worcester aforesaid for the said County of Worcester on the Tuesday next preceeding the last Tuesday of April indicted for that, the said William Brooks resident of Charlestown in the County of Middlesex Laborour, James Buchannon of the same Charlestown Laborour and Ezra Ross of Ipswich in the County of Essex Laborour not having GOD before their Eyes, but being moved and seduced by the Instigation of the Devil on the first day of March last past, with force and Arms, at Brookfield in the County of Worcester aforesaid, feloniously, Willfully and of their Malice aforethought in and upon Joshua Spooner of said Brookfield then and there in the Peace of GOD, and of the said Government and People being, an Assault did make, and that the aforesaid William Brooks with his right Fist, the said Joshua Spooner to and against Ground then and there feloniously, Willfully and of his malice aforethought did Strike down, and the same Joshua Spooner so on the Ground lying, he the said William Brooks with both his Hands and feet of him the said William Brooks in and upon the back, Head, Stomach, Sides and Throat of him the said Joshua Spooner, then and there feloniously, willfully, and of his Malice aforethought did Strike, beat, and kick, giving to him the said Joshua Spooner as well by the stricking down of him the said Joshua Spooner to the Ground as aforesaid as also by the stricking, beating and kicking the said Joshua Spooner in and upon the back, Head & Stomach, Sides and Throat, of him the said Joshua Spooner as aforesaid with both the Hands and feet of him the said William Brooks in manner aforesaid, Several Mortal Bruizes, of which said Several mortal Bruizes in the said Joshua Spooner, there instantly died . . . and that James Buchannon aforesaid and Ezra Ross aforesaid feloniously and of their Malice aforethought then and there were present, aiding, Assisting abetting, Comforting and maintaining the aforesaid William Brooks to the felony and Murther aforesaid, in form aforesaid to be done and Committed and that the said William Brooks, James Buchannon and Ezra Ross the aforesaid Joshua Spooner at Brookfield aforesaid, in Manner and form aforesaid feloniously, Willfully and of their Malice aforethought killed and Murthered against the Peace of the Government and People aforesaid, and the Law of this State in such Case made and provided — And that Bathsheba Spooner of Brookfield in the County of Worcester, Widow, late Wife of the said Joshua Spooner, not having GOD before her Eyes but being seduced by the Instigation of the Devil, before the Felony and Murther aforesaid by the aforesaid William Brooks, James Buchannon and Ezra Ross in manner and Form aforesaid done and Committed, that is to say on the Twenty eighth day of February last Past, the aforesaid Bathsheba Spooner at Brookfield aforesaid in the County of Worcester aforesaid, the Felony and Murther aforesaid in manner and form aforesaid to be done and committed Maliciously, Willfully, and of her Malice aforethought did incite, move, abett, Counsel and procure against the Peace of the Government and People aforesaid — To which the said William Brooks James Buchannon Ezra Ross, and Bathsheba Spooner pleaded <u>not Guilty,</u> and were by Verdict, of our Jurors, for our said County of Worcester Convict and thereupon the said William Brooks, James Buchannon, Ezra Ross, and Bathsheba Spooner were by our Justices of our said Court adjudged to Suffer the Pangs of Death as to Us appears by a Copy of Record of said Court hereunto annexed whereof Execution doth still remain to be done:

We Command you therefore that on Thursday the fourth day of June next between the Hours of twelve and four of the Clock in the afternoon, You Cause the said William Brooks, James Buchannon Ezra Ross and Bathsheba Spooner to be conveyed from our Goal in Worcester aforesaid where they now are, in your Custody to the Usual Place of Execution in our said County of Worcester, and there to be hanged by the Neck until their Bodies be dead, for which this Shall be your Sufficient Warrant—Fail not at your Peril and make return of this Writ with your doings therein into the Secretary's Office of said State at Boston on the tenth Day of June next:

Witness the Major Part of our Council at Boston this Eighth day of May, In the Year of our Lord, One thousand Seven hundred and Seventy Eight—

By their Honors Order
    John Avery Dy. Secy.
Jer. Powell, Artemas Ward, Jedidiah Preble, T. Cushing, John Whetcomb, S. Holten, B. White, Benj. Austin, H. Gardner, Moses Gill, D. Hopkins, N. Cushing, A. Fuller, Josiah Stone, Oliver Prescott

ORDER FOR SUSPENSION OF SENTENCE

The Government and People of the Massachusetts Bay in New England
To the Sheriff of our County of Worcester

Greeting, Whereas William Brooks resident at Charlestown in the County of Middlesex Labourer James Buchannon of the same Charlestown Labourer/and Ezra Ross of Ipswich in the County of Essex Labourer and Bathsheba Spooner of Brookfield in the County of Worcester Widow/now Prisoners in our Goal in said Worcester in our said County of Worcester, were at our Superiour Court of Judicature, Court of Assize & General Gaol Delivery held at Worcester in and for our said County of Worcester on the Tuesday next preceding the last Tuesday of April convicted of Murder and was thereupon adjudged to suffer the Pains of Death: and a Warrant issued out by the major part of the Council of our State aforesaid requiring you to put the Sentence thereof in Execution the fourth day, June next: but it hath been represented to us that the said William Brooks, James Buchannon, Ezra Ross, and Bathsheba Spooner are desirous of further time being allowed them to prepare for Death—We of our special

Grace and favour do hereby direct and Command you to suspend and delay the Execution of the Sentence of our said Court until Thursday the Second Day of July next—at which Time you are to proceed to Execute the said Warrant in manner and form as therein is Directed.

Witness the Major Part of our Council at Boston this twenty eighth Day of May in the year of our Lord 1778.

By Their Honors Order

John Avery, Depy. Secy.

Jer. Powell, Artemas Ward, Walter Spooner,* Jabez Fisher, Moses Gill, Benj. Austin, Dan Davis, L. Danielson, N. Cushing, Oliver Prescott, A. Fuller, Josiah Stone, John Pitts, Sam. Baker, Oliver Wendell.

RETURN OF THE SHERIFF
(FIRST EXAMINATION WRIT)

Worcester. In strict compliance with the within directions and warrant I have summoned two men midwives and twelve lawful matrons and caused the said matrons to be under oath and in my proper person with the said men midwives and matrons attended on the said Bathsheba Spooner they have made the searches as required in the within writ—The verdict of the above matrons is that the said Bathsheba Spooner is not quick with child.

Given under our hand & seals, this eleventh day of June, A.D. 1778.

William Greenleaf, Sheriff, [Seal]

Josiah Wilder, Midwife, [Seal

Elijah Dix, Midwife, [Seal]

A list of the Matrons—
Elizabeth Rice
Mary Todman
Hannah Perry
Zurbilch Stowell
Christian Walker
Ezebel Quigley
Margaret Brown

---

*no relation to Joshua

Mary Bridge
Lidia Ball
Hannah Brooks
Mary Sternes*
Sarah Jones

[Endorsed]

Warrant for examining Bathsheba Spooner respectg her being quick with child with the return of the Sheriff of the County of Worcester thereon also, enclosing her petition not granted. June 23, 1778.

OPINION OF MIDWIVES
(SECOND EXAMINATION)

Worcester, June 27, 1778

To the Honour. Board of Councillors
for the State of Massachusetts Bay —

May it please your honours:

We, the subscribers have examined the Body of Mrs. Bathsheba Spooner (by her Desire) to find whether she is quick with Child or not, & altho' it was our and the Jury of Matrons Opinion on the examination of the 11th Instant that she was not quick with Child at that time, yet upon this further examination, we would inform your Honours, that we must give it as our Opinion that we have reason to Think that she is now quick with Child.

John Green	
Josiah Wilder	Midwives
Elijah Dix	
Hannah Mower	Woman Midwife

Worcester, June 27, 1778

To the Honbl. Board of Councillors
for the State of Massachusetts Bay —

Whereas we, the Subscribers, Matrons on the Examination of Mrs. Bathsheba Spooner, on the 11th Instant did give it as Our Opinion on

---

*[Stearns]

Oath, that she was not quick with Child at that time, have again this day at her request examined her present Circumstances and give it as our Opinion that she is not even now Quick with child.

Elizabeth Rice

Molly Tattman

FINAL RETURN OF THE SHERIFF

Worcesters. In obediance to the within Directions: I suspended the Execution of Wm. Brooks James Buchannon Ezra Ross & Bathsheba Spooner from the forth June last, till July The Second Day which was on Thursday last; Then Carried The abovesaid Wm. Brooks James Buchannon Ezra Ross with Bathsheba Spooner to the place of Execution and there hanged them Each By The Neck untill They were dead; between the houres of twelve & four of the Clock in the Afternoon, as Directed by a warrant to me from the Major Part of The Council bearing Date The Eighth Day of May last in the year of our Lord One Thousand seven hundred and seventy Eight.

Willm. Greenleaf Sherriff

Lancaster July 6 AD 1778

NOTES

Introduction

1. *Massachusetts Spy,* 5 March 1778.
2. Parkman, "The Adultress Will Hunt for the Precious Life."
3. Chandler, "The Trial of Mrs. Spooner and Others," *American Criminal Trials,* vol. 2, 54.
4. Crafts, "The Spooner Genealogy," 1913–1922.
5. Paine, Minutes of Trial and Law Cases, 1777–1782, Robert Treat Paine acted as the prosecutor in the Spooner murder trial. Though his notes substantially follow the more widely known trial notes written by Associate Justice Jedediah Foster ("Notes on the Trial of Bathsheba Spooner, 1778"), they also include some intriguing additional testimony such as this characterization of Joshua's drunkeness. For future references to the Paine minutes, see appendix C.
6. Sargeant, "Indictment of William Brooks, James Buchanan, and Ezra Ross." Sargeant was one of five judges who sat at the Spooner trial (the other four were Chief Justice William Cushing, Jedediah Foster, David Sewall, and James Sullivan). A transcription of Sargeant's case notes, which offer more detailed testimonies than all other known accounts, are included in appendix D. For future references to the Sargeant notes, see appendix D.

2. By the Lot of Providence

1. According to Peleg W. Chandler (*American Criminal Trials,* vol. 2, no. 10) "The venerable Major Benjamin Russell, who then lived in Worcester, recollects seeing Ross and Mrs. Spooner riding on horseback together before the murder; he states that the former was a fine-looking youth, and that the beauty of the latter, who was a remarkable horsewoman, has not been exaggerated in the least by traditionary accounts." Listings in the *Massachusetts Soldiers and Sailors of the Revolutionary War* describe two Ross brothers as dark-complected, suggesting that Ezra's coloring was probably dark, as was Bathsheba's.

2. Petition of Jabez and Johana Ross, 26 May 1778. For future references to this document, see appendix H.

3. From a Ross family Bible in the *Ipswich, Massachusetts, Vital Records,* we know the following information about the Jabez Ross family. The children whose names are in boldface are known to have survived at the date of the Rosses' petition.

> Father, Jabez b. 1705, d. 2 December 1801
> Mother, Johana
> 1. Abner b. 1 August 1740; d. 3 April 1758
> 2. Lydia b. 24 July 1742
> 3. David b. 20 January 1744
> 4. Ruth b. 30 December 1745; d. 1745
> 5. **Joanna** b. 3 March 1746
> 6. **Kneeland** (Neeland) b. 3 April 1748
> 7. Martha b. 12 March 1749; d. 19 September 1773
> 8. **Jabez Jr.** b. 3 March 1750
> 9. **Timothy** b. 30 January 1751
> 10. Lucy b. 30 December 1753; d. 15 May 1761
> 11. Jedediah b. 16 March 1755
> 12. Huldah b. 24 December 1757
> 13. Lucy b. 16 January 1759
> 14. **Ezra** b. 20 July 1761; hanged 2 July 1778
> 15. Susan b. 5 June 1762

Benjamin and Nathaniel Ross are not listed in the *Ipswich Vital Records,* but are listed in the Minute Men Enlistments (Captain Nathaniel Wade's Company, 1/24/75) along with Jabez Jr. and Kneeland, suggesting these are the two of seventeen children missing from the *Vital Records* listing. The Minute Men Enlistments are to be found in Thomas Franklin Waters' *Ipswich in the Massachusetts Bay Colony 1700–1917,* 2:317.

4. For a full account of what came to be called "The Ipswich Fright," see Waters, *Ipswich,* vol. 2, 320–23.

5. Ibid., 321–22.

6. About which Thomas Paine wrote his famous words in "The American Crisis": "These are the times that try men's souls. The summer soldier and the sunshine patriot will, in this crisis, shrink from the service of their country; but he that stands it now deserves the love and thanks of man and woman."

7. The distance reported by Ross at Rowley, Mass., April 1777. *Massachusetts Soldiers and Sailors of the Revolutionary War,* vol. 13.

8. From the Reverend Thaddeus Maccarty, "Account of the Behaviour of Mrs. Spooner" and also the 7 May 1778 issue of the *Massachusetts Spy.*
9. See Ketchum, *Saratoga,* 84.
10. Waters, *Ipswich,* vol. 2, 339.
11. Lamb, *Occurrences During the Late American War,* 193.

3. A Bad Conjugal Example

1. Chandler *American Criminal Trials,* vol. 2, 8, 9.
2. The seven Ruggles children listed in Helen Bourne Joy Lee's *Bourne Genealogy* and also in Chandler's *American Criminal Trials* are:

> Martha b. 10 August 1737, m. John Tufts of Brookfield November 1765, d. 1813
>
> Timothy b. 7 January 1739, m. Sarah Dwight, d. Granville, Nova Scotia, 1831
>
> Mary b. 10 February 1741, m. John Green of Worcester March 1762, d. 1814
>
> John b. 30 September 1742, m. Hannah Sackett, d. Wilmot, Nova Scotia, 1830
>
> Richard b. 4 March 1744, m. Wealthia Hathaway 1771, d. Clements, Nova Scotia, 1834
>
> Bathsheba b. 15 February 1746, m. Joshua Spooner of Brookfield, 8 January 1766, d. 7/2/1778
>
> Elizabeth b. 15 May 1748, m. Gardner Chandler of Worcester, 18 August 1772.

3. Shipton, *Sibley's Harvard Graduates,* vol. 9 (1731–1735) provides a comprehensive account of Ruggles's early life and political and military career.
4. Ruggles, *The Offering,* 30.
5. Lee, *The Bourne Genealogy,* 29. See also Paige, *History of Hardwick.*
6. Shipton, *Sibley's Harvard Graduates,* vol. 9, 199.
7. See The Mayflower Descendants, 58.
8. *The Group* was never dramatized, or, perhaps, intended to be dramatized; it is a set of monologues with no dramatic tension or movement. Parts were published in the *Boston Gazette* and the January 1775 *Massachusetts Spy.* John Adams, then a close friend and mentor to Mercy Warren, rushed the play into print as it was being written and quickly disseminated it around patriot circles in both Philadelphia and Boston.
9. Great Britain's rigid class system suffered a sea change in the provinces, particularly in the mid- to late eighteenth century with the proliferation

of American colleges turning out great numbers of professionals and cultivated men. For a fee of £10 per year for four years, sons of artisans, tradesmen, and farmers were able to rise from the ranks of yeomen to become gentlemen.

10. In Jedediah Foster's trial notes, Prudence, a black woman who worked at Walker's tavern, testified that when Sergeant Buchanan offered her his handkerchief, Bathsheba said, God damn the handkerchief, I will not touch it.

11. Lovell, *Sandwich: A Cape Cod Town,* 157.

12. John Adams, *Life and Works* (Boston: 1850–56), 67; quoted in Paige, *History of Hardwick,* 78.

13. A painting of the Ruggles house in Hardwick by Winthrop Chandler, *Homestead of General Timothy Ruggles,* is reproduced in Lipman and Armstrong, eds., *American Folk Painters.*

14. Blake, *History of the Town of Princeton,* 55–58.

15. Ruggles, *The Offering,* 30.

16. Ibid.

17. Record 51497, Timothy Ruggles, 1777 Hardwick Administration, Worcester Probate Court. The entire estate was confiscated by the state in 1777.

18. *Boston Evening-Post,* 13 February 1775. Quoted in Shipton, *Sibley's Harvard Graduates,* vol. 9, 210.

19. Upon Lt. Gen. Thomas Gage's remark at Bunker Hill that the rebels would disperse at the sight of a cannon, Ruggles had answered, "These are the very men who conquered Canada. I have fought with them side by side; they will fight bravely. My God! Sir, your folly has ruined your cause."

20. John Adams, *Life and Works* (Boston: 1850–56), 67. Quoted in Paige, *History of Hardwick,* 78.

21. Marriages in the eighteenth century were often arranged among families and considered to be akin to business arrangements. Benjamin Franklin, for example, dickered with his prospective in-laws for a larger dowry before consenting to wed. When he didn't get the sum he wanted, negotiations broke off.

22. Joshua Spooner had a mortgage on one-half interest in the "Olivers Mills" property in Middleborough, Massachusetts, which belonged to three of Judge Peter Oliver's sons (nephews to Andrew Oliver, the stamp tariff collector hanged in effigy on the Liberty Tree). The property, which included a saw mill, forge, coal house, iron house, grist mill, cider mill, and about fifty acres of land, was confiscated by the American government in 1775, leaving the title in dispute. Ultimately the Spooner children appear to have received one-half of the rents and of the sale price for

Olivers Mills when that portion of Spooner's estate was finally settled in 1797.

4. *Irrevocably Joined in Marriage*

1. Ehrlich, *Ehrlich's Blackstone,* 83.
2. Andrew Oliver was also the brother-in-law of Royal Gov. Thomas Hutchinson (and appointed lieutenant governor under Hutchinson). Hutchinson, Oliver, and Timothy Ruggles were the top three names on the list of those Loyalists banished for life from Massachusetts.
3. Joshua Spooner Letterbook, 1741–1742, American Antiquarian Society, Worcester, Mass. John Spooner owned at least one ship himself, the *Elizabeth,* presumably named after his first wife.
4. Crafts, "The Spooner Genealogy."
5. From the will of John Spooner.
6. The John Spooner portrait hangs in the Reynolda House Museum of American Art, Winston-Salem, North Carolina.
7. A bill listing John Spooner Jr.'s funeral expenses may be found in the Spooner Papers at the Massachusetts Historical Society: "Strong double-lid ruff elm coffin, covered with fine black cloth, two rows and one round the edge of the lid brass nails struck close and dotted with gilt ornaments & metal plate of inscription finely chast, Chinese handles gilt & chast To a strong leaded coffin wall, a lead plate of inscription the inside Lined and ruffled with fine crape & a fine crape mattress for the bottom — To a superfine shroud sheet pillow & case, Velvet Pall, a set of black ostrich feathers, 2 conduction with horses silk coverings, hatbands and gloves, a hearse & 3 coaches & cloaks, Fethers & Velvets for the hearse and horses, a man in mourning to carry the Led Feathers, 10 men in D to attend the coaches, gloves & favors for D, 2 clergymens best rich armozeen silk scarves, 15 best rich allamode silk hatbands, 15 pair of mens best lace looped gloves, 2 pr. of womens purple kid, 3 crape hatbands for servants, crape hatband 7 gloves for the sexton, 10 gentlemans fine new cloaks, dues to Fulham, paid for a bottle of wine 2 shillings."
8. From the Brookfield Town Records Collection, American Antiquarian Society, Worcester, Mass.
9. Deeds for Brookfield land amounting to over eighty acres bought by Joshua Spooner in 1767 and 1769 are on file, but whether it was woodlands, pasture, or a house lot is not specified.
10. Robert Wilder, who has excavated the site, found evidence of a dump at the northeast corner. The inventories, taken in 1778 and in 1792, when the estate was finally settled, were as follows:

Worcester Probate, Inventory of the real and personal Estate of
Joshua Spooner, March 16, 1778, (Appraised by John Hamilton,
Phineas Upham, Francis Foxcroft, all of Brookfield):

Arms of wearing apparel	£101.11
Furniture in the West Parlour	150.13.6
Furniture in the East Parlour	45.12.6
Books in —— d	59.12
Plate	178.1
In the Pantry	15.10
Furniture in the West Chamber	66.16
Furniture in the East Chamber	39.5
Furniture in the kitchen, grain & c	139.9.9
Farming Tools	96.0.6
Hay	3.0
Livestock	247.10
Linnen	15.12
Farm & Appurtenances	1809.
Pew	40.
Saddle & Bridle & c	5.10
Sundries	8.11
Pencilcase & Spoon	.6
	£3039.11.2

March 30, 1782 Appraisal:

The Homestead, Farm & buildings situate in the South Parish in said Brookfield, containing about 100 acres . . . with the privileges and appurtances thereof	£480.
A Pew in the third Precinct meetinghouse	20.
A tract of meadowland situate in the South side of the River supposed to contain 5 or 6 acres	15.
	515.

A leased parcel in the Great Swamp on the South Side of the River	7.10

11. Fiske, "A Sermon Preached at Brookfield, March 6, 1778, on the Day of the Interment of Mr. Joshua Spooner," 17.

12. Peleg Chandler described it as: "still standing (1843) unchanged, except by the waste of years. It was a plain, but large and respectable dwelling, two stories in height and constructed after the fashion of those times, when comfort was considered more than show in the economy of living. It is situated on the north side of the old [Post] road from Brookfield to

Worcester, about half a mile eastward of the meeting house of the South Parish, in the former town. In front, and nearly opposite, on the south side of the road, are stately elms. The buildings are unpainted, dilapidated, and falling to decay." (Chandler, *American Criminal Trials*, 4.) The house's last appearance on a map was in 1885 (Geo. Walker Atlas).

13. Marvin, *History of Worcester County,* "The Spooner Case," 56.

5. Seduced from Virtue and Prudence

1. According to *Massachusetts Soldiers and Sailors of the Revolutionary War,* Ross joined Capt. Robert Dodge's company in Col. Samuel Johnson's regiment. In the four months of duty in the north, Dodge's company served under Generals Seth Warner, Benjamin Lincoln, and Horatio Gates. His term of service began 15 August 1777 and he was discharged 14 December 1777.

2. Massachusetts Historical Society *Collections*, vol. 2.

3. *Massachusetts Spy,* "State of Massachusetts Bay Proclamation," 30 October 1777; notice of The order of Congress, 27 November 1777.

4. Foster, "Notes on the Trial of Bathsheba Spooner," American Antiquarian Society, Worcester.

5. Ibid.

6. A good half of Ebenezer Parkman's diary, from 1719 to 1755, transcribed by Francis G. Walett (1974), is available through the American Antiquarian Society, Boston, Mass. The remainder, in manuscript form, may be found in the Parkman Family Papers collection there.

7. The long account of the murder and trial, published in the 7 May issue, was also published in *Powers' and Willis's Independent Chronicle,* 30 April.

8. Maccarty, "Account of the Behavior of Mrs. Spooner."

9. Riedesel, *Baroness von Riedesel and the American Revolution,* 70.

10. Mohr, *Abortion in America,* 6–7.

11. Shipton's *Sibley's Harvard Graduates* provides a detailed explanation of Ruggles's problems with the British high command.

12. Levi Lincoln made a strong case for Bathsheba's insanity in her defense. An account of his arguments supporting it may be found in appendix E.

13. The description of Joshua's behavior is from Alexander Cummings, Foster trial notes (appendix B).

14. Temple, *History of North Brookfield,* 238. Jabez Crosby was apparently wealthy and owned a larger house than the Spooners' (according to the 1798 direct tax). Crosby's son Oliver built a mansion in 1791, which still stands in Brookfield today.

15. Loved Lincoln's testimony in Foster's and Sargeant's notes puts the date "at about" the first of February, though in Sargeant's notes he said they left on Tuesday, which would have been 3 February.
16. *Massachusetts Spy*, 7 May 1778.

6. Burgoin People

1. Accounts vary as to the number of British prisoners taken. Burgoyne himself claimed to have only 3,500 men left before Saratoga (see Marvin Brown's foreword to Riedesel, *Baroness von Riedesel and the American Revolution*, xxxii), but he was inclined to be untrustworthy in order to avert blame for the defeat; the 16 May 1778 issue of the *Massachusetts Spy* reported that 5,752 "prisoners and deserters before surrender" were taken. Ketchum, *Saratoga*, 437, puts the number of British and Germans who surrendered on 17 October at 5,895.
2. Lamb, *An Original and Authentic Journal of Occurrences during the Late American War*, 196.
3. According to the *Spy* article, the barracks were designed to be: "140 feet in length, 40 feet wide, with a hip roof, two stories high, eight feet in the clear, the sides, and ends, boarded and clapboarded, to have three long entries through, and a stair case in each of said entries, twelve rooms in each story 20 feet square, with double floors and plank petitions, ten cabins in each room, eight stacks of chimneys, four of which are to be double, the jams to be three feet deep, the fronts and backs four and a half feet deep; two windows each room containing twelve squares each ten by eight glass."
4. Lamb, *Memoir of His Own Life*, 242–45.
5. According to William Young's testimony in Paine's trial notes (appendix C).
6. A public confession of guilt served a very important spiritual purpose in the public spectacle of eighteenth-century capital punishment, which was intended as a deterrent to sin as well as to crime. The confession of guilt was central to the Calvinistic drama of repentance and redemption, but only true repentance would earn the possibility of eternal life for such a heinous sin as murder. The three male prisoners fervently hoped for forgiveness and eternal life, and (according to Maccarty) their whole imprisonment was spent "resolved to lie at God's feet" in prayer and reading and discoursing upon the bible. In their own words at the confession's conclusion: "We desire to give glory to God by free and full confession of our heinous guilt. We trust we have with deep penitence and contrition of soul consigned it to God, hoping . . . that our scarlet

and crimson guilt may be done away, that we may be saved from eternal damnation which we know we justly deserve, and obtain eternal life and salvation." Thus Buchanan, Brooks, and Ross had everything to gain by telling the whole truth as they remembered it in their confession (the possibility of eternal life), and everything to lose (eternal damnation) by lying.

7. Alexander Cummings's testimony in Paine's trial notes, appendix C.

8. Ibid.

9. Ibid. Cummings also testified that Bathsheba promised to "make a man of him" if he would kill Mr. Spooner for her (in both Paine's and Foster's notes [appendix C, appendix B]). If Cummings was telling the truth, Bathsheba's willingness to grant sexual favors in exchange for murdering Joshua is an indication of her increasing desperation.

10. Buchanan's account in "The Dying Declaration" presents a confusing time frame. He cites the specific day (8 February) he and Brooks arrived at the Spooners, with a certainty that seems reliable. He is vaguer about Joshua's arrival: "Having tarried ten or eleven days, as nearly as can be recollected, her husband came home." By working through his time references backwards from the murder, however, Sunday, 15 February, appears to be the date Joshua returned from Princeton, ironically on Bathsheba's thirty-second birthday. If, however Alexander Cummings is to be believed, according to Foster's and Sargeant's notes, Joshua returned Monday night.

11. "You are already acquainted with the character of Mrs. Spooner which has long labored under Aspersions highly to her disadvantage and is now complected as one of blackest and most detestable." Letter from Dwight Foster of Brookfield to J. Clarke, Thursday 5 March 1778. J. Clarke was possibly the Reverend Jonas Clarke, at whose parsonage in Lexington Paul Revere warned John Hancock and Sam Adams on the night of 18 April 1775 that the Regulars were out.

12. The Spooners' neighbors: to the north, the widow of Jabez Upham; east, Samuel and Abigail Hinkley; south (across the post road), Dr. Francis Foxcroft, Dr. Jonathan and Abigail King, and someone named Swift; west, Obadiah Cooley and Joshua Upham. (Courtesy of Robert Wilder, Brookfield.)

13. Though Martha was nine years older than Bathsheba, they married within two months of each other (Martha, November 1765; Bathsheba, January 1746) both to Brookfield gentlemen. At the time of the murder, Martha and John had four children: Patty, age five; twins John and Joseph, age three; and Gardner, eight months. The Tuftses' house was more modest than the Spooners' — one-storied with seven windows, oc-

cupying 856-square feet of land with fifty-nine acres of farmland, compared to the Spooners', which was two-storied with eighteen windows, occupying twelve hundred square feet of land with one hundred acres of farmland (1798 direct tax records).

14. Excerpted from Dwight Foster letter to J. Clarke.

15. U.S. Revolution Collection (January–March 1778), American Antiquarian Society, Worcester, Mass.

16. Special files were needed for white smith's finishing work, according to Robert Wilder, a Brookfield historian.

17. Prudence's testimony is recorded in Foster's trial notes (appendix B). We can only speculate as to whether this is the same handkerchief that Buchanan sent Brooks to retrieve from the other British soldier a week earlier.

18. See Mohr, *Abortion in America*, 6–7.

19. Mary Walker's and Prudence's testimony, Foster's trial notes (appendix B).

20. Mary Walker's testimony, Foster's trial notes (appendix B).

7. *"His Time Is Come"*

1. In 1778, John Jones Spooner of Roxbury (who would become the Spooner children's guardian) listed among his debts against Joshua Spooner's estate:

> October 24, 1778:
> For bringing Mr. Spooner's son from Ipswich 2.10
> 65 weeks board for Josh[a] a 13/14, 43.6.8.

In the eighteenth century it was common for upper-class male children to attend grammar schools away from home, but it is unclear from this account if Joshua boarded in Roxbury with his uncle or in Ipswich.

2. *Massachusetts Spy*, 7 May 1778.

3. The location has been identified by Robert Wilder, a Brookfield historian.

4. This appears to be an error on Buchanan's part, or the time of an earlier plan. On Saturday afternoon, Mary Walker overheard them agree on Sunday at 11 o'clock (from Foster's and Sargeant's notes).

5. "The Widow Stratton . . . was in the kitchen when the murder was done (and whose conscience must witness whether she was before, privy to this hostile design against the life of a man who found her bread) . . ." (*Massachusetts Spy*, 5 May 1778).

6. From the Warrant of Execution, 8 May 1778 (appendix I). The Bill of

Indictment, describing the crime in detail, was incorporated within the Warrant of Execution almost word for word.

7. This exchange was reported in the *Massachusetts Spy*, 7 May 1778. Secondary accounts of the murder have perpetuated some confusion over whether Joshua was beaten with a club or with Brooks's fist. Justice Sargeant's notes quote Dr. Jonathan King as testifying, "I saw a Club which was found standing up, and supposed to be what they knocked him down with." Perhaps in consequence, the Brookfield coroner's report stated that Spooner had been beaten with a club. But Brooks confessed that he had kicked and beaten Joshua with his fist. The Indictment and Death Warrant describe at length Joshua's being beaten with Brooks's hands, but neither mentions a club. In Sargeant's notes Prudence also testified that Brooks's hand was "swelled all up."

8. Alexander Cummings's testimony, Foster's notes (appendix B).

9. Ibid. The quote is substantially the same in Paine's notes.

10. Sarah Stratton's testimony, Foster's notes.

8. The Hands of Justice

1. As of June 1776, Brookfield's population was 2,670 compared to Worcester's 2,000.

2. The description of eighteenth-century Worcester, its buildings, and the location of the jail comes from Spears, *Old Landmarks and Historic Spots of Worcester, Massachusetts;* Massachusetts Historical Society *Collections*, vol. 1, "Topographical Description of Worcester" (ca. 1790); Wall, "Reminiscences of Worcester from the Earliest Period"; and a 1795 map of Worcester by Francis E. Blukes (Massachusetts State Archives, Boston).

3. Isaiah Thomas first established his *Massachusetts Spy* newspaper in Boston, but because of its inflammatory patriotic content the paper was in danger of being seized by the British. In 1775 Thomas moved the whole printing operation to Worcester, where the *Spy* was ultimately leased to Anthony Haswell until July 1778. Thomas again took over the paper's publication, arriving just in time for the hanging of Joshua Spooner's murderers.

4. The progression of events has been reconstructed from Curtis's, Whitney's, and Ball's testimony in Foster's and Paine's notes.

5. The coroners jury apparently had been summoned by Ephraim Cooley. The formal coroner's jury report is dated the next day, 3 March, declaring before Thomas Gilbert, Gentleman (coroner) that Joshua Spooner was feloniously assaulted near his own door by one or more persons

unknown. It is signed by Jonathan King, Obadiah Cooley (Ephraim's father), Richard Whellen, Francis Foxcroft, Moses Dorr, Seth Bannister, Benjamin Jennings, John Waite, Elias Staples, Adoninam Walker, James Upham, William Hincher, Asa Bigelow, and Comfort Olds, "good and lawful men of Brookfield" (Record books of the Superior Court).

6. See Morris, *Fair Trial*, 106.

7. The 3 March issue of the *Massachusetts Spy* said that "Mrs. Spooner . . . and the rest of her associates were seized and on Tuesday evening brought to this town and confined in gaol." However, Ephraim Cooley speaks of bringing her to Brown's tavern, and Samuel Brown's itemized bill dated Monday, 2 March, includes only one night's charges.

8. Samuel Brown submitted a bill dated 2 March 1778 to the County of Worcester "for what was Expended at my House in the Examination of the Murderers of Mr. Spooner by the Guard &C." The bill included "8 suppers, 4 mugs sider, 5 breakfasts, liquor, and provisions for the Guards' horses [and totaled] . . . £2 / 16." (Revolutionary Council Papers, 1777–1778, Massachusetts State Archives, Boston).

9. The first two quotations are from Obadiah Rice's testimony as recorded in Foster's notes; the last statement from Bathsheba is found in Sargeant's notes.

10. Elisha Hamilton's testimony is in both Foster's and Paine's notes.

11. Jesse Parker (another Spooner servant) was brought to jail at the beginning of April (according to Joseph Wheeler's testimony in Foster's notes) as a material witness. British Sgt. Samuel Woods was also jailed until after the trial because he was present at Walker's tavern when the plot was being discussed and was a friend of Bathsheba's (see chap. 6). He apparently had nothing sufficiently incriminating to offer, because there is no record of his appearance as a witness.

12. *Diary,* 1771, Nathan Fiske Papers 1750–1799.

13. Salary receipt and notebook, Nathan Fiske Papers 1750–1799.

14. Fiske, "Sermon on the Tragical Death of Mr. Spooner."

15. Born in Boston, Robert Treat Paine was forty-seven at the date of the trial and a prominent Massachusetts patriot. He had been a signer of the Declaration of Independence and member of the Continental Congress, as well as attorney general of the state from 1777 to 1790. His notes on the trial testimony are in appendix C.

16. Record books of the Superior Court.

17. The jurors' names were Ephraim May, Jonathan Phillips, Ebenezer Lovel, David Bigelow, Benjamin Stowell, Samuel Forbush, Joseph Herrington, John Phelps, Manasseh Sawyer, Elisha Goddard, Abraham Bachelor, and Mark Bachelor (Record books of the Superior Court, 227–28).

18. William Cushing replaced John Adams, who was appointed chief justice of Massachusetts. Adams, however, was far too busy with the work of the Continental Congress to sit as a judge and resigned the position. In 1770 Adams had successfully defended the British perpetrators of the "Boston Massacre," and he might well have lent a greater degree of impartiality to these proceedings had he kept his place at the bench. Cushing held the position of Massachusetts supreme justice until his promotion to the U.S. Supreme Court in 1789.

   Jedediah Foster had been a justice of the peace in Brookfield since 1754 and was an ardent patriot. He was a member of the Provincial Congress of 1774 and a colonel in the Brookfield militia. He was appointed a judge of the Superior Court in Worcester after the flight of Loyalist judges in 1775, and he would later serve as a member of the convention that drafted the state constitution. Jedediah Foster's "Notes on the Trial of Bathsheba Spooner, 1778" is in appendix B.

19. Maccarty, "Account of the Behaviour of Mrs. Spooner."

20. Lincoln's notes on his summary to the jury are in appendix E.

21. During the trial itself two inequities were in fact noted and apparently ignored. In Robert Treat Paine's minutes a Mr. Sprague testified that "the pris. suffer by being tryed all together because they charged one another," and also that "[Ross's participation] only makes him an acces. after fact." Another obvious inequity was the choice of the young and untried Levi Lincoln as defense attorney, pitched against, presumably, the best lawyer in the state.

9. Petitions to the Council

1. Shipton, *Sibley's Harvard Graduates*, vol. 10.

2. *Murder Most Foul*, 18.

3. Maccarty's "appendix" was published by Isaiah Thomas, who printed an advertisement seeking subscribers for it in the *Massachusetts Spy*, 16 July 1778.

4. Maccarty, "Account of the Behaviour of Mrs. Spooner."

5. Parkman, "The Adultress Will Hunt for the Precious Life."

6. See Mohr, *Abortion in America*, 3.

7. The other eleven matrons were: Elizabeth Rice, Mary Todman (or Tattman), Hannah Perry, Zurbilch Stowell, Christian Walker, Ezebel Quigley, Margaret Brown, Mary Bridge, Lidia Ball, Hannah Brooks, and Sarah Jones. (Documents associated with the midwives' examinations as well as Bathsheba's petition are in appendix I.)

8. Maccarty, "Account of the Behaviour of Mrs. Spooner."

9. This body had evolved from the former Royal Governor's Council to which Brig. Timothy Ruggles had been briefly appointed a member. Ruggles's acceptance of the appointment to the Royal Governor's Mandamus Council in August 1774 resulted in his banishment from Hardwick and ultimately Massachusetts.

10. Shipton, *Sibley's Harvard Graduates*, vol. 12, 326.

11. Paul Revere, perhaps the best known Son of Liberty, joined Ruggles's long list of detractors in 1768, when Ruggles voted to recind a proposed boycott of British manufactured goods. Revere engraved a copper plate entitled "A Warm Place — Hell," depicting the seventeen members of the legislature (dubbed The Recinders) who voted against the boycott marching into the maw of hell; they were led by Brig. Gen. Timothy Ruggles.

12. From Worcester Courthouse Probate Record #55243.

13. Record books of Superior Court of Judicature, 227–28.

14. John Avery Jr. held a position of eminence in Massachusetts politics until his death in 1806. He became Massachusetts's first secretary of state and upon his death was given a state funeral.

10. Dreadful Scene of Horror

1. "A Mournful Poem: . . ," stanza 6.

2. Ebenezer Parkman apparently was not among them, because in his diary entry that day he said, "concerning ye poor woman, it is with me uncertain whether she is hanged or not, or what has become of her."

3. A detailed account of the execution was published in the 6 August issue. The 9 July issue published only a brief notice that the execution had taken place on the appointed date. An editor's note introducing the fuller account in the 6 August issue stated that "the following paragraph would have been published in season, had it not been . . . mislaid." One can't help wondering if Isaiah Thomas, shrewd entrepreneur that he was, had purposely "mislaid" it in order to sell more papers to a public hungry for news of this celebrated event.

4. The location of the jail and gallows as well as the ostrich plume anecdote may be found in Spears, *Old Landmarks and Historic Spots of Worcester.* The anecdote about the wedding dress is courtesy of Harriet Sanders Shealy, a descendant of Martha and John Tufts, Bathsheba's sister and brother-in-law. Tufts family tradition has it that Bathsheba's wedding ring was given to her sister Martha, who passed it down to her youngest son, Francis, who in turn passed it to his daughter, Lou Tufts. Lou Tufts never married and died in 1934, at which time the ring disappeared. If the family tradition is

true, we can only speculate as to the degree of irony Bathsheba's decision to wear her wedding dress might have represented. A few of her quotes suggest that she wasn't adverse to irony, but it also may have been simply the most practical choice. Bridal dresses were then made from various materials and hues, and worn repeatedly. Some high-waisted styles from the 1770s have survived, suggesting that she might have worn it simply to accommodate her pregnancy.

5. Information on the construction of gallows, procedural matters and other hanging lore came from Teeters and Hedblom, *Hang by the Neck,* 46–47, 66, 153, 173–184.

6. The description of Bathsheba creeping up the ladder on her hands and knees has beggared the imaginations of historians since it was written. Because it would have been nearly physically impossible as well as extraordinarily difficult to ascend a ladder while wearing skirt and petticoats in such fashion, it must be ascribed to poetic license on the part of the reporter. Another instance of poetic imagination is the description of Bathsheba's taking the sheriff by the hand after her arms had been pinioned. These lapses in veracity provoke one to wonder whether this account reflects what actually took place or a romanticized version in keeping with the elevated tone of execution literature of that period.

7. Rush, *Medical Inquiries and Observations Upon the Diseases of the Mind,* 96.

11. Remains

1. See Teeters and Hedblom, *Hang by the Neck,* 305.

2. From a letter written by Gen. William Heath of Roxbury in February 1792 in support of the application of his son, William Heath Jr., to administer the Joshua Spooner estate. Probate Court Records, Worcester, Mass.

3. Quoted in *Sibley's Harvard Graduates,* vol. 9, 222.

4. *History of Worcester County,* 65.

BIBLIOGRAPHY

Manuscript Sources

Coroner's jury report, 3 March 1778. Miscellaneous Manuscripts Collection. American Antiquarian Society, Boston.

Cushing, Chief Justice William. "Notes of cases decided in the Superiour and Supreme Judicial Courts of Massachusets, from 1772–1789, Worcester, April Term, A.D. 1778." MS 2141, MSS Bound Manuscript Collection. Harvard Law School Library, Cambridge, Mass.

Deeds for property bought by Joshua Spooner, 1767, 1769. Brookfield Town Hall Records, Brookfield, Mass.

Fiske, Nathan. Diary, 1771; Notebook; Salary receipt. Nathan Fiske Papers. Box F, Octavo vol. American Antiquarian Society, Worcester, Mass.

Forbes, Esther. Notes. Esther Forbes Papers. Miscellaneous manuscript collection. American Antiquarian Society, Worcester, Mass.

Foster, Dwight. Letter to Mr. J. Clarke, 5 March 1778. Foster Family Papers. Box 1, Folder 3. American Antiquarian Society, Worcester, Mass.

Foster, Judge Jedediah. "Notes on the Trial of Bathsheba Spooner, 1778." Foster Family Papers. Box 1, Folder 3. American Antiquarian Society, Worcester, Mass.

Funeral charges, Mr. John Spooner. Spooner Family Papers, 1645–1834. Massachusetts Historical Society, Boston.

Indictment. April Term, 1778. Superior Court Records. Massachusetts State Archives, Boston.

Letter to the Massachusetts Council at Boston from the Brookfield Committee of Safety, 8 March 1778. Brookfield Town Records. American Antiquarian Society, Worcester, Mass.

Lincoln, Levi. "Minutes in the Case of the Murder of Mr. Spooner." Lincoln Family Papers, 1776–1820. Octavo vol. 50. American Antiquarian Society, Worcester, Mass.

Maccarty, Thaddeus. Reverend Maccarty's final plea to the Council supporting Bathsheba's pregnancy, 26 June 1778. Executive Council Records. Massachusetts State Archives, Boston.

Massachusetts direct tax census, 1798. Schedules A, B, C, D, E, F. Research library of Old Sturbridge Village, Sturbridge, Mass.

Opinion of Midwives, second examination, 27 June 1778. Executive Records, Revolutionary Council Papers, 1777–1778. Massachusetts State Archives, Boston.

Order for Suspension of Sentence, May 28, 1778 to Thursday, the 2nd day of July. Executive Records, Revolutionary Council Papers, 1777–1778. Massachusetts State Archives, Boston.

Paine, Robert Treat. Minutes of Trial and Law Cases, 1777–1782. Robert Treat Paine Papers. Massachusetts Historical Society, Boston.

Parkman, Rev. Ebenezer. "The Adultress Will Hunt for Precious Life," sermon preached at Westborough, 5 July 1778. Parkman Family Papers, Octavo vol. 5. Box 1, Folder 7. American Antiquarian Society, Worcester, Mass.

———. Diary, April–July 1778. Parkman Family Papers. Octavo vol. 5. Box 1, Folder 7. American Antiquarian Society, Worcester, Mass.

Petition of Bathsheba Spooner, 16 June 1778. Executive Records, Revolutionary Council Papers, 1777–1778. Massachusetts State Archives, Boston.

Petition of the Prisoners for a Reprieve, 20 May 1778. Executive Records, Revolutionary Council Papers, 1777–1778. Massachusetts State Archives, Boston.

Petition of Ross Family, 26 May 1778. Executive Records, Revolutionary Council Papers, 1777–1778. Massachusetts State Archives, Boston.

Record book of the Executive Council, refusal to grant Bathsheba's petition for a stay of execution, 23 June 1778. Executive Records, Revolutionary Council Papers, 1777–1778. Massachusetts State Archives, Boston.

Record books of the Superior Court of Judicature, 1775–1780. Executive Records, Revolutionary Council Papers, 1777–1778. Massachusetts State Archives, Boston.

Records from the Worcester, Mass. Probate Court. Ruggles, Timothy, Hardwick, 1777. Administration (#55257, Series A); Spooner, Elizabeth, Bond of Guardianship (#55243); Spooner, Joshua, Brookfield, 1778. Administration (#55257, Series A).

Return of the Sheriff, First Examination Writ, 6 July 1778. Executive Records, Revolutionary Council Papers, 1777–1778. Massachusetts State Archives, Boston.

Sargeant, Nathaniel Peaslee. "Indictment of William Brooks, James Buchanan, & Ezra Ross for the Murder of Joshua Spooner on the 1st Day of March at Brookfield & Bathsheba Spooner as accessory before the fact." Nathaniel Peaslee Sargeant Casebook. Peabody-Essex Museum, Salem, Mass.

Warrant of Execution, 8 May 1778; 28 May 1778; Final Return of the Sheriff, 6 July 1778. Executive Records, Revolutionary Council Papers, 1777–1778. Massachusetts State Archives, Boston.

Will of John Spooner, probated 26 December 1763. Suffolk County Probate Records. Massachusetts State Archives, Boston.

Writ De Ventre Inspiciendo, 28 May 1778. Executive Records, Revolutionary Council Papers, 1777–1778. Massachusetts State Archives, Boston.

Published Sources

Anthony, Katharine. *First Lady of the Revolution: The Life of Mercy Otis Warren.* New York: Doubleday, 1958.

Berg, Fred Anderson. *Continental Army Units.* Harrisburg, Pa.: Stackpole Books, 1972.

Blake, Francis Everett. *History of the Town of Princeton.* Princeton, Mass., 1915.

Bobrick, Benson. *Angel in the Whirlwind: The Triumph of the American Revolution.* New York: Simon & Schuster, 1997.

Boorstin, Daniel J. *The Americans: The Colonial Experience.* New York: Random House, 1958.

Brookfield, Mass. *Vital Records of Brookfield, Mass.* Worcester, Mass.: Franklin P. Rice, 1909.

Brown, Alice. *Mercy Warren.* New York: Scribners, 1896.

Bullock, Chandler. *The Bathsheba Spooner Murder Case.* Worcester, Mass.: American Antiquarian Society, 1939.

Butterfield, L.H., ed. *Adams Family Correspondence,* vol. 1, December 1761–May, 1776. Cambridge: The Belknap Press, 1963.

———. *The Adams Papers: The Earliest Diary of John Adams.* Cambridge: Harvard University Press, 1966.

Chandler, Peleg W. *American Criminal Trials.* Vol. 2. "Trial of Mrs. Spooner and Others." Boston : T.H. Carter, 1844, 2–58.

Cohen, Daniel A. *Pillars of Salt, Monuments of Grace.* New York: Oxford University Press, 1993.

Demos, John. *The Unredeemed Captive.* New York: Alfred A. Knopf, 1994.

Drake, Francis S. *The Town of Roxbury: Its Memorable Persons and Places.* Roxbury, Mass., 1878.

Dwight, Timothy. *Travels in New England and New York.* Cambridge: The Belknap Press, 1969.

"The Dying Declaration of James Buchanan, Ezra Ross, and William Brooks, Who were executed at Worcester, July 2, 1778, for The Murder of Mr. Joshua Spooner." (In quarto and broadside editions: "The Last Words and Dying Speech of James Buchanan, Ezra Ross, and William Brooks, who were executed at Worcester for the murder of Mr. Joshua Spooner.) Early American Imprints Series. American Antiquarian Society, Worcester, Mass.

Ellis, Joseph J. *Passionate Sage: The Character and Legacy of John Adams.* New York: Norton, 1993.

Erlich, J.W. *Erlich's Blackstone.* Westport, Conn.: Greenwood Press, 1959.

Fennelly, Catherine. *The Garb of Country New Englanders, 1790–1840.* Old Sturbridge Booklet Series. Meriden, Conn.: Meriden Gravure Co., 1966.

Fischer, David Hackett. *Paul Revere's Ride.* New York: Oxford University Press, 1994.

Fiske, Nathan, A.M. "A Description of the Town of Brookfield" and "Historical Account of the Settlement of Brookfield." *The Massachusetts Historical Society Collections,* vol. 1. 1806. Reprint, Boston: Munroe & Francis, 1792, 271–74.

———. "Sermon on the Tragical Death of Mr. Spooner," 6 March 1778. Boston: Thomas and John Fleet, 1778.

Forbes, Esther. *The General's Lady.* New York: Harcourt Brace, 1938.

———. *Paul Revere and the World He Lived In.* Boston: Houghton Mifflin, 1942.

Friedman, Lawrence M. *Crime and Punishment in American History.* New York: HarperCollins, 1993.

Garrett, Elizabeth Donaghy. *At Home: The American Family 1750–1870.* New York: Harry N. Abrams, Inc., 1989.

Geib, Susan. *Changing Works: Agriculture and Society in Brookfield, Massachusetts 1785–1820.* Ph.D. diss. University of Michigan, 1981. Ann Arbor: University of Michigan International Dissertation Services, 1981.

Green, Samuel Swett. "Bathsheba Spooner: Incidental remarks made at the annual meeting of the American Antiquarian Society, Worcester, October 22, 1888." Worcester, Mass., 1889.

Halttunen, Karen. *Murder Most Foul.* Cambridge: Harvard University Press, 1998.

Hull, Natalie E. H. *Female Felons: Women and Serious Crime in Colonial Massachusetts.* Urbana: University of Illinois Press, 1987.

Ipswich, Mass. *Vital Records of Ipswich, Mass.* Vols. 1 and 2. Salem, Mass.: Essex Institute, 1910.

Jones, E. Alfred. *The Loyalists of Massachusetts.* London: St. Catherine Press, 1930.

Kerber, Linda K. *Women of the Republic.* New York: W.W. Norton, 1986.

Ketchum, Richard M. *Saratoga.* New York: Henry Holt, 1997.

Lamb, Roger. *Memoir of His Own Life.* Dublin, 1811.

———. *An Original and Authentic Journal of Occurrences during the Late American War.* 1809. Reprint, New York: Arno Press, 1968.

Langguth, A.J. *Patriots: The Men Who Started the American Revolution.* New York: Simon & Schuster, 1988.

Larkin, Jack. *The Reshaping of Everyday Life, 1790–1840.* New York: Harper & Row, 1989.

Lee, Helen Joy. *The Bourne Genealogy.* Chester, Conn.: The Pequot Press, 1972.

Lipman, Jean, and Tom Armstrong, eds. *American Folk Painters of Three Centuries.* New York: Simon and Schuster, 1980.

Lovell, Russell A., Jr. "Annals of the Revolution — Timothy Ruggles. Parts 1–3. *The Acorn* (Sandwich Historical Society): 1 (Nov. 1974); 2 (Feb. 1975); 3 (May 1975).

———. *Sandwich A Cape Cod Town.* Sandwich, Mass.: Archives and Historical Center, 1984.

Maccarty, Thaddeus. "The Guilt of Innocent Blood Put Away." Sermon preached 2 July 1778, with appendix, "Account of the Prisoners after their Commitment, Trial, and Sentence," and "Account of the Behaviour of Mrs. Spooner after her Commitment and Condemnation for being Accessory in the Murder of her Husband at Brookfield, March 1, 1778." Early American Imprint Series. American Antiquarian Society, Worcester, Mass.

Maier, Pauline. *From Resistance to Revolution.* New York: W.W. Norton, 1991.

Marvin, Abijah P. *History of Worcester County, Massachusetts.* Boston: C.F. Jewett, 1879.

Massachusetts General Court. *Journals of the House of Representatives of Massachusetts.* Vol. 54. Boston: Massachusetts Historical Society, 1989.

Massachusetts. Office of the Secretary of State. *Soldiers and Sailors of the Revolutionary War.* Vol. 13. Boston: Wright and Potter, 1898.

Massachusetts Spy, Worcester, Mass., 5 March, 7 May, 2 June, 11 June, 25 June, 2 July, 9 July, 6 August 1778. Early American Newspapers Collection. American Antiquarian Society, Worcester, Mass.

Masur, Louis P. *Rites of Execution: Capital Punishment and the Transformation of American Culture, 1776–1865.* New York: Oxford University Press, 1989.

Miller, Andrew. *Ingenious Pain.* New York: Harcourt Brace, 1997.

Mohr, James C. *Abortion in America.* New York: Oxford University Press, 1978.

Morris, Richard B. *Fair Trial.* New York: Alfred A. Knopf, 1952.

"A Mournful Poem: Occasioned by Sentence of Death being pass'd upon William Brooks, James Buchanan, Ezra Ross and Bathsheba Spooner, of Brookfield, and who were all executed at Worcester on Thursday the 2nd Day of July 1778." Early American Imprints Series. American Antiquarian Society, Worcester, Mass.

Nylander, Jane C. *Our Own Snug Fireside.* New York: Alfred A. Knopf, 1993.

Paige, Lucius R. *History of Hardwick and Genealogical Register.* Boston: Houghton Mifflin, 1883.

Paine, Thomas. "The American Crisis, 1." Broadside. Boston: John Gill, 1776.

Reynolda House. *American Originals: Selections from the Reynolda House Museum of American Art.* New York: Abbeville Press, 1990.

Reidesel, Baroness Fredericka Charlotte Louisa von. *Baroness von Riedesel and the American Revolution: Journal and Correspondence 1776–1783.* Trans. Marvin Brown Jr. Chapel Hill: University of North Carolina Press, 1965.

Ruggles, James L. *The Offering, or The Blind Man's Tribute: A Collection of Prose and Poetry.* Hardwick, Mass., 1848.

Rush, Benjamin. *The Autobiography of Benjamin Rush.* Ed. George W. Comer. Princeton, N.J.: Princeton University Press, 1948.

———. *Medical Inquiries and Observations Upon the Diseases of the Mind.* New York: Hafner Publishing Co., 1962.

Sandrof, Ivan. "Forgotten Giant of the Revolution." Vol. 3, no. 6. Worcester, Mass: Worcester Historical Society, 1952.

Sheldon, Asa. *Yankee Drover 1788–1870.* Reprint, Hanover, N.H.: University Press of New England, 1988.

Shipton, Clifford K. *Sibley's Harvard Graduates.* Vol. 9. Boston: Massachusetts Historical Society, 1945.

Spears, John Pearl. *Old Landmarks and Historic Spots of Worcester, Massachusetts.* Worcester, Mass: Commonwealth Press, 1931.

Stanton, Elizabeth Cady. "The Fatal Mistake that Stopped the Hanging of Women in Massachusetts. *New York World,* 1899.

Steele, Richard C. *Isaiah Thomas.* Worcester, Mass.: Worcester Bicentennial Commission, 1975.

Teeters, Negley K., and Jack H. Hedblom. *Hang by the Neck.* Springfield, Ill.: Charles C. Thomas, 1967.

Temple, J. H. *History of North Brookfield, Massachusetts.* Illinois, 1887.

Ulrich, Laurel Thatcher. *Good Wives: Image and Reality in Northern New England.* New York: Oxford University Press, 1983.

———. *A Midwife's Tale.* New York: Alfred A. Knopf, 1990.

Wall, Caleb. *Reminiscences of Worcester from the Earliest Period.* Worcester, Mass.: Tyler and Seagrave, 1877.

Ward, Christopher. *The War of the Revolution.* 2 vols. New York: Macmillan, 1952.

Warren, Mercy Otis. *The Plays and Poems of Mercy Otis Warren.* Comp. Benjamin Franklin V. New York: Scholars' Facsimiles & Reprints, 1980.

Waters, Thomas Franklin. *Ipswich in the Massachusetts Colony 1700–1917.* 2 vols. Ipswich, Mass.:Ipswich Historical Society, 1917.

Wheeler, Richard. *Voices of 1776.* New York: Penguin Books, 1972.

ACKNOWLEDGMENTS

This book owes much of its accuracy and authority to the generous efforts of historians, scholars, archivists, and friends over a period of twenty years. Many of the primary sources on which this work is based were found at the American Antiquarian Society, Worcester, Massachusetts. I am especially grateful to Thomas Knoles and Marie Lamoureux for help in locating manuscripts and to Richard Anders, who provided the time of sunset and phase of the moon for 1 March 1778, the night Joshua Spooner was murdered. Mr. Knoles, director of reference services and curator of manuscripts, devoted many hours to verifying and correcting my transcriptions of Jedediah Foster's and Levi Lincoln's trial notes, included in the appendix.

The Massachusetts Historical Society also contributed a great deal, of source material as well as the expertise of its staff. My thanks to Conrad E. Wright, Ford Editor of Publications, Virginia H. Smith, research librarian, and especially to Edward W. Hanson, senior associate editor of publications. The transcription included here of the portion of Robert Treat Paine's "Minutes of Trial and Law Cases" that pertains to the Spooner murder owes much of its accuracy and clarity to Hanson's transcription, which will be included among other writings of Robert Treat Paine to be published in a forthcoming volume of the Massachusetts Historical Society *Collections*. Mr. Hanson made another important contribution to this book by acquainting me with the existence of Associate Justice Nathaniel Peaslee Sargeant's case notes (located in the Essex Peabody Museum archives), which provide the most detailed account of the Spooner trial testimony discovered to date.

Other institutions and people to whom I am indebted for making their resources available are: the Worcester Historical Society; the Worcester Probate Court; the Quaboag Historical Society and Pat Turner, Will Earley, and Marguerite Geis; the Merrick public library in Brookfield and Mrs. Reta Warman; the West Boylston Historical Society and Ed and Dot Whitcomb; the Hardwick Historical Society and its president, Leon Thresher (a Timothy Ruggles descendant); the Old Sturbridge Village research library, with special thanks to Ed Hood for describing an eighteenth-century well and to Jack Larkin for estimating the current value of Joshua Spooner's inheritance; the

Massachusetts Supreme Judicial Court, Department of Archives and Records Preservation, and Elizabeth C. Bouvier, Head of Archives, and Bill Milhomme; the New England Historic Genealogical Society, Scott A. Bartley and Ed Johnson in particular; The Peabody Essex Museum and Jane Ward, curator of manuscripts; the Harvard Law School library and Mary L. Person, reading room supervisor; the Worcester Art Museum and Laura K. Mills, Curatorial Assistant, American Art; David R. Brigham, Curator of American Art, and Julia Green for permission to use Winthrop Chandler's painting of the Ruggles Homestead; the Dimond Library of the University of New Hampshire; and the Reynolda House, Museum of American Art, Winston-Salem, North Carolina.

I owe a great debt to individual historians who have shared their knowledge and material, especially to fellow Bathsheba Spooner researcher Bojan Jennings of Plymouth, Massachusetts. Jennings read and criticized this manuscript and contributed information on such particulars as the mortgage deed between Joshua Spooner and Peter, Daniel, and William Oliver; various actions of the Plymouth Probate Court regarding the title to Joshua Spooner's Middleborough property; information on eighteenth-century abortion methods, the medicinal dosage of calomel, and the medieval ordeal by touch; and details on the construction of Worcester's jail from Caleb Wall's *Reminiscences of Worcester from the Earliest Period*. It was Mrs. Jennings who acquainted me with the existence of the Robert Treat Paine manuscript trial notes in the Massachusetts Historical Society archives. Her generosity in sharing her research and her fine critical eye contributed immeasurably to this effort.

Over the last twenty years, Russell A. Lovell Jr. of Sandwich, Massachusetts, has most generously shared his research and resources from his own work on Timothy Ruggles, Bathsheba Bourne Ruggles, and the Bourne family. His book, *Sandwich, A Cape Cod Town* (published by the Town of Sandwich in 1984 and updated in a new third edition in 1996) has been particularly useful. I am especially grateful for his unstinting support and for first encouraging me to write this book.

My gratitude also to Robert Wilder of Brookfield for enthusiastically sharing his vast knowledge of the history and physical landmarks of his town; for providing deeds to, and a map, of the Spooner property and abutters; and for his creation of a 1778 map of Brookfield and a diagram of the Spooner house especially for this book.

Thanks also to Peter Terry of Brookfield for finding the picture of the Spooner barn; to Harriet Shealy, a direct descendant of Martha Ruggles Tufts, for sharing her family history, "Tufts Family of Georgia"; and to Jane Cram of Ipswich, who allowed me access to the Linebrook parish records.

I am greatly indebted to Vincent J. Fuller, who brought his many years of experience as a noted Washington, D.C., defense attorney to bear on an assessment of the legal proceedings in this case.

Thank you to my brother-in-law, Dr. Ned Lund, and to Dr. Harry Ainsworth, a pathologist at St. Luke's Hospital in New Bedford, Massachusetts, for advising on the appearance of Joshua Spooner's corpse; to Craig West for information on the merits of nitric acid as a poison; and to Jay Goldspinner, professional storyteller and fellow Bathsheba Spooner enthusiast.

And to Jane Garrett, John Demos, Bruce Wilcox, Ella Kusnetz, and John Yount for their part in bringing this book to publication, thank you.

DEBORAH NAVAS has written and published fiction and non-fiction and worked as a magazine editor for twenty years. She has published a collection of short stories (Southern Methodist University Press) entitled *Things We Lost, Gave Away, Bought High and Sold Low,* as well as eighteen stories in literary magazines including the *North American Review, South Dakota Review, Northeast, Carleton Miscellany,* and *Fiction Network.* She has also published an article on the Bathsheba Spooner execution in the Massachusetts Historical Society's *Proceedings* 108.

She won the New Hampshire Writers' Project 1994 Emerging Writer award based on her short story collection, and two stories won PEN Syndicated Fiction awards and were recorded for National Public Radio's "The Sound of Writing."